Shanie Jacobs' Crochet Book

Shanie Jacobs' Crochet Book

by Shanie Jacobs

Illustrated by David Jacobs
Photographs by Stanley K. Patz

The Bobbs-Merrill Company, Inc.
Indianapolis / New York

Copyright © 1979 by Shanie Jacobs

All rights reserved, including the right of reproduction
in whole or in part in any form
Published by The Bobbs-Merrill Company, Inc.
Indianapolis   New York

Designed by Rita Muncie

Manufactured in the United States of America

First printing

Library of Congress Cataloging in Publication Data

Jacobs, Shanie.
   Shanie Jacobs' Crochet book.

  1. Crocheting.   I. Title.   II. Title: Crochet book.
TT820.J32   746.4'34   78-11202
ISBN 0-672-52381-7

To Davie, whose wisdom has been my guiding light

Acknowledgments

The author gratefully acknowledges the assistance of the following companies in providing the yarns for the projects in this book:

Bernat, Emile & Sons Co., Uxbridge, Mass.
Brunswick Worsted Mills, Inc., Pickens, S.C.
Coats and Clark, Inc., Stamford, Conn.
The D.M.C. Corp., Elizabeth, N.J.
Lion Brand Yarn Co., New York, N.Y.
Spinnerin Yarn Co., Inc., South Hackensack, N.J.
Tahki Imports Ltd., Teaneck, N.J.
Ulmann, Bernhard, New York, N.Y.
William Unger & Co., Inc., New York, N.Y.

The author wishes to thank the editors of *Woman's Day* and *Good Housekeeping* magazines for permission to use some of her designs which originally appeared in their publications, and Adel Rootstein (U.S.A.), Inc., for the use of the mannequins.

The author also expresses her deepest appreciation to the following people for their creative assistance in producing this book:

Dorothy Holohan, Lori Levine, Julie Marschner, Gloria Morales, Andie Taras, Priscilla Brownlee, Honey Wolters, Robert Cohen, Margaret Drekauen, Alice Delman, and Linda Greene.

Table of Contents

Foreword — xi

Preface — xiii

Part I General Crochet Instructions

General Notes	1
The Slip Knot	1
The Chain Stitch	3
The Single Crochet	3
The Slip Stitch	5
The Half-Double Crochet	6
The Double Crochet	6
The Triple Crochet	7
The Double-Triple Crochet	9
Increasing	9
Decreasing	10
The Hazelnut Stitch	10
The Loop Stitch	11
The Reverse Stitch	12
The Lover's Knot	13
Casting into Fabric	14
Treble Crochet Casting into Fabric	15
Picking Up a New Ball and Changing Colors	15
Changing Colors in Mid-Row	16
Ribbed Crochet	16
Knotting and Cutting	17
Finishing	17
Joining	18
Tassels and Fringes	18
Loop Fringes	19
Unwinding from Both Ends	19
Pom-Poms	20
Looped Pom-Poms	21
Crochet Notation	21
Glossary of Abbreviations	23
Table of Crochet Hook Equivalents	24

Part II Crocheted Inserts and Additions to Fabric

Lotus T-Shirt	27
Sleeveless Tank Top	29
One- or Two-Sleeve Lotus T-Shirt	31
Long-Sleeved Net Topping	33
Sleeveless Tank Top Dress	36
Long-Sleeved Net-Topped Evening Gown	40
Tricolor Rosette Leotard/Tights	43
Poncho Dress Ensemble	45
Net Hat	48
Evening Purse Bag	51
Sturdy Tote Bag	53
Window Sunburst	55
Scallop Ruffle Kerchief	59
Rosette-Bordered Skirt	60
Teens' Bolero Top	63
Evening Shoulder Bag	65
Bridesmaids' Trailing Coverlet	66
Costume Leotard	68

Part III Ladies', Men's and Children's Wear

Whirlpool-Motif Overblouse	73
Barbary Coast Halter	75
Cotton Mini-Poncho	77
Striped Demi-Cloche	78
Three-Pouch Belt	79
One-Piece Sunsuit	81
Basic Brimmed Hat	83
Hand Warmer Muffler	85
Mini-Tank Halter	86

Cotton Sweater-Blouse	88	Mesh Rosette-Bordered Shawl	135
Winter Booties	89	Men's Winter Gloves	137
Multicolor Full Poncho	91	Toddlers' Hooded Coat	139
Patchwork-Motif Sweater	93	Disco Scarf	141
Glitter Coverlet	98	Summer Playsuit	143
Fluffy House Slippers	99	Ladies' Three-Season Gloves	146
Medieval Belt and Choker	100	Men's Ski Sweater	148
Men's Lounge Jacket	102	Boys' Hooded Sweater	150
Two-Piece Bikini	105		
Doily Camisole	107	**Part IV Crochet for the Home**	
Multicolor Ski Muffler	111		
Winter Sweater, Skirt and Hat Ensemble	112	Fruit Basket	155
		Op-Art Bedspread/Wall Hanging	156
Fan Shawl	116	Grid Curtain	160
Children's Striped Pullover	118	New York Skyline Wall Hanging	161
Oriental Tote and Slippers	120	Scintillating Blanket/Wall Hanging	163
Men's Cardigan	123	Oval Floor Mat	166
Victorian Blouse	125	Shopping/Laundry Bag	168
Men's Cossack Hat	129	Jute Planter	169
Rainbow Hooded Cape	130	Show Kitchen Towel	171
Deco Clutch	133	Interwoven Tablecloth	172

Foreword

Ever since the crafts boom began in the middle to late 1960s, the idea of creating with one's hands has brought hundreds of designers to my office at *Woman's Day*. The work they present covers many areas of crafts, from batik, embroidery and macramé to clay, weaving and wood. But if someone were to ask me what the most popular craft has been, I would say crochet. It is a medium that has enabled a lot of people to express themselves in a simple yet creative way. It is a technique that was borrowed from our grandmothers and then became an expression of its times with shawls, afghans, vests and granny squares turned out by the thousands. Its popularity is understandable, since it uses only one tool—the hook—to produce creations for wear or for use in the home, creations such as those in *Shanie Jacobs' Crochet Book*.

Shanie Jacobs was already an outstanding designer when she first came to my office in 1973 to show me a wonderful bias-striped poncho she had crocheted and which we subsequently presented in our February 1974 issue. She had just returned to New York City after six work-filled months of communal living with two friends and their seven children in an old wood-heated house in upstate New York. The three women had set up a rotating daily schedule that enabled one woman to carry out the household duties and care for the children while the other two crocheted. It was here that Shanie, who had never crocheted before joining the commune, really learned the basis of her craft in an environment of shared experiences where each gave of her specialty.

With time and experience she so finely honed her crochet techniques that she was able to teach herself to write concise instructions. She has also acquired the ability to convert knitting patterns to crochet, thereby widening her horizons. Since 1974 she has created thirty-six original designs for us and several more for *Good Housekeeping*'s *Needlecraft Quarterly* and *Cosmopolitan* magazine. In 1977 she opened a successful crochet and crafts gallery boutique in Soho in New York City which carries editions of her work and one-of-a-kind pieces. She now approaches her crochet as an artist would, or perhaps a sculptor. First, there is her interest in texture and pattern as in her tablecloth on page 172; then her unusual feeling for the body, as in her sleeveless tank top on page 29. She understands the human form and knows how to enhance it. One can almost call her garments "body wear." Underlying this feeling for form, whether it be one of her tops or a bedspread, is the basic understanding of its construction.

This, therefore, is a book whereby Shanie leads you step-by-step through the crochet process, beginning at the most elemental starting point—the slip knot. From there she takes you through all the basic stitches, plus some not so basic, and then into projects that will enable you to make such things as a fabulous tank top, a halter, a wall hanging or a sweater.

If you are a beginner, you will be able to learn to crochet from this book; the diagrams and instructions are clear and concise. If you are experienced, you will have a collection of beautiful and unique projects. So no matter what your skills are, I hope you will be as inspired as I am by Shanie Jacobs' crochet designs.

Theresa Capuana
Needlework and Crafts Editor
Woman's Day Magazine

Preface

Shanie Jacobs' Crochet Book has been published with the hope of sharing some of the immeasurable fulfillment that the practice of this wonderful craft provides. As experienced crocheters already know, the fact that crochet can produce fashionable garments or breathtakingly beautiful home decorations eventually becomes secondary to the hours of serenity it introduces into our rather hectic everyday lives. Happily, the portability of the craft affords us the opportunity to experience these times even when we are away from home.

In my desire to encourage the craft I have spared nothing in providing explicitness in Part I of this book. This is a "how-to" section designed to educate, and thus capture, the beginner in the basics of crochet, an area where other publications may have failed. The General Notes at the very beginning set the proper mood for learning to crochet; they present hints that will dispel the annoying obstacles which can frustrate and stop the beginner. Illustrations are given for each step of the basic techniques, not only demonstrating what to do, but assuring the novice that she has done her work correctly.

Similarly, the individual project instructions contain a minimum of abbreviations and condensed notations and a maximum of illustrations and explanatory text so that a beginner, having once practiced the pertinent basics explained in Part I, can confidently tackle any project in this book with the expectation of good results.

The various crocheted articles have been chosen to satisfy a broad spectrum of tastes. Emphasis has been placed on the classic approach, so that the ensuing years will not detract from the usefulness of the items produced. Part II is an exclusive section involving crocheting into fabric, which provides the striking qualities of hand crochet without the necessity for crocheting the entire garment. Part III contains a complete selection of wear that is fully crocheted, ranging from the nostalgic to the contemporary, the practical to the frivolous, the easily modified to the highly exacting. Part IV presents lengthy projects, a few of which sacrifice explicit instructions for personal creativity.

I trust you will make good use of this book in the years to come, taking full advantage of the paths it opens to the joys of crochet.

S.J.

Part I
General Crochet Instructions

General Notes

The instructions in Part I contain descriptions and illustrations of the various crochet stitches used in this book. There are some basic habits that you would do well to develop at the onset. These will enable you to practice and, subsequently, learn more easily, ultimately ensuring evenness and consistency in the completed projects you'll be making later.

1. Practice the basic stitches presented in Part I with a size J or K crochet hook on heavy, four-ply wool or acrylic yarn in a light color.

2. Every crochet hook has a flat, wide ridge section about one-quarter of the distance from the hooked end. Get into the habit of moving *every* loop you take on your hook (even including the basic slip knot) onto the *center* or widest part of this ridge (Figure I-1), by sliding your hook forward and then backward to remove the loop. Do this for *every loop of every stitch you make*. This operation should become second nature to you; it will guarantee a perfect and consistent stitch size for all of your work, as well as provide ease for entering each stitch as you work.

3. Unwrap a generous amount of yarn from the ball or skein from which you are working so that you are assured of a tension-free supply while crocheting. As soon as you feel the slightest tension, let out another generous supply of loose yarn.

4. Similarly, the immediate supply of yarn for your crocheting is provided by the length between your work and the turns on your left index finger (Figure I-6). To start with, you may feel comfortable with two or three turns on your index finger; later on, perhaps only one. In either event, this supply length should have *just* the amount of tension required to prevent the length of yarn from sagging—no more, no less. The look of your completed garment depends in great part on the control of this tension.

5. Learn to twist your hook before pulling your yarn loops through the crocheted stitches. You will quickly discern how much twist is needed to keep the desired loops caught, yet allowing the hook to pass smoothly through the crochet spaces without catching any unwanted loops or partial strands.

6. The text and illustrations in Part I of this book are intended for right-handed crocheters. They can easily be converted for left-handers by reading "left hand" for "right hand" and vice versa in the text and by observing all illustrations through a mirror propped up perpendicular to the pages of the book.

The Slip Knot

Most crochet begins with a series of chain stitches that are generated from the basic slip knot (*abbreviated: sl kn*). A simple way to form this knot is to start by wrapping the yarn around the first two fingers of the left hand, with the loose end crossing in front, as shown in Figure I-2. The loose end should be about 6" long, unless otherwise specified by instructions. Holding the crochet hook vertically, as illustrated in Figure I-3, slip the hook behind the yarn at the upper index finger and in front of the yarn at the lower part of this finger. Then swing the back of the hook downward so that it ends up still in a vertical position, but with the hook end pointing upward, as shown in Figure I-4. Catch the loop thus

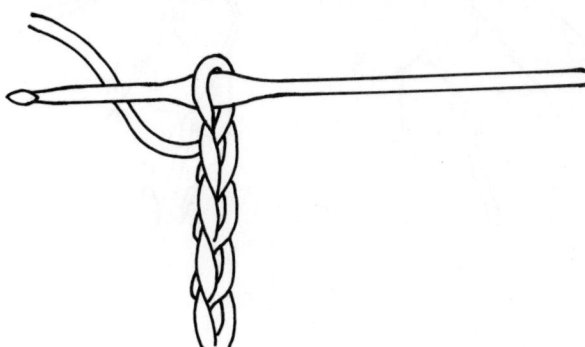

Figure I-1

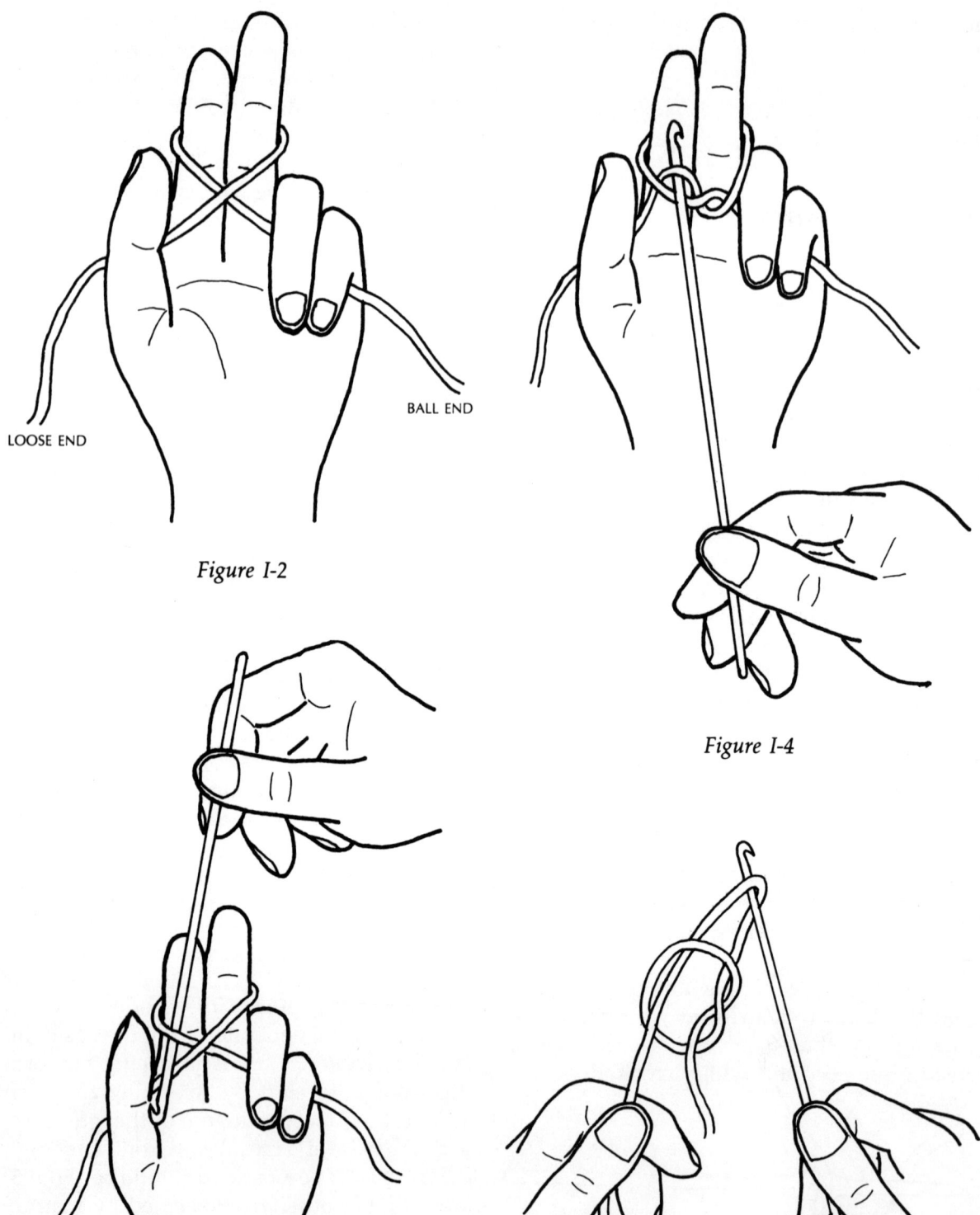

LOOSE END BALL END

Figure I-2

Figure I-4

Figure I-3

Figure I-5

formed with the hook and bring the knot onto the body of the hook by pulling upward, as depicted in Figure I-5, making sure to maintain your hold on the loose end with your left thumb.

The Chain Stitch

After making a slip knot, your crochet instructions will usually specify a certain number of chain (*abbreviated: ch*) stitches, i.e., ch 25. This chain, often called the "foundation chain," will determine the basic length of the rows of crochet work that follow.

To construct the chain, wrap two or three turns of yarn from the ball end firmly around the left index finger; grasp the knot part of the slip knot on your hook between the thumb and middle finger of your left hand, as shown in Figure I-6. With a motion of your left index finger, catch the yarn on the hook from behind, as shown in Figure I-6. This operation is called "yarn-over-hook" (*abbreviated: yoh*) and is often specified this way in crochet instructions. Still holding the knot firmly, draw the hook to the right, bringing the yarn through the loop for a distance great enough

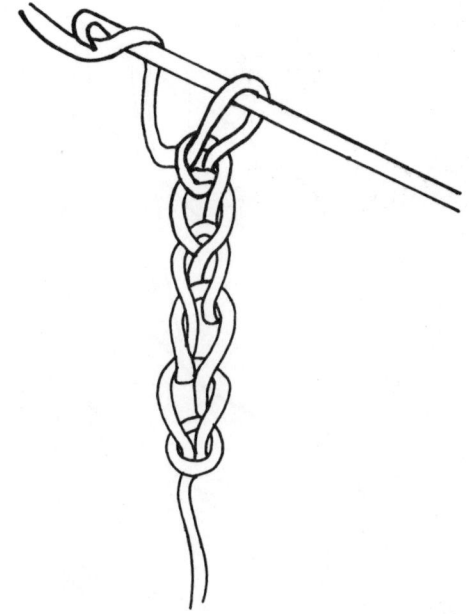

Figure I-7

to fit over the center of the ridge of the hook. This operation is termed "pull through loop."

To form additional chains, yarn-over-hook again, pull through loop, yarn-over-hook, etc., supplying new yarn around your index finger every few chains as needed. Your chain row should appear as in Figure I-7. When counting chains, count only the completed loops, not the loop remaining on your hook.

The Single Crochet

The single crochet (*abbreviated: sc*) is the simplest and most often used of all crochet stitches. Several of the projects in this book are made almost exclusively with this stitch, but the variations of pattern accomplished through color changes provide for a startling appearance of complexity in the look of the finished product.

To practice the single crochet, first make a chain. Holding the chain between the thumb and middle finger of the left hand, wrap two or three turns of yarn around your left index finger, as shown in Figure I-8. Not counting

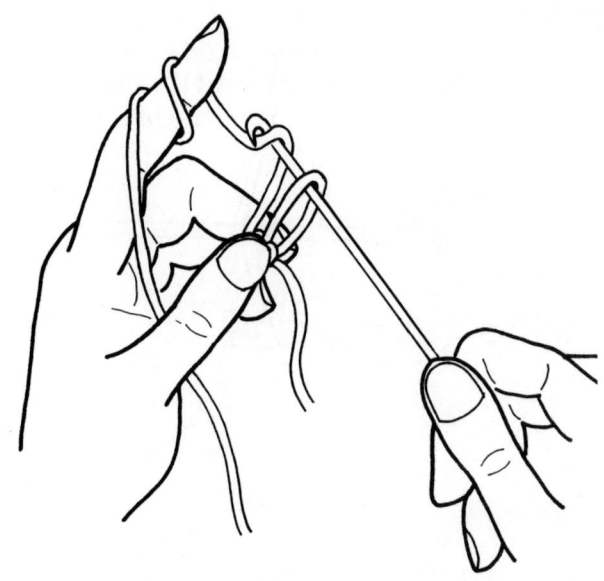

Figure I-6

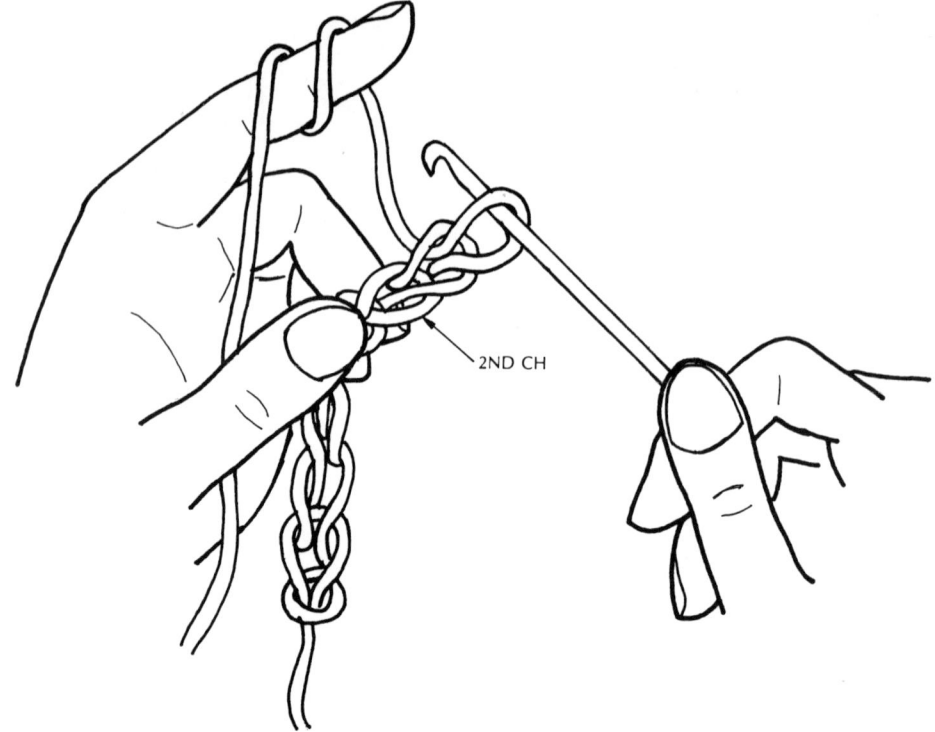

Figure I-8

the loop on your hook, locate the second chain from the hook, as indicated in Figure I-8; then insert the hook through this stitch, as shown in Figure I-9, being sure to keep two strands on top, one on bottom. With a movement of your left index finger, bring the yarn over the hook and catch it (yarn-over-hook) as depicted in Figure I-9. Draw the yarn

Figure I-10

arrow in Figure I-11, and repeat the preceding steps. Your row of single crochet should

Figure I-9

through the stitch (pull through loop), leaving you with two loops on your hook, as shown in Figure I-10. Yarn-over-hook again and pull through two loops, completing the single crochet.

To begin the next single crochet, insert hook in the next chain, as indicated by the

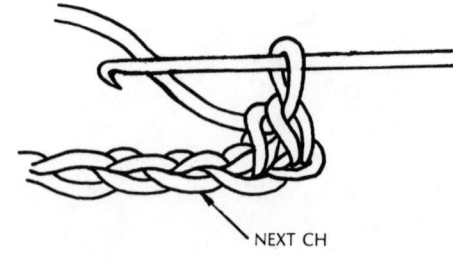

Figure I-11

appear as in Figure I-12. Note from Figure I-12 that the tops of the single crochet row are actually chains; you should have no trouble single-crocheting into your row of single

GENERAL NOTES 5

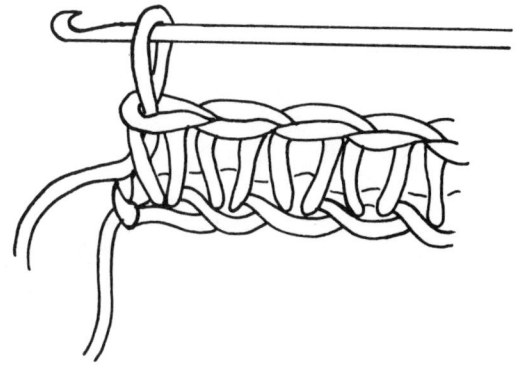

Figure I-12

crochet. If you wish to practice single-crocheting into a row of single crochet, complete your single crochet row, chain one, and turn work so that you will be heading in the same direction as before, as illustrated in Figure I-13. Then insert hook in first single crochet, as indicated by the arrow in Figure I-13.

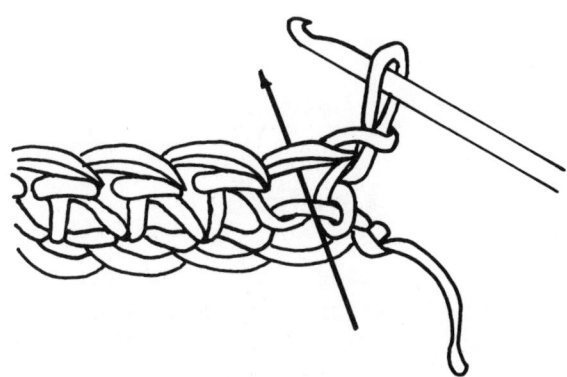

Figure I-13

The Slip Stitch

The slip stitch *(abbreviated: sl st)* is used to join the end of a row to the beginning in order to form a ring or tube, to reinforce edges of crochet work, or often to retrace your steps back down a row so that you can branch off from another point.

To make the slip stitch, first make a chain; begin by holding it in the position shown in Figure I-8, which is actually the best standard position for holding all crochet work, even after many rows have been completed. Insert

the hook in the second chain from the hook, as shown in Figure I-14; yarn-over-hook and pull through both loops, completing the slip stitch, as shown in Figure I-15.

Figure I-14

Figure I-15

To make a slip stitch on a single crochet row, simply insert your hook in the first stitch of the row, as shown in Figure I-13, yarn-over-hook, and pull through stitch and loop,

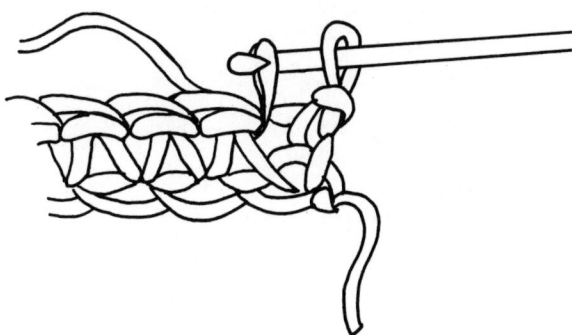

Figure I-16

as shown in Figure I-16. When the slip stitch is to be used to join the beginning of a chain row to the last chain just made, insert the hook through the first chain, as shown in Figure I-17, yarn-over-hook, and pull through stitch and loop, completing the slip stitch.

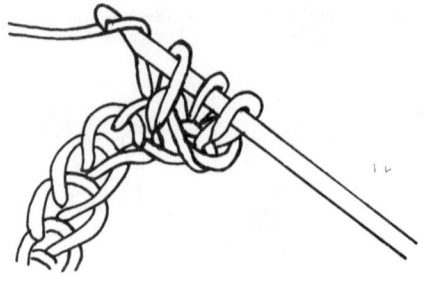

Figure I-19

pull through all three loops, completing the half-double crochet (*abbreviated: hdc*), as shown in Figure I-20.

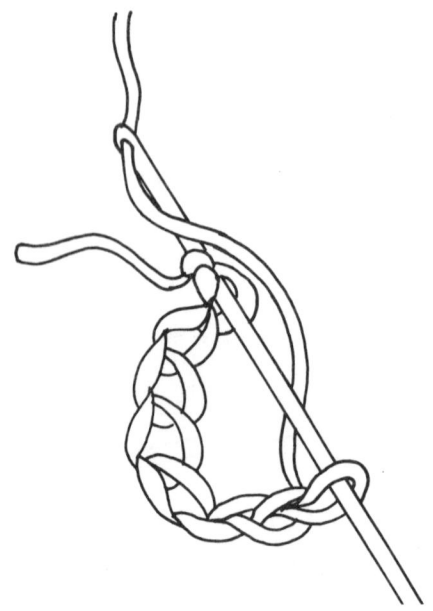

Figure I-17

Figure I-20

The Half-Double Crochet

With a foundation chain on your hook and holding your work in the standard position (Figure I-8), yarn-over-hook first and then insert hook in third chain space (*abbreviated: ch sp*) from hook, as indicated in Figure I-18.

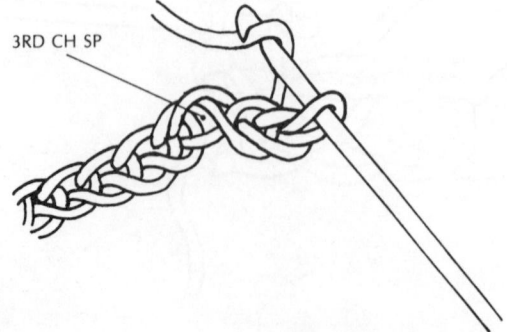

Figure I-18

Yarn-over-hook and pull this loop onto your hook, which gives you the three loops shown in Figure I-19. Now yarn-over-hook again and

The Double Crochet

The double crochet (*abbreviated: dc*) is a variation of the single, twice as high. The saving in space that it affords is made up for by the sacrifice in firmness.

It's best to practice the double crochet on a row of single crochet. First, chain three, giving you the configuration shown in Figure I-21; then turn your work around so that it is

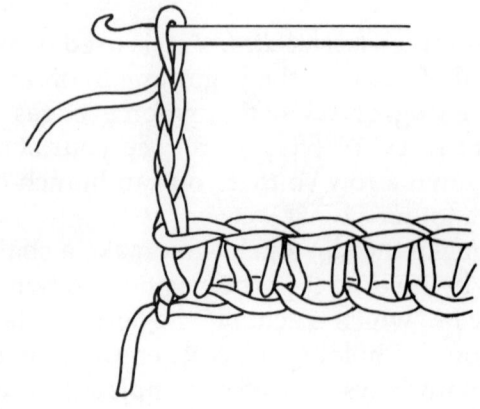

Figure I-21

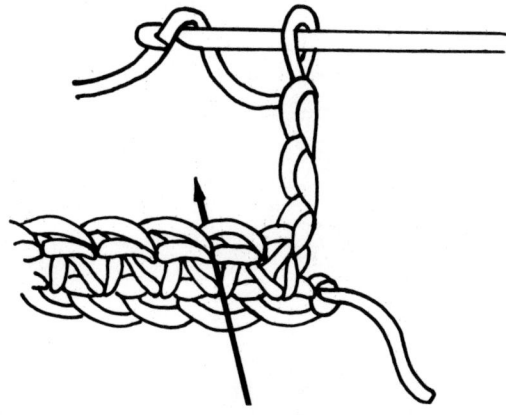

Figure I-22

Yarn-over-hook again and pull through the first two loops on your hook *only*, leaving you with two loops left on hook (Figure I-25). Yarn-over-hook for the last time and pull through these two loops, completing the double crochet (Figure I-26). To start your next double crochet, yarn-over-hook and insert hook through the second single crochet, etc.

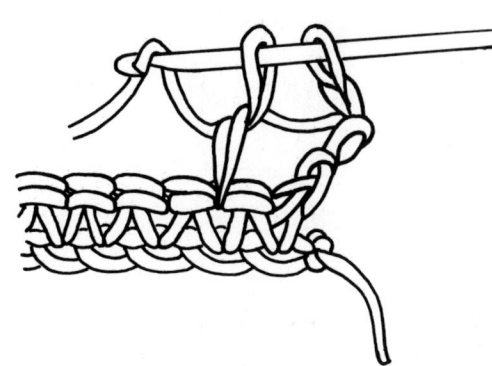

Figure I-25

in the position shown in Figure I-22. This turning operation is simply specified in crochet instructions as "turn." Now yarn-over-hook and insert hook through first single crochet, as illustrated by the arrow in Figure I-22. You must always catch the two top loops of *any* stitch, unless otherwise specified by instructions. Yarn-over-hook again (Figure I-23) and pull through the stitch and the two loops on your hook, leaving you with three loops on hook (Figure I-24).

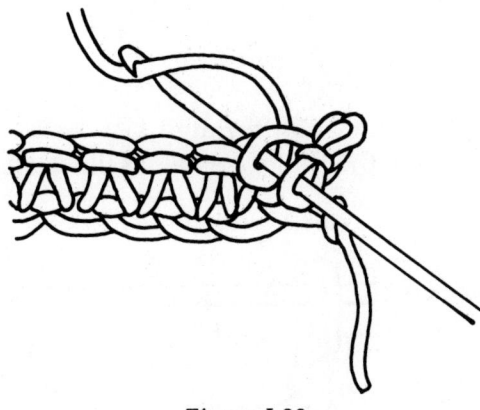

Figure I-23

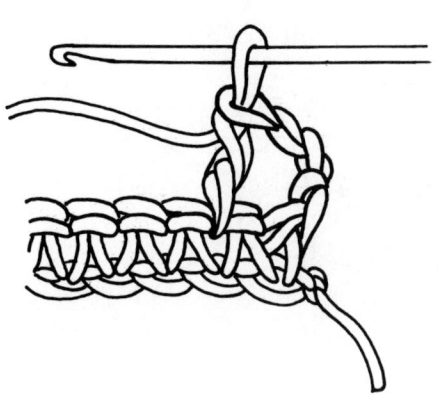

Figure I-26

The Triple Crochet

The triple crochet (*abbreviated: trc*), like the double, is simply a higher extension of the single. In its basic form, it comes out three rows (of single crochet) high, so you will be chaining four to turn at the end of your rows. A variation of the triple crochet, called the "long triple" is often made to match the height of five or more chains, and is also described in this section.

To make the triple crochet over a row of single crochet, chain four at the end of the row, turn, and yarn-over-hook *twice*, as

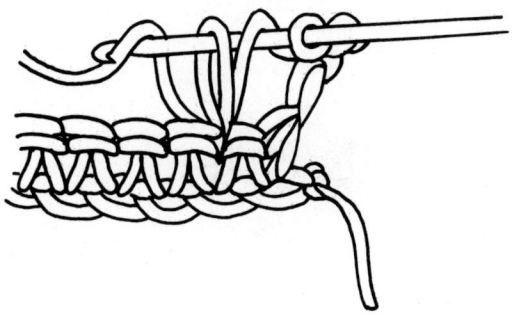

Figure I-24

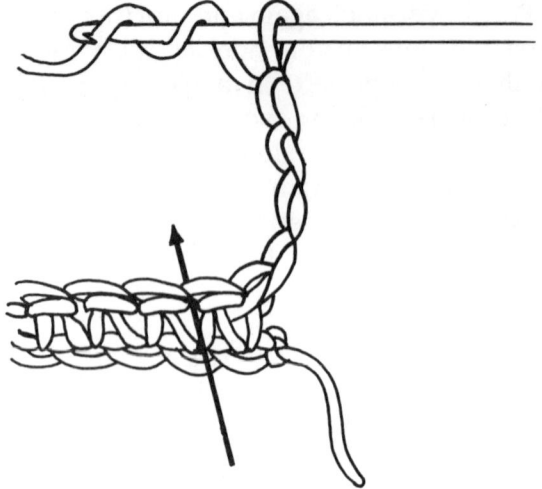

Figure I-27

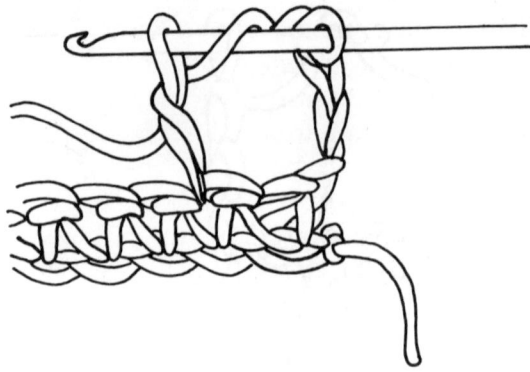

Figure I-29

shown in Figure I-27. Insert your hook through the second single crochet of the previous row, as indicated by the arrow in Figure I-27, yarn-over-hook again, and pull through, giving you four loops on your hook, as shown in Figure I-28.

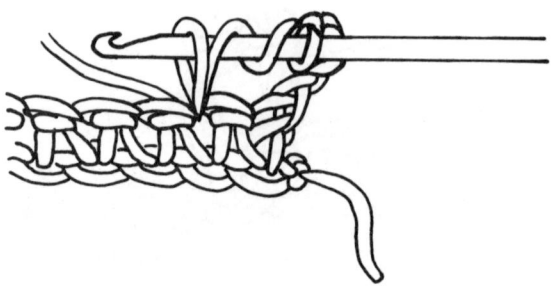

Figure I-28

For a long triple crochet of a chain-five height or more, at this point you would take exception to one of the rules given in General Notes. Instead of bringing every loop to the center ridge of your hook to give it its proper size, you would draw out the loops nearest the hook end to the distance to match your chain, keeping the body of your crochet hook parallel to your previous row.

To continue either type of triple crochet, yarn-over-hook and pull through the first two loops on your hook, giving you the configuration shown in Figure I-29—three loops on hook. Then yarn-over-hook and pull through two loops again, leaving you with the two loops shown in Figure I-30. Finally, yarn-

Figure I-30

over-hook and pull through last two loops, completing the triple crochet, as illustrated in Figure I-31.

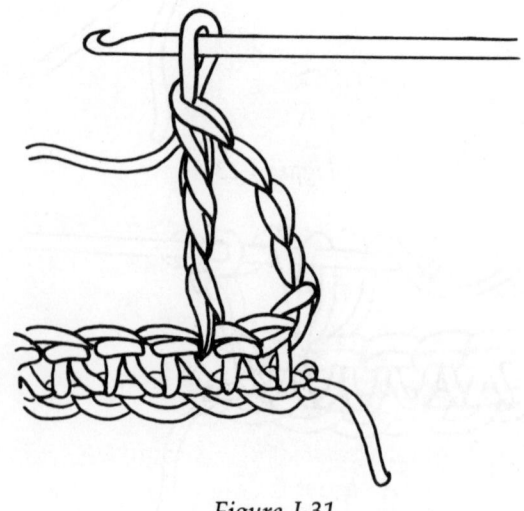

Figure I-31

To continue practicing the triple crochet, yarn-over-hook twice and enter the next single crochet of your previous row, etc. Do not forget to chain four before turning at the end of each row. You may then want to practice the long triple crochet by chaining six at the end of a row and raising your loops to match its length, as previously described.

The Double-Triple Crochet

A still taller extension of the triple crochet is the double-triple crochet (*abbreviated: dbl trc*), requiring a chain-five to turn at the end of a row to match its height. To make the double-triple crochet, yarn-over-hook three times and insert hook through the next stitch in the previous row. Yarn-over-hook again and pull through stitch, giving you five loops on your hook. Then continue as for triple crochet: yarn-over-hook and pull through two loops, yarn-over-hook and pull through next two loops, etc., until you have one loop left on hook, as shown in Figure I-32.

example, when working from the waistline of a sweater to the bustline, where more fullness is needed. Increasing may be done at the beginning, end, or at one or more points in the row of crochet; your specific instructions will tell you how many stitches to increase, and where.

The technique of increasing is the same for any of the basic crochet stitches—single crochet, double crochet, half-double crochet, etc.—and simply consists of making two or more stitches in the same space that you would ordinarily make one. Working two stitches in this space would be considered an increase of one stitch, making three stitches, an increase of two. When you reach these stitches on your next row of crochet, treat each one as an individual stitch; hence the length of your working row is increased.

See Figure I-33 for an example of increasing one stitch in the center of a single crochet row. At the point shown, you would yarn-over-hook and enter the hook where the arrow

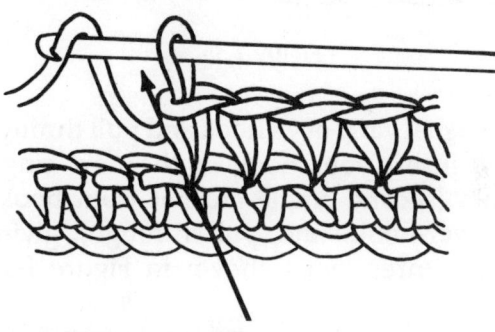

Figure I-33

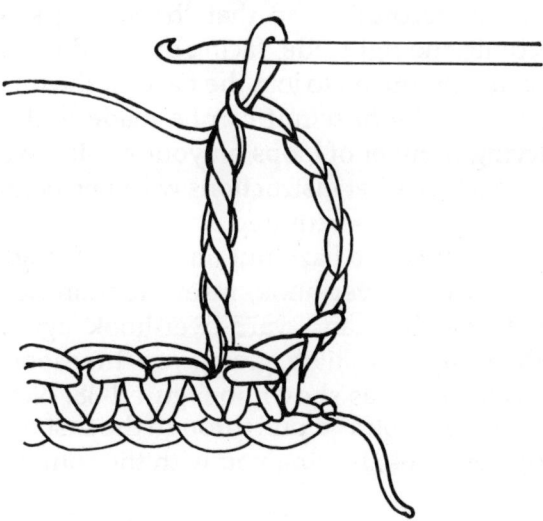

Figure I-32

Increasing

An increase (*abbreviated: inc*) is required when a row of crochet must be made longer than a previous row. This would be necessary, for

indicates, which is the same space in which you have just single-crocheted. After completing the single crochet, the two stitches would have the appearance of Figure I-34.

Figure I-34

Decreasing

Similarly, a decrease (*abbreviated: dec*) takes place where your next row must contain fewer stitches than your working row, such as when you are tapering the wrist end of a sleeve. Decreasing may also take place at either end of a row, or at one or more places within a row.

To decrease one stitch at the center of a single crochet row, begin a conventional single crochet by inserting your hook in the next single crochet from your hook, yarn-over-hook, and pull through, giving you the two loops shown in Figure I-35. Now, instead

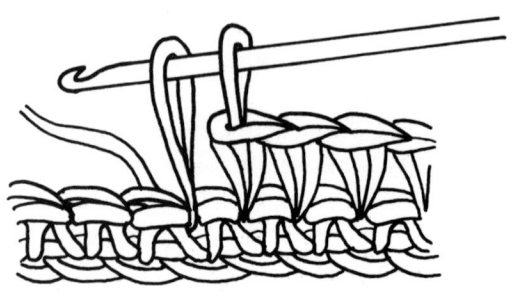

Figure I-35

of the usual yarn-over-hook and pull through loops, insert your hook in the next single crochet (second single crochet from hook), yarn-over-hook, and pull through, giving you the three loops shown in Figure I-36.

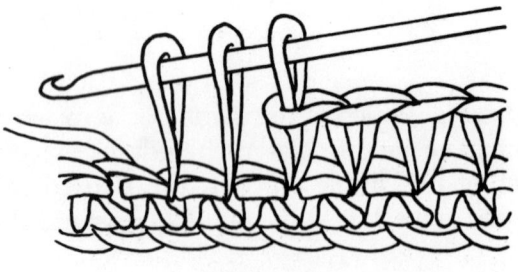

Figure I-36

Then yarn-over-hook again and pull through all three loops, completing the decrease, as shown in Figure I-37.

Decreasing a row of double crochet or triple crochet is similarly accomplished by making a conventional stitch up to the point where you have two loops on your hook, which, in each case, is the next-to-last step. Instead of performing the last step, make another

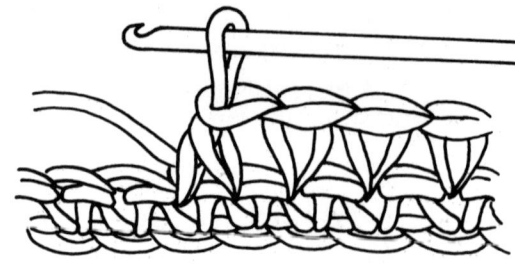

Figure I-37

double crochet or triple crochet in the next stitch, up to the point where there are three loops on your hook. Then yarn-over-hook and pull through all three loops to complete the decrease.

The Hazelnut Stitch

This stitch produces knobby clusters that rise in relief on the wrong side of your work. The effect is decorative, so that the wrong side becomes the right side, facing outward when you are instructed to join the parts of the final garment. The hazelnut can be made with a varying number of loops on your hook. Your particular crochet instructions will specify the amount of loops required.

To practice the hazelnut on a row of single crochet, yarn-over-hook, insert hook in next single crochet, and yarn-over-hook again. Pull through the stitch, giving you three loops on your hook, as shown in Figure I-38. Now yarn-over-hook and pull through the first two loops on hook, leaving you with the configu-

Figure I-38

GENERAL NOTES 11

ration shown in Figure I-39. Thus far you have done the equivalent of a double crochet minus the last step. To continue the hazelnut,

Figure I-39

yarn-over-hook again, insert hook in the same space as before, yarn-over-hook again, and pull through stitch. This leaves you with the four loops shown in Figure I-40. Then, as before, yarn-over-hook and pull through first two loops on your hook.

Figure I-40

To close the hazelnut at this point, yarn-over-hook and pull through all three loops, as shown in Figure I-41. The final appearance is illustrated in Figure I-42. A hazelnut thus made would be specified in your instructions as "a hazelnut with three loops to close,"

Figure I-41

Figure I-42

since it had three loops on the hook before the closing step. If your instructions specify a hazelnut with four, five, or more strands (or loops) on your hook, you would repeat the process—yarn-over-hook, insert hook in stitch, yarn-over-hook, pull through stitch, yarn-over-hook, pull through first two loops on hook—as many times as necessary to produce the specified number of loops on your hook. Then, to close, yarn-over-hook and pull through all loops.

The Loop Stitch

The loop stitch creates a pile effect, the depth of which can be varied by the height of a loop controlled by your left index finger.

To make the loop stitch on a row of single crochet, chain one at the end of your row, turn, and wrap the yarn over your left index finger from back to front, as shown in Figure I-43. Insert your hook in the first single

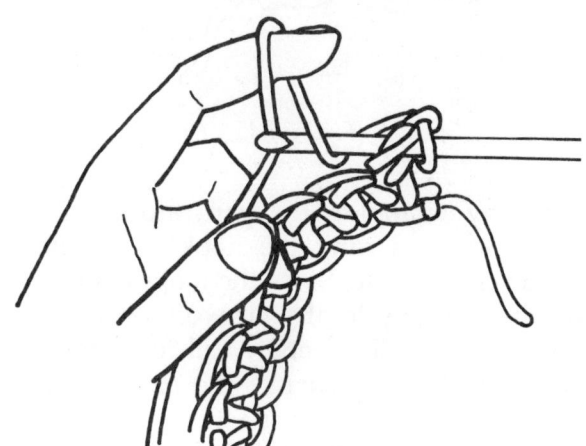

Figure I-43

crochet, passing it behind both strands of the loop on your finger. Then catch *both* strands of the loop and pull through the stitch, giving you the three loops on your hook shown in Figure I-44. Yarn-over-hook and pull through all three loops to complete the stitch, as illustrated in Figure I-45. Start your next loop

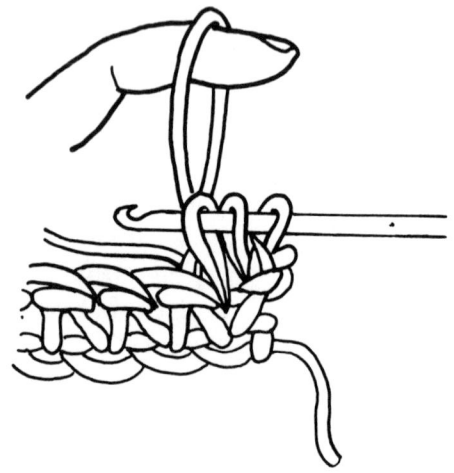

Figure I-44

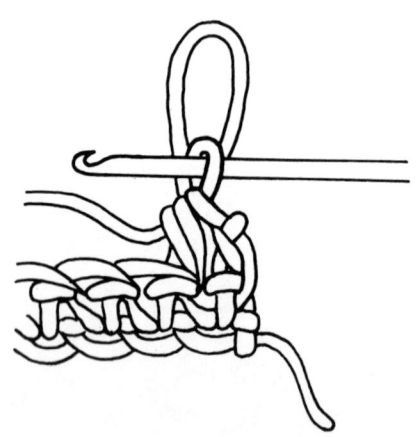

Figure I-45

stitch by wrapping the yarn around your finger and inserting the hook in the next single crochet, etc. Since the loops come out on the wrong side of your work only, your instructions will generally call for a row of single crochet to separate the rows of loop stitches. The loop stitch is actually a variation of the single crochet, so you should have no trouble recognizing the two top strands forming the individual stitches, when working into your loop stitch row.

The Reverse Stitch

The reverse stitch is a single crochet that is worked from right to left, that is, in the opposite direction from your usual work. It is almost exclusively used to bind the edges of crochet, such as the bottom of a sweater, the neckline, wristline, etc. It has the effect of strengthening an edge so that it cannot be stretched past its original length.

When your instructions call for a reverse stitch, it may have to be made into a finished row, with a starting point somewhere in the center of this row. To enter a finished single crochet row, make a slip knot on your hook and insert it in any single crochet on the row; then yarn-over-hook, as shown in Figure I-46.

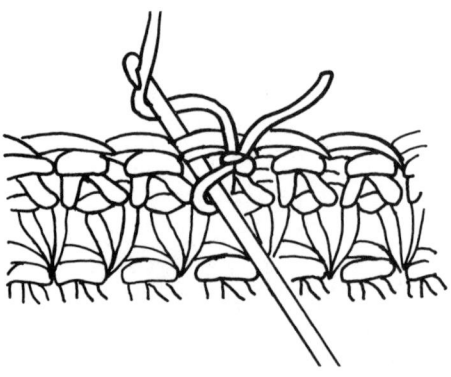

Figure I-46

Pull through the stitch, giving you two loops on your hook, as shown in Figure I-47. Yarn-over-hook again and pull through these two loops, thus completing a conventional

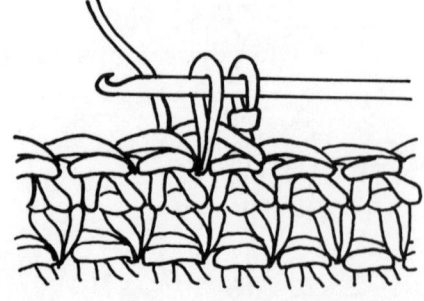

Figure I-47

single crochet (Figure I-48). Now insert your hook in the single crochet before your working stitch, as indicated by the arrow in Figure I-48. Yarn-over-hook from behind, as shown in Figure I-49, pull through the stitch, yarn-over-hook again, and pull through the two loops on your hook, completing the reverse stitch, as illustrated in Figure I-50. To start your next reverse stitch, insert your hook in the stitch before the working stitch, yarn-over-hook, etc.

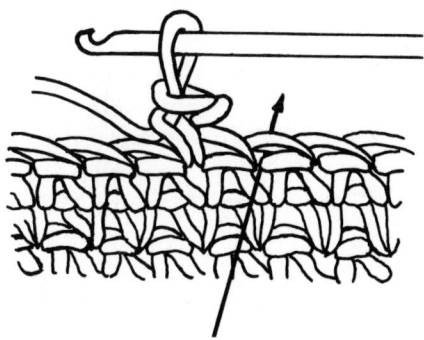

Figure I-48

Figure I-49

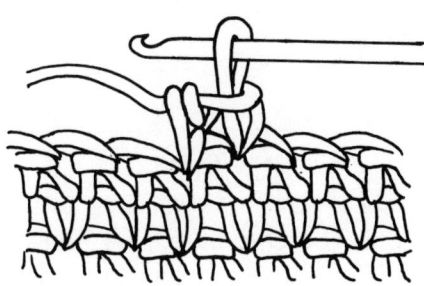

Figure I-50

The Lover's Knot

The lover's knot creates an open, lacy effect for shawls, capes, etc., simply by extending the first loop of a basic single crochet. To practice it, make a slip knot and chain one. Now pull the loop on your hook out to a distance of about 1½". Yarn-over-hook and pull through loop, as illustrated in Figure I-51. Insert your hook in the space between your original chain-one loop and the strand just drawn through it, as indicated by the arrow in Figure I-51. Yarn-over-hook and pull through loop, giving you the two loops shown in Figure I-52. Yarn-over-hook again and pull through these two loops to complete the lover's knot, as depicted in Figure I-53.

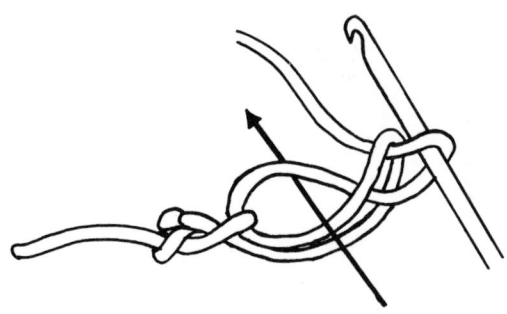

Figure I-51

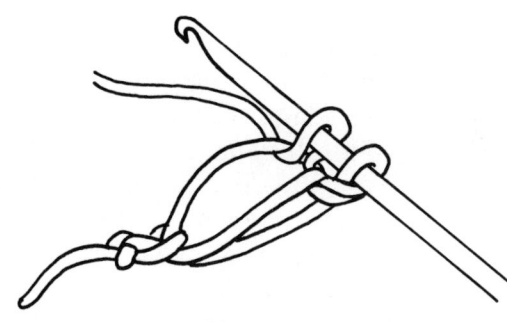

Figure I-52

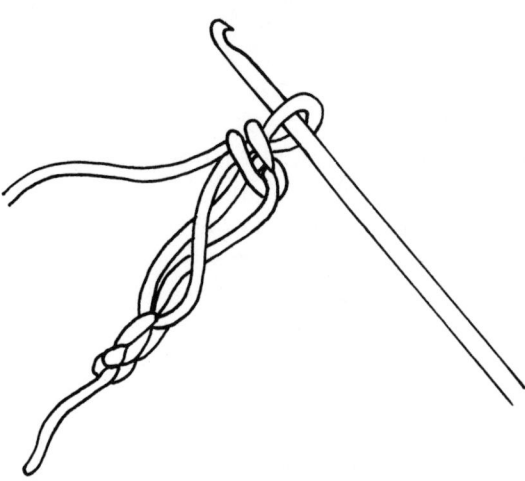

Figure I-53

The loop on your hook can now be drawn out again for your second stitch. To practice joining the lover's knot, as you will be required to do in your second and later rows of crochet, make a few more lover's knots, turn, and insert the hook through the two top strands of the knot part of the second lover's knot from your hook, as indicated by the arrow in Figure I-54. Single-crochet to this knot: yarn-over-hook, pull through stitch, yarn-over-hook, and pull through two loops.

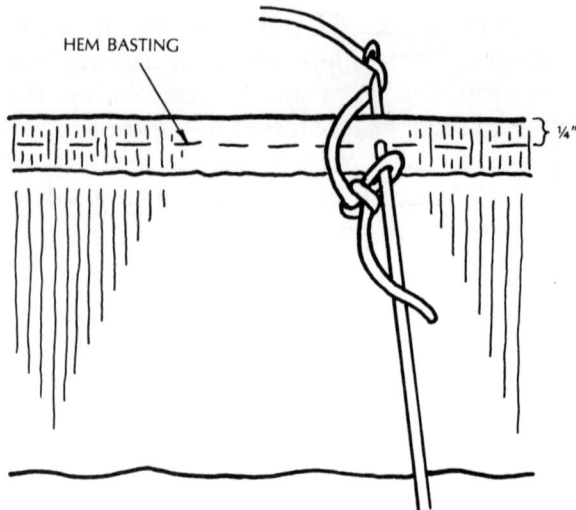

Figure I-55

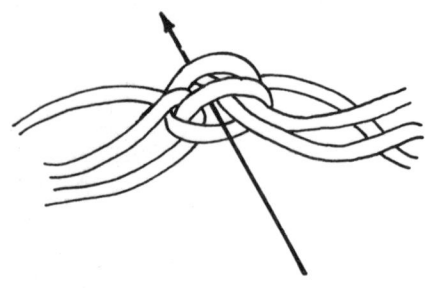

Figure I-54

Casting into Fabric

All of the projects in Part II of this book require casting into the material of a garment to produce the foundation of crochet into which the various designs are to be inserted. To practice this simple process, baste a ⅜" to ½" hem into the end of a scrap piece of ribbed cotton fabric for about 6" or so. Instead of using a large crochet hook and heavy yarn as suggested for the previously described stitches, you must use a number 13 steel hook and fairly fine yarn, such as number 5 pearl cotton, for casting into fabric.

Make a slip knot, and, holding your work so that you are facing the inside of the hem, insert your hook into the fabric at a distance of about ¼" from the edge, as shown in Figure I-55. The insertion of the hook should be accomplished with a gentle, vibratory motion, with your left index finger backing up the fabric so as to prevent "stabbing" the material and thereby producing a large hole. Yarn-over-hook and pull the loop through the material, giving you two loops on your hook, as shown in Figure I-56. Yarn-over-hook again and pull through the two loops,

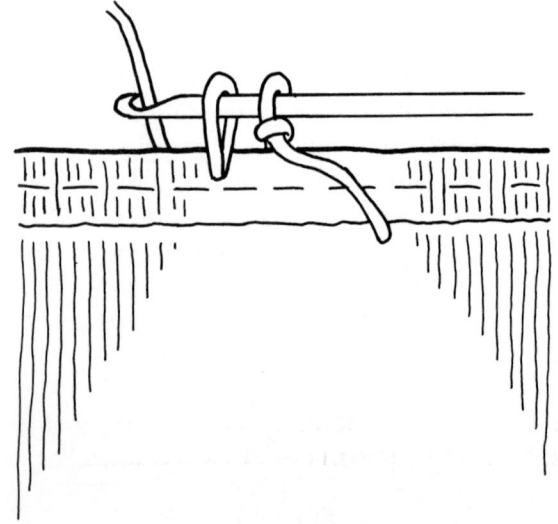

Figure I-56

completing the cast stitch, as illustrated in Figure I-57. As you can see, the cast stitch is basically a single crochet, using the hole in the material as a loop. Enter the material for your next stitch at the same distance from the edge, about ⅛" or slightly more from your first point of entrance.

GENERAL NOTES 15

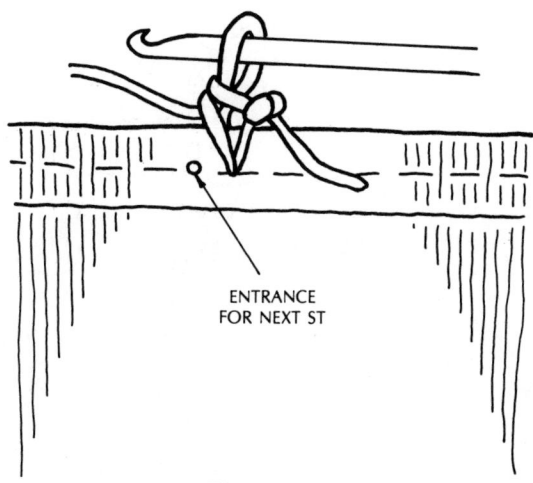

Figure I-57

Treble Crochet Casting into Fabric

A variation of the single crochet type of cast is the treble crochet cast. It begins in the same manner as the single crochet type of cast, but after the first stitch is completed, a chain is then made to the length specified in your particular instructions. Then yarn-over-hook twice, insert hook through material in the proper place for your second stitch, yarn-over-hook again, and pull through material, bringing the loop out to match the length of your chain. The remaining steps are the same as for the long triple: yarn-over-hook, pull through the first two loops, yarn-over-hook, pull through two loops, yarn-over-hook, pull through the last two loops. For your next stitch, yarn-over-hook twice and insert the hook through the material as before, etc.

Picking Up a New Ball and Changing Colors

If you find yourself running out of yarn while crocheting, don't wait too long before bringing in a new ball. When the ball end is about 12" long, take the start of a new ball and match it tip-to-tip to the old ball end. Then, taking both strands together, tie a firm single knot about 4" from the tips. You may then continue crocheting right past the knot, hiding the loose ends later.

Introducing a new color usually takes place at the end of a crochet row. If this row is a single crochet row, insert your hook in the last stitch of the previous row, yarn-over-hook, pull through the loop, and then yarn-over-hook with your new color, as shown in Figure I-58. Pull through the last loop with the new color, completing the single crochet, as illustrated in Figure I-59.

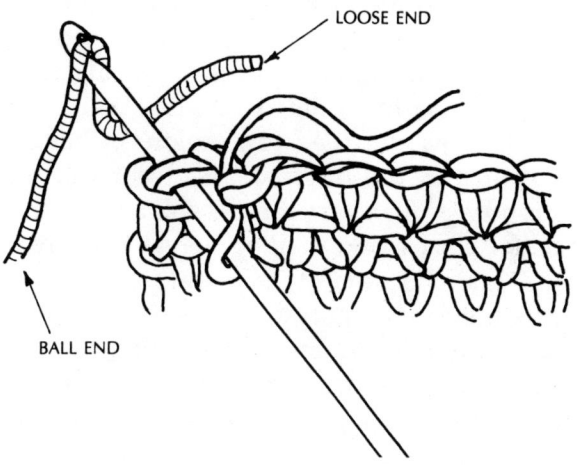

Figure I-58

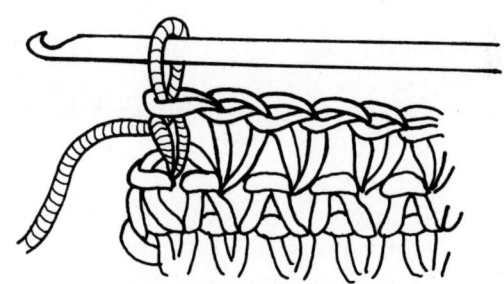

Figure I-59

The length of the loose end of your new color when yarning over hook should generally be the same length as that you will be instructed to cut the old color loose end. If the instruction calls for an irregularly long end (greater than 6"), it probably is going to be used in a joining operation, so you should limit your new color loose end to 5". If you are instructed to change color at the end of a row that is other than single crochet, begin the last stitch with the old color and bring it to the next-to-last step. Then yarn-over-hook with the new color, as previously described, and complete the stitch, just as for the single crochet.

Changing Colors in Mid-Row

Rarely will you be instructed to change colors in mid-row unless your project calls for an inserted pattern of one or more new colors against the background of your original color. Where the pattern calls for no more than 2" or so per row of the new color(s), before returning to the original, the technique of "stranding" (carrying the old color along the back of your work, making it available to be used again as needed) can save you a good deal of time and energy. This is so because it does away with the need for cutting the old color, hiding its loose end, reintroducing the old color with a slip knot, and then having to hide its loose end. Without stranding, this process would have to be repeated for each row that requires a color change. What is being sacrificed for this saving? Nothing but a series of loose yarn loops on the wrong side of your work.

The technique of changing colors in mid-row is the same as that described in the previous section for changing at the end of a row: you simply complete your stitch by yarning over hook with the new color. The important fact to remember in this case is that your next stitch, which is done completely in the new color, is counted as the first stitch of the new color. Similarly, the last stitch of the new color is closed by yarning over hook with the original color.

To practice stranding on a single crochet row, change to a new color somewhere in mid-row and make three single crochets with the new color, allowing the ball end of the original color to hang down out of the way. Then complete the fourth single crochet by yarning over hook with the original color. The loose strand should have just enough tension to prevent it from sagging, but not enough to bind your crochet work, as illustrated in the back view of Figure I-60.

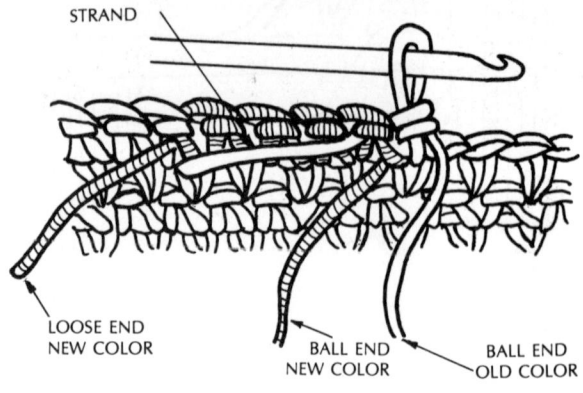

Figure I-60

Ribbed Crochet

Some instructions call for crocheting in the back loop only, which is contrary to the general rule of always catching the two top strands of a chain or stitch. This variation produces a ridged, or ribbed, effect in the texture of your work. The arrows in Figure I-61 indicate the points of hook insertion in a chain and single crochet row for ribbed crochet. The remainder of the stitch is performed in the same manner as the conventional stitch.

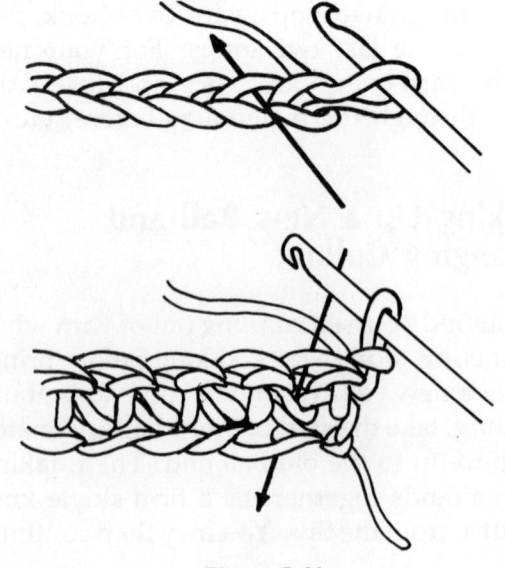

Figure I-61

Knotting and Cutting

When your instructions call for knotting yarn and cutting (sometimes referred to as "breaking off"), the knotting is done with your crochet hook, not by hand. The knot is formed by yarning over hook and pulling a loop (as long as specified) for your end length through the loop on your hook. This operation amounts to nothing more than a chain-one with a long loop, which is then cut at its peak with sewing scissors, as shown in Figure I-62. The ball end of the yarn is then gently withdrawn.

time. The process itself consists of threading the end through the yarn needle, bringing the end to the wrong side of your work, and then weaving the yarn back through each individual stitch of the row from which the end emanates. This is done for a distance encompassing about eight stitches, at which point a single knot is tied directly to a crocheted stitch, as shown in Figure I-63. After knotting, the yarn is "hidden" again by weaving through three more stitches; then the yarn is cut right at the level of the crochet with sewing scissors.

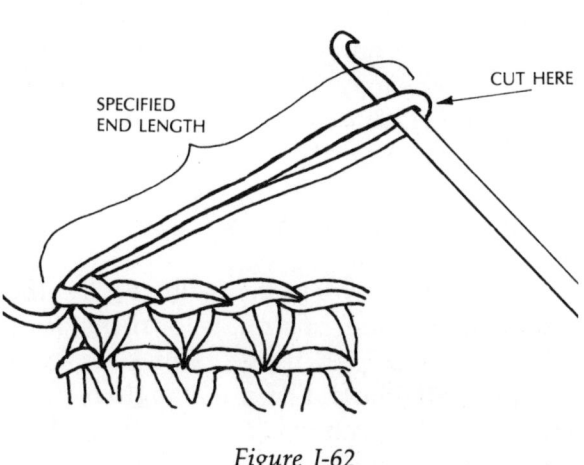

Figure I-62

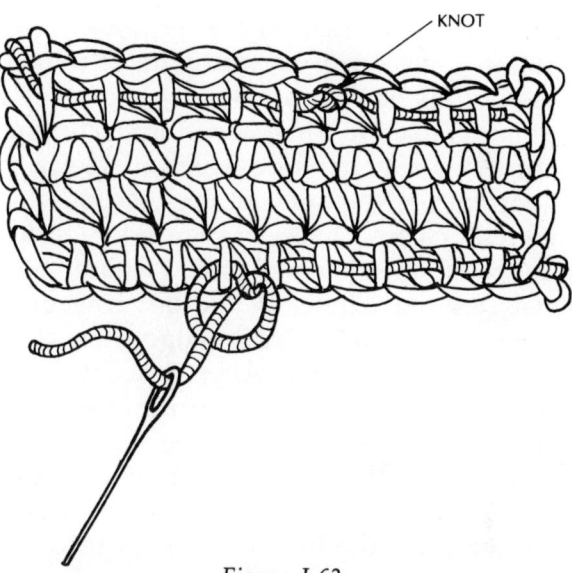

Figure I-63

Finishing

After completing a crocheted project, you will be left with a number of loose ends which, in some cases, may amount to a good many. Try to avoid the feeling that now, since the crochet work is completed, you can rush through the finishing process. Remember that the appearance and strength of the final product relies greatly on the care taken during finishing. Indeed, a project involving many color changes may require more time for finishing than it will for the actual crocheting, but will be well worth the effort.

Finishing is accomplished through the use of a yarn or tapestry needle that has an eye wide enough to allow facile threading of the yarn ends. The needle should be at least 2" long, the longer lengths saving you some

When you are finishing a slip knot end that began a chain row, hide it behind the vertical loops of your first row of crochet, as illustrated at the bottom of Figure I-63. When hiding the end of a last row, travel it through the vertical loops of this row, as depicted at the top of Figure I-63. When finishing the different-colored ends of a color-change row, first take each end in either hand and, by a gentle pulling action, "steer" the last stitch into position, so that the colors are properly aligned. Then finish each end as described above in the row of its color.

The tension for your running stitches should be firm enough to keep the yarn snugly against the crochet but not so tight as to cause binding.

Joining

Joining is accomplished with the use of the yarn needle in a somewhat similar manner to finishing. The length of yarn needed to join two sections of crochet for any given distance amounts to about three times this distance; many of the projects in this book instruct you to leave such ends as provision for the finishing operation. Where these ends are longer than one yard or so, you may find it tedious to have to weave the entire length through your crocheted stitches at the beginning of the join. Instead, you may want to cut such ends to a length of one yard and then reenter a new piece of yarn when the first runs out, as described below.

Joining, like finishing, is performed on the wrong side of your work, which is especially important if you are joining sections of different colors, since it allows for easier hiding of the joining yarn. Figure I-64 illustrates the joining of the last row of a single crochet section to the edge of another single crochet section. After threading the loose end of your joining yarn through the yarn needle, cross over the border, weave down the second piece, cross back over the border, weave down the first piece, etc., as depicted in Figure I-64. Always try to catch two loops of each piece to provide for strength, and avoid passing over spaces, or else your joining yarn will show on the right side.

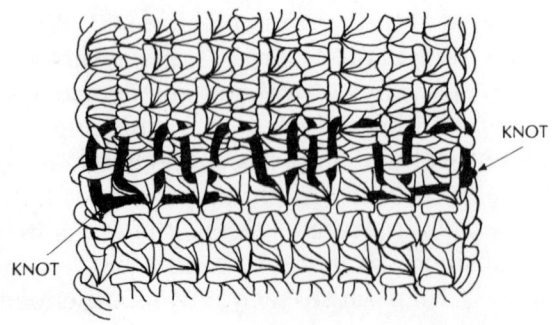

Figure I-64

End the join by single-knotting to the last stitch with your yarn needle (as shown in Figure I-63) and traveling the yarn for three more stitches to hide it before cutting, just as for finishing. If your seam ends at the very end of a crocheted piece, the hiding operation should be performed back along the direction from which you just finished the join (Figure I-64). Similarly, if the pieces you are to join do not have a loose end left that is long enough for this purpose and you must start your join with a new piece of yarn, travel it for three stitches first and then single-knot it to the stitch at the beginning of your join. If the seam is to begin at the very edge of the crochet, this direction of initial travel will be opposite to the direction of joining.

The tension of your joining stitches should be firm enough to prevent separation of the joined pieces when wearing the garment but not so tight as to distort the crochet at either side of the seam.

Tassels and Fringes

Your crochet instructions will specify the length and number of strands (or turns) for a particular tassel or fringe. Either is constructed with the aid of a rectangular cardboard template, about 2" in width and ½" longer than the specified length of tassel or fringe. After making the template, wrap it lengthwise with the proper number of turns of yarn, as shown in Figure I-65. The final

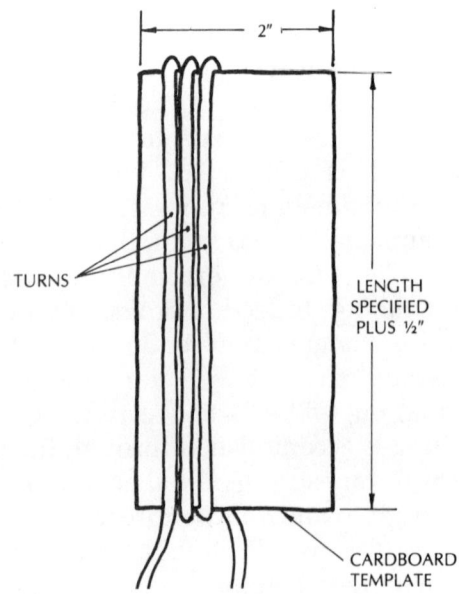

Figure I-65

number of strands will be twice the number of turns on your template. Then slip the yarn off the template and, while holding the top strands firmly together, cut the bottom strands off with sewing scissors, about ¼" from the end.

With the wrong side facing you, catch all of the strands with a crochet hook of a large enough size through the last two loops at the end or edge of your crochet, as shown in Figure I-66. Yarn-over-hook with all the strands at their centerpoint, as shown in Figure I-66, and pull through the loops.

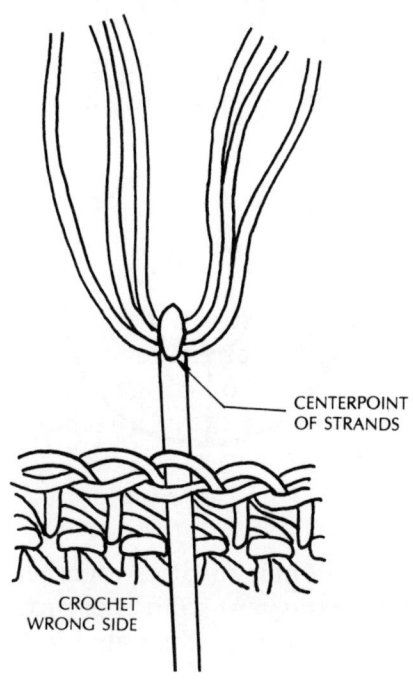

Figure I-66

Yarn-over-hook again with all the strands, as illustrated in Figure I-67, and pull completely

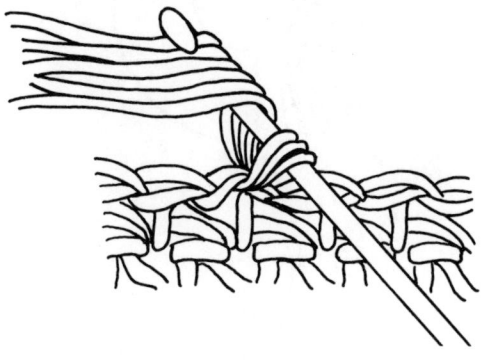

Figure I-67

through the loop, finishing the attachment, as shown in Figure I-68.

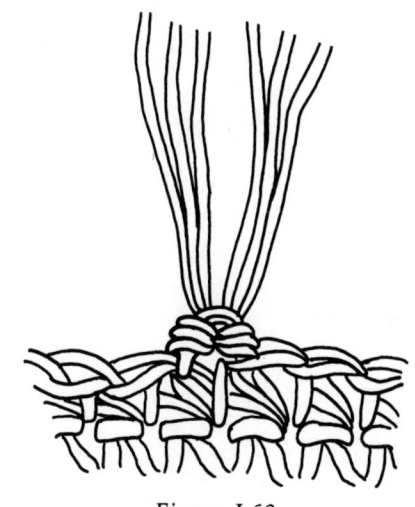

Figure I-68

Loop Fringes

An easy way to attach a fringe continuously along a border of crochet is by means of a loop fringe, which does not require a template or any cutting. Worked with the wrong side of your work facing you, it consists simply of the loop stitch made with the proper number of strands and pulled out to the specified length. After completing a border with this stitch, the ends may be cut off to provide the effect of a conventional fringe.

Unwinding from Both Ends

In those cases when your instructions call for a small amount of crochet using two strands of the same color, you may save yarn by using the inner and outer ends of your ball or skein simultaneously. If you cannot get to the inner end, as in the case of a bobbin, wind your own ball for the amount of yarn required.

To wind a tangle-proof ball that will allow you to use yarn from the inside and outside simultaneously, start by grasping a 12" loose end between your right thumb and index finger. Then wind about six turns around your index and middle fingers, as shown in Figure I-69. Slip these turns off your fingers withdrawal. You can wind such a ball from your skeins or bobbins before starting to crochet and secure the outer end by hiding it under one or two strands on the outer surface of your ball.

Pom-Poms

Pom-poms are an alternative to tassels for finishing tie ends. They also make decorative lampshade and light bulb pulls just by themselves. To make a pom-pom, cut two circles out of a piece of light cardboard to the diameter specified in your instructions. Then slit these discs and cut out internal circles ¾" in diameter, as shown in Figure I-71.

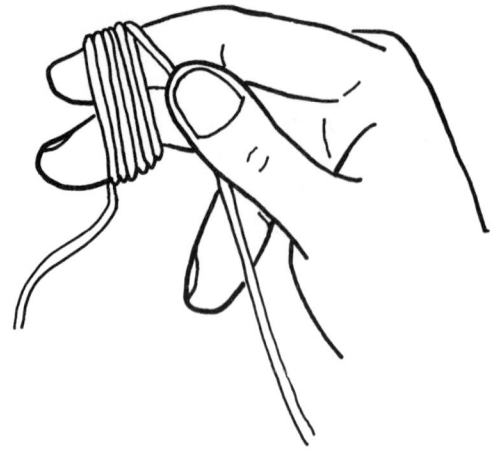

Figure I-69

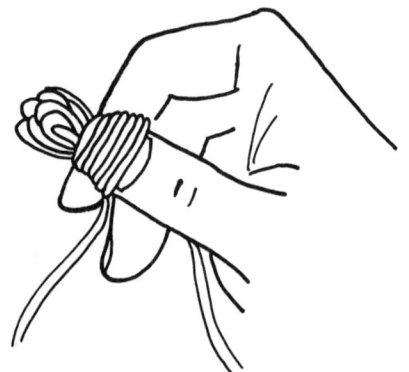

Figure I-70

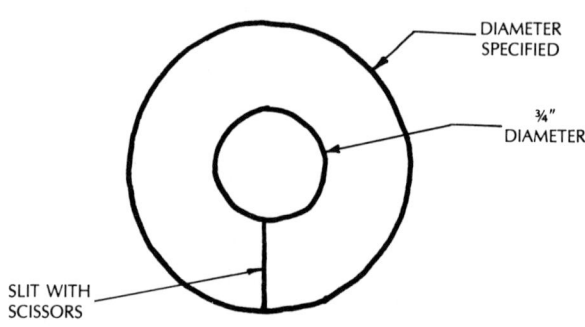

Figure I-71

and, keeping your thumb grasp still firm on the initial loose end, wind a dozen turns at right angles to your original turns, as shown in Figure I-70, allowing them to overlap onto your thumb. This action will begin to form a cuplike indentation in the ball around your thumb. Turn the ball to a slightly different angle and wind another dozen turns, allowing them to overlap your thumb. Continue in this manner, turning the ball at different angles and allowing the yarn to overlap your thumb. If a large enough ball is wound this way, your thumb will be completely hidden inside it. When completed, the removal of your thumb will expose a hollow "well" from which the initial loose end can be withdrawn without any danger of tangling.

This method of ball winding can also be applied to crochet where only one strand is required. It can save you a good deal of time during crocheting by virtue of its ease of yarn

Hold the pair of discs together and start wrapping the yarn strands of proper color(s) for your project, as illustrated in Figure I-72.

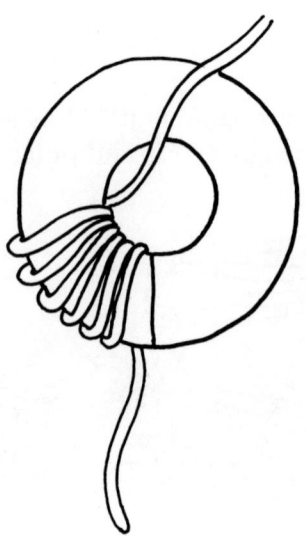

Figure I-72

Be sure the slits in both pieces are lined up so that you can get your yarn through the opening for each turn. Continue wrapping all around discs and then back until the central hole is filled with yarn.

Using sharp sewing scissors and starting at the outside circumference, cut the yarn along a circular line which would be the extension of the edge of the discs. When you reach the edge of the discs, slip the blade of your scissors between the discs to aid in cutting. At this point hold the yarn securely at the center, using your thumb and forefinger. When finished cutting all strands, take a length of yarn and run it between the discs around the centers of the yarn wraps, tying a tight double knot to secure them. Then slip discs off the pom-pom.

Looped Pom-Poms

An interesting pom-pom variation is made with the use of a four-tined fork as a template. Begin by draping a 12" section of the proper color yarn in half in the center opening of the fork (Figure I-73). This section of yarn will be used to tie the pom-pom when completed.

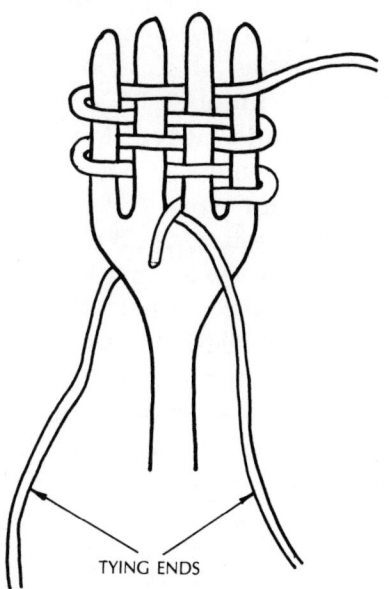

Figure I-73

Then, using the strand(s) of proper color(s), thread through the same center notch, leaving the shortest end possible, and weave through the tines in the fashion illustrated in Figure I-73. Hold the short end firmly against the fork with your thumb and forefinger.

When the fork tines are tightly filled with the yarn wraps, bring the tying ends over in a single knot at the top of the fork. Pull this knot tighter and tighter as you lift the wraps off the tines, and tie it double when completed. Use the tying end to attach the pom-pom to your work.

Crochet Notation

This section explains the meaning of the terms and symbols in general crochet use, both in this book and in others, and, together with the Glossary of Abbreviations which follows, should enable you to comply with any crochet instruction.

* The asterisk introduces a portion of crochet that is to be repeated a number of times. The end of this portion is indicated by the word "repeat."

Row and round A row is a complete line of crochet that is usually ended by a turning chain and then worked back on itself. Sometimes the turning chain is given in the beginning of the next row of instructions. A round is worked in one direction only to give a circular or tubular format to the crochet, and often requires the use of a safety pin as a marker to aid you in keeping track of its beginning.

Chain space The space between the two top strands and bottom strand of a chain stitch, into which a crochet stitch is worked.

Chain-1 space, chain-2 space, etc. The space formed by one, two, or more chains is often treated as a loop in itself. You crochet into it by inserting your hook directly into this space.

Row space The spaces left at either end of crocheted rows as a result of the loops formed by the turning chains, or the chain-one space itself, may be treated as stitches in order to crochet along such edges.

Stitch gauge A stitch gauge is given at the beginning of most instructions to ensure that the dimensions of your finished piece will coincide with those of the designer. It gives the number of stitches and rows per inch, using the hook and yarn specified. If you are using a yarn of a different thickness than that specified, you may use a hook one or two sizes up or down from the specified size to achieve the correct gauge. As stated in General Notes, the habit of slipping every loop onto and then off the ridge of your hook will assure that you attain the proper gauge with the proper yarn.

Even row (or round) Sometimes notated as "work even," this term simply means to work a row (or round) without increasing or decreasing.

Turning chain A turning chain is the chain you make at the end of a row of crochet to bring the following row to the proper height for the stitches it requires. For a row of single crochet, it is usually a chain-one; for half-double crochet, a chain-two; for double crochet, a chain-three; etc. For all rows *except* a single crochet row, the turning chain counts as the first stitch of the new row; hence you will usually be instructed to "skip first stitch" of the previous row. When ending a row, your last stitch will be worked into the top of the turning chain, thus retaining the proper number of stitches in each row.

2 Strands Where crochet instructions specify the use of two or more strands, these are held together and treated as one throughout all aspects of crochet, including changing of colors, knotting, cutting, joining, etc.

2 Single crochet, 3 double crochet, etc. When a number precedes the abbreviation for a stitch, work that many stitches into the same space where you would normally work one.

( ) Parentheses are used similarly to the asterisk pairs to define a complex stitch pattern that you will be asked to repeat a number of times, as in: (trc in next dc, ch 1, trc twice in next sc) 6 times . . . ; or used to give a title to a particular pattern, as in: . . . dc 4 times in same sp (shell made) . . . ; or to describe a special way of increasing, i.e.: . . . hdc twice in next trc (inc made) . . . ; or also used to assure you or correct you as to the number of stitches to be made in a particular row, as in: . . . sl st to first sc (42 sc made). When the parentheses enclose a pair of numbers separated by a comma, the instructions you are following include information for three different sizes. The smallest size is usually outside the parentheses, then the next largest, then the largest. Where a garment can be worn by both men and women, the women's Small, Medium and Large sizes are given first with the use of parentheses; then the men's sizes follow, with the similar use of brackets.

Picot Any looped or scalloped pattern which is usually based on a chain that is joined back on itself at some point is called a picot. It is often used as a decorative border for crochet. Since such borders call for repetition of this pattern, it will be most often defined after a set of instructions by parentheses, as in: . . . sc in next loop, ch 7, sc in 5th ch from hook (picot made). Make 12 picots . . . .

Marker pins A small brass safety pin fastened to a loop in the last stitch of a round and then moved to the last stitch of the ensuing rounds is often required to keep track during crocheting in the round. Where there are to be increases or decreases in one or more places in a series of rows or rounds, the corresponding number of safety pins are similarly used and moved. Markers are also used to indicate where a sleeve or pocket is to be joined to your work.

Break off and fasten Also notated as "fasten off," this phrase is simply telling you to cut the yarn and knot it to the work. The General Crochet Instructions in Part I call for knotting with your crochet hook, so the specific project instructions require that the knotting be performed first, then the cutting.

Right and wrong sides When your crochet work consists of special stitches, such as the hazelnut, loop, or two-row patterns, it will be obvious to you which side is "right," or facing outward when the garment is to be worn. Otherwise, patterns or stitches that are repeated row after row have no basic right or wrong sides; you may choose either one for hiding loose ends, joining, etc., as long as you remain consistent with it. Some instructions will define the right or wrong side when presenting the pattern for the first row of crochet.

End row (or round) 2, 3, etc. Where a crochet pattern is made up of two or more rows (or rounds) of individual stitch patterns and your instructions do not call for a given number of rows (or rounds) for a portion of the work, but, rather, specify working to a certain length or leave it up to your particular fit preference, you may find this notation at the end of the portion. This means that you must end your portion with the stitch pattern specified in that particular numbered row (or round).

Base of stitch You may sometimes be required to crochet into the base of a stitch, rather than into the usual two top strands. In some cases this is done to achieve a strong connection to the crochet, as for a tie end, or simply as a decorative variation of a conventional stitch. Consult the arrows in Figure III-23 of Boys' Hooded Sweater in this book to indicate the proper hook insertion for crocheting into the base.

Compensation Many of the projects in Part II of this book involve loops of chain stitches. To be assured that they end up with an even appearance, you will be asked to stop crocheting at various intervals and count your remaining stitches. A chart will then be presented, instructing you to alter the pattern you have been following for the next few loops, in order to gradually compensate by gaining or losing one chain in these loops. In other projects, when making the foundation chain you may be instructed to be sure your chain is a multiple of two, three, etc. This is done to ensure that the ensuing stitch pattern, which repeats itself every two, three, or more stitches, will end in your last chain.

Glossary of Abbreviations

beg	beginning
ch	chain
ch sp	chain space
dc	double crochet
dbl trc	double-triple crochet
dec	decrease
hdc	half-double crochet
inc	increase
lp	loop
p	picot
pat	pattern
pr r	previous row
pr rnd	previous round
ptl	pull through loop
reg	regular
rem	remaining
rep	repeat
rnd	round
row sp	row space
sc	single crochet
sk	skip
sl kn	slip knot
sl st	slip stitch
sp	space
st(s)	stitch(es)
tog	together
trc	triple crochet
trp trc	triple-triple crochet
ws	wrong side
yoh	yarn-over-hook

Table of Crochet Hook Equivalents

The crochet hooks in general usage today are made of aluminum, steel or plastic, each having its own gauge-numbering or -lettering system. All of the hooks specified by letter in this book refer to aluminum hooks; all those by number are for steel hooks. If you wish to use plastic hooks, the table given in Figure I-74 will provide you with the proper equivalent.

ALUMINUM	N	M	L	K	J	I	H		G	F	E	D	C		B	
PLASTIC				10½	10	9	8	7	6	5	4	3	2			
STEEL												00	0	1	2	3–14
DIAMETER (IN.)	3/8	5/16	9/32	1/4												

Figure I-74

Part II
Crocheted Inserts and Additions to Fabric

26 SHANIE JACOBS' CROCHET BOOK

Lotus T-Shirt

Materials

long- or short-sleeved round neck T-shirt in color and size of your choice, preferably 100% cotton knit, ribbed
1 ball (53 yds.) of No. 5 pearl cotton yarn in matching or contrasting color to T-shirt
1 No. 13 crochet hook (steel)
1 size B crochet hook
stiff cardboard or oaktag for template
compass
ruler
felt-tipped pen or chalk
scissors
sewing scissors
straight pins
sewing needle and thread
safety pins
yarn needle

Preparation

1. Lay out T-shirt on flat surface with both side seams lying at extreme edges.
2. Prepare template by scribing a circle 3¾" in diameter on cardboard or oaktag for Small or Medium T-shirt, 3⅞" in diameter for Large. Cut out template directly on scribed line.
3. With pen or chalk make a reference mark at a distance of 1½" below lowest point of neckline hem, as shown in Figure II-1.
4. Place circular template on T-shirt with uppermost point at reference mark. Measure distance from extreme right and left edges of template to corresponding underarm seam along the lines shown in Figure II-1; adjust template until both are equal. Be sure that top edge of template is still at the level of the reference mark.
5. When template is centered, mark around it with pen or chalk; then cut the marked circle out of the T-shirt, cutting just outside the marked line.
6. Turn T-shirt inside out and fold back the raw edge of the circle, forming a hem ⅜" to ½" deep. Starting at the top, carefully line up the center straight ribs of the hem with their corresponding ribs in the body of the T-shirt

Figure II-1

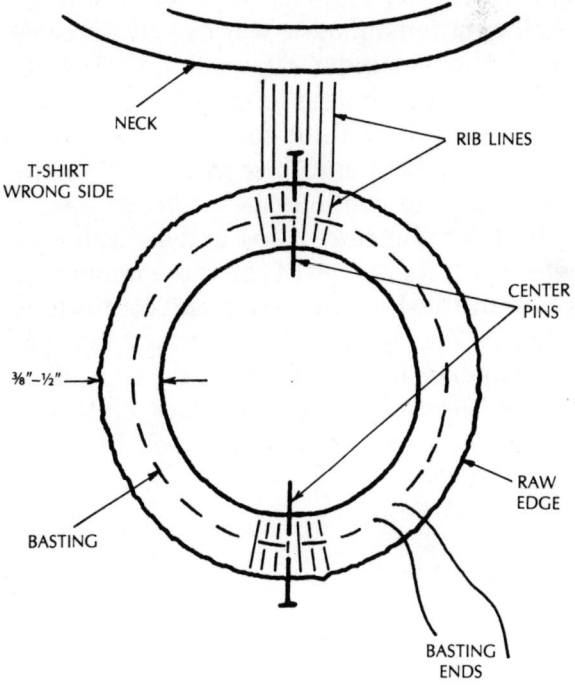

Figure II-2

and then pin in place. Repeat for the center bottom of the circle (Figure II-2). Now work between pins, gently molding the hem flat as you go, so that it falls naturally in place all around the circle, without pulling or stretching. Add a few more pins as needed.

7. Baste around hem with sewing thread, as shown, leaving a 2" to 3" length of thread at the start and finish, for easy thread removal later.

Crochet

Using No. 13 hook and pearl cotton yarn, cast into circular hem, as described in Casting into Fabric in Part I. Remove basting thread by gently pulling loose end. This pat is worked in rnds of chs, sc and sl sts. Sl sts are used only for the first lp of each rnd. A small safety pin may be used in each first ch of each new rnd to indicate where the sl sts must begin.

Round 1 Using size B hook, * ch 9, sk 8 sc which have been cast into material and sc in the 9th. Repeat from * until three-fourths of the circle has been completed with ch-9s and sc. Count remaining sc which have been cast into the material and divide this number by 9. You will now be left with a quotient and a remainder of 1, 2, 3, etc., up to 8, or 0, if the number of remaining sc was exactly divisible by 9. If the remainder is 0, continue as before. Otherwise, continue as follows: If the remainder is 1, sc in 10th st for the next lp and continue as before; if 2, sc in 10th st for the next 2 lps and continue as before; if 3, sc in 10th st for the next 3 lps and continue as before; if 4, for the next 4 lps; if the remainder is 8, sc in 8th st for the next lp and continue as before; if 7, sc in 8th st for the next 2 lps; if 6, for the next 3 lps; if 5, for the next 4 lps. This process ensures that your last ch-9 will contain 9 sts on your cast-on hem. End first rnd with ch-9.

Round 2 Sl st in first ch sp of your first lp of ch-9s (to connect first rnd) and sl st for the next 3 chs (4 sl sts in total), sc in 5th ch sp, which is the center of first lp of ch-9s. * Ch 7, sc in 5th ch sp. Repeat from * until end of rnd, ending with ch-7.

Round 3 Sl st in first ch sp of first lp of ch-7s (to connect 2nd rnd) and sl st for the next 2 chs (3 sl sts in total), sc in 4th ch sp, which is the center of your first lp of ch-7s. * Ch 5, sc in 4th ch sp. Repeat from * until end of rnd, ending with ch-5.

Round 4 Sl st in first ch sp of first lp of ch-5s (to connect 3rd rnd) and sl st for 1 more ch, sc in 3rd ch of your first lp of ch-5s. * Ch 3, sc in 3rd ch of lp of ch-5s. Repeat from * until end of rnd, ending with ch-3.

Round 5 Sl st in first ch of your first lp of ch-3s (to connect 4th rnd) and sc in 2nd ch. * Ch 1, sc in 2nd ch of lp of ch-3s. Repeat from * until end of rnd, ending with ch-1.

Round 6 Sl st to st before first ch of 5th rnd (to connect 5th rnd), sc in ch-1 sp, and do not ch any more, but * sc in ch-1. Repeat from * until end of rnd. Sl st to first sc to join.

Round 7 * Sk 1 sc and sc in next sc, turning garment as necessary. Repeat from *, decreasing to the end as the circle closes. Knot and cut, leaving an end not less than 12" long.

Finishing

Using a yarn needle or No. 13 hook, bring end and beg of yarn to wrong side of shirt. Using yarn or tapestry needle, travel the finishing end through the crocheted sts, taking the shortest possible path in the direction of the hem. Knot gently to first available st under hem, being sure that thread has a minimum of tension behind the knot. Hide end further by running it beyond the knot for approximately 12 sts under hem; then cut. Hide beg thread in a similar manner, traveling it in opposite direction to end thread.

Sleeveless Tank Top

Materials

T-shirt in color and size of your choice, preferably 100% cotton knit, ribbed
1 ball (53 yds.) of No. 5 pearl cotton yarn in matching or contrasting color to T-shirt
1 No. 13 crochet hook (steel)
1 size D crochet hook
ruler
felt-tipped pen or chalk
yardstick
straight pins
sewing scissors
sewing needle and thread
yarn needle

Preparation

1. Lay out T-shirt on flat surface with seams lying at extreme edges.
2. Measure ¾" down from point where side seam joins underarm seam and place a reference mark on shirt, using pen or chalk (Figure II-3). Repeat for other side.
3. Lay bottom edge of yardstick or other straightedge across shirt so that it connects both reference marks, as shown.
4. Using this bottom edge as a guide, mark a gentle arc with pen from one reference mark to the other, dipping below the straightedge about ¼" at center (Figure II-3). If you lack confidence in your ability to draw this arc freehand, you may use the straightedge as a guide and mark the line straight across.
5. To aid in cutting, place a few straight pins through the front and back of the shirt, parallel to the marked line and about 1" above it, being careful not to allow side seams to overlap out of line while working.
6. Cut entire top off T-shirt just below marked line, cutting front and back simultaneously.
7. Remove pins and turn shirt inside out. Fold back raw edge to form a ⅜" to ½" hem and pin in place, working your way around top of

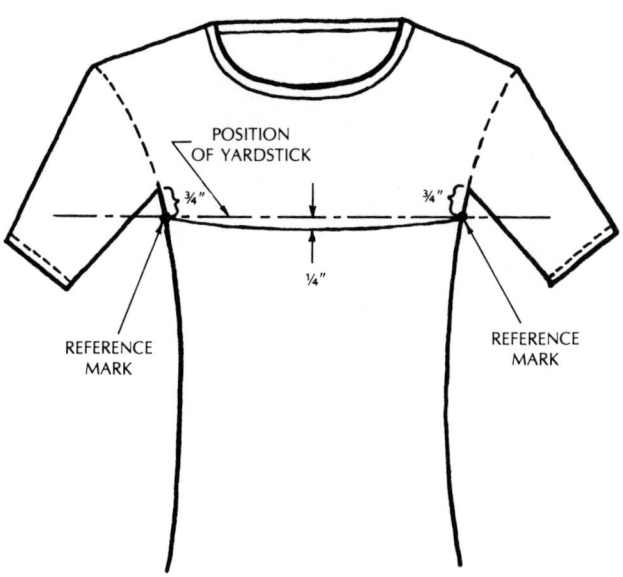

Figure II-3

shirt and carefully lining up ribs in hem with ribs in body of shirt.

8. Baste hem with sewing thread and needle, leaving a 2" to 3" end of thread at start and finish for easy thread removal later. Remove pins.

Crochet

Using No. 13 hook and pearl cotton yarn, cast 7 sts per inch into hem of T-shirt, starting at a distance of ½" in front or behind either side seam and following instructions set out in Casting into Fabric in Part I. After casting all around top of shirt, sl st into first sc, using size D hook. From this point the front and back of the shirt are worked separately.

Front
Row 1 Working toward the opposite side seam from which you started, * ch 9, sk 7 sts, sc in 8th. Repeat from * until halfway to next seam, then count remaining sts which have been cast into hem and subtract 3 from this number. Divide this result by 8, which will give you a quotient and a remainder of 1, 2, etc., up to 7 sts, or 0, if the number of remaining sts (minus 3) is exactly divisible by 8. If the remainder is 0, continue as before. If it is other than 0, sc in 9th st for the number of steps equal to your remainder. This method ensures that your last ch-9 will leave you with 3 sts before the seam. After the proper number of steps, continue from * as before.
Row 2 Turn, sl st to first 4 chs, sc in 5th. * Ch 9, sc in 5th ch sp of next lp. Repeat from * across.
Rows 3–5 Repeat 2nd row.
Row 6 Repeat 2nd row. Knot yarn and cut, leaving a 12" end.
Back Make a sl kn on hook, leaving a 5" end, and sc in 3rd st on cast-on hem of Back.
Rows 1–5 Repeat as for Front.
Row 6 Repeat 2nd row. After sc in last lp, turn, sl st 4 chs, then ch 24 for Small, 26 for Medium, or 28 for Large sizes. Sc in 5th ch of corresponding lp of ch-9s on Front to join first shoulder strap. Turn, * ch 5, sc in 5th ch sp of next lp of 6th row of Front. Repeat from * to end of row, then ch 24 (26, 28) as for first strap, and join to corresponding lp on Back to form second shoulder strap. Turn; repeat from * above, ending with sl st to sc at base of first shoulder strap. Knot yarn and cut, leaving a 12" end.
Finishing Bring loose ends at hem to wrong side, using yarn needle or No. 13 hook. Knot gently to first available st under hem, then travel for approximately 12 more sts under hem and cut. Using yarn needle, travel the 12" ends through crocheted chs, taking shortest path to hem. Bring under hem, knotting to first available st, then travel for approximately 12 more sts under hem and cut.

One- or Two-Sleeve Lotus T-Shirt

This design may be crocheted on either one or both sleeves of a long- or short-sleeved T-shirt. Combined with the Lotus T-Shirt (page 27), it will give you as many as three beautiful lotuses on one shirt.

Materials

The same materials as for Lotus T-Shirt (page 27) except: long- or short-sleeved (minimum length of 8" from bottom of sleeve to sleeve seam), round neck T-shirt in color and size of your choice, preferably 100% cotton knit, ribbed (The 53-yard ball of yarn will provide for 2 lotuses)

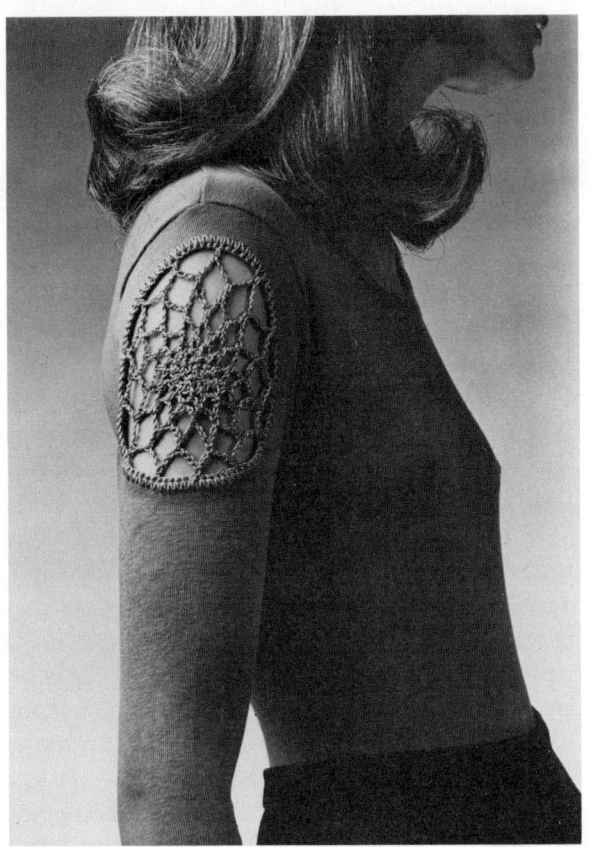

Preparation

1. Place T-shirt on a flat surface with the bottom of the sleeve you will be working on pointing toward you and the rest of the T-shirt away from you.

2. Gently grasp each edge of the top of the sleeve between the thumb and forefinger of each hand and carefully roll the fabric so that the seam along the side of the sleeve is facing you and is centered between outside edges of the sleeve. You may measure the distance from the seam to either edge to assure centering. Pin underside of sleeve to top side, as shown in Figure II-4.

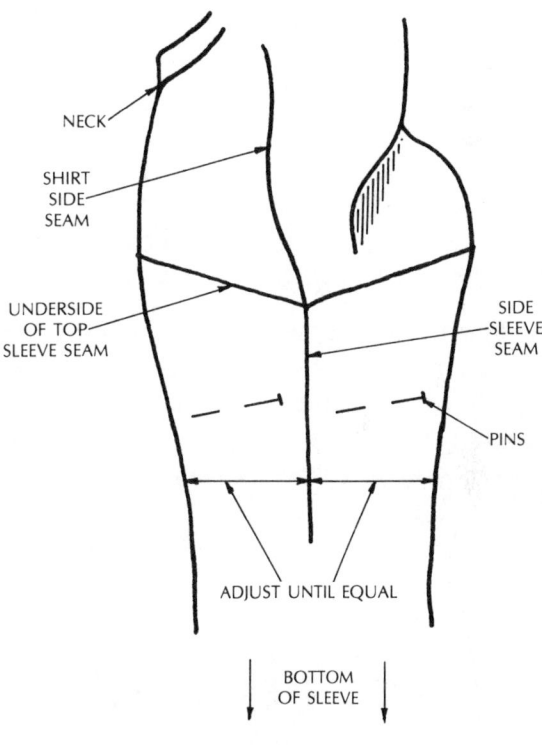

Figure II-4

3. Turn sleeve over so that it is in the position shown in Figure II-5, again with the bottom of the sleeve pointing toward you and the rest of the shirt out of the way. This time the top of the sleeve will be facing you.

4. Prepare template by scribing a circle $3\frac{9}{16}$" in diameter on cardboard or oaktag for Small and Medium shirt, $3\frac{3}{4}$" in diameter for Large. Cut out template on scribed line.

5. Using felt-tipped pen or chalk, place a reference mark in line with the top seam and

1" below the point where it meets the sleeve seam (Figure II-5).

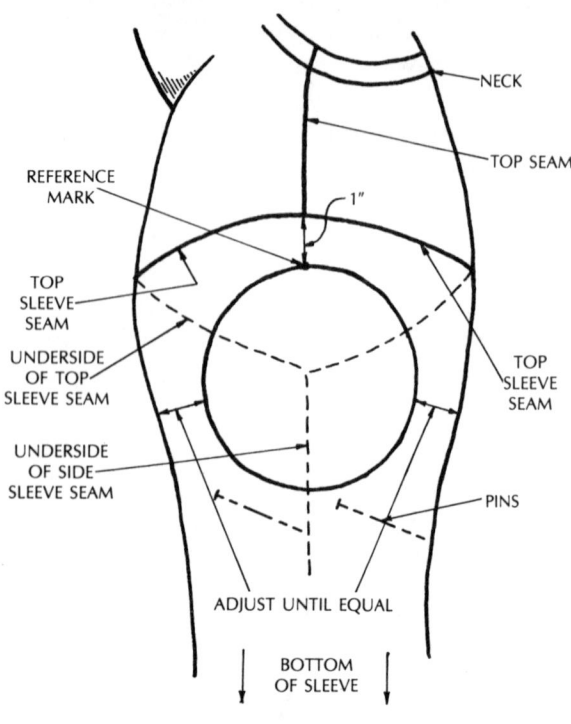

Figure II-5

6. Place template on the sleeve with top edge of circle on reference mark and adjust template so that extreme right and left edges of circle are at equal distances from corresponding edges of sleeve, as shown in Figure II-5.

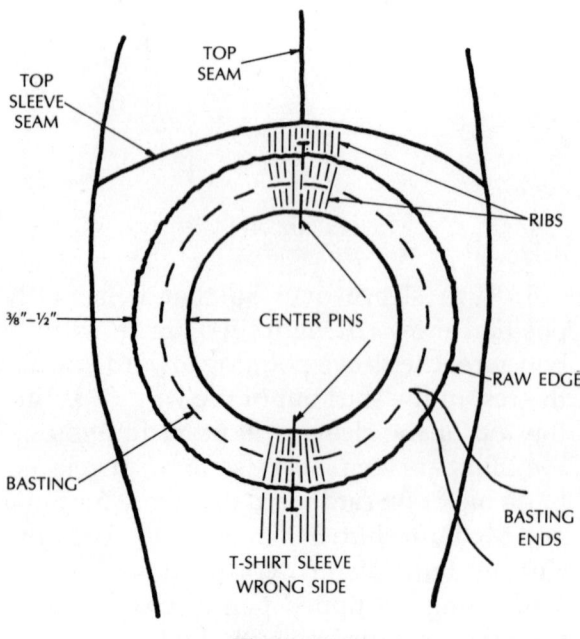

Figure II-6

7. When template is centered, mark around it with pen.

8. Remove pins and cut circle out of top face of sleeve, just outside the marked line, being careful not to nick underside of sleeve with scissors.

9. Turn T-shirt inside out and fold back the raw edge of the circle to form a hem 3/8" to 1/2" deep. Start at the top and carefully line up the center ribs of the hem with their corresponding ribs in the sleeve, then pin in place (Figure II-6). Repeat for the center bottom of the circle. Now work between pins, gently molding hem as you go, so that it falls naturally in place all around the circle, without pulling or stretching. Add a few more pins as needed.

10. Baste around hem with sewing thread, leaving a 2" to 3" length of thread at start and finish for easy thread removal later. Remove pins.

11. Repeat from step 5 for other sleeve, if desired.

Crochet

Cast into circular hem, using No. 13 crochet hook and pearl cotton yarn, as described in Casting into Fabric in Part I. Remove basting thread by pulling gently at loose end. This pat is worked in rnds of chs, sc, and sl sts. Sl sts are used only for the first lp of each rnd. A small safety pin may be used in each first ch of each new rnd to indicate where the sl st must begin.

Round 1 Using size B hook, * ch 7, sk 6 sts which have been cast into material, and sc in the 7th. Repeat from * until three-fourths of the circle has been completed with ch-7s and sc. Count remaining sc which have been cast into the material and divide this number by 7. You will get a quotient and be left with a remainder of 1, 2, 3, etc., up to 6, or 0, if the number of remaining sc was exactly divisible by 7. If the remainder is 0, continue as before. Otherwise, continue as follows: If the remainder is 1, sc in 8th st for the next lp and continue as before; if 2, sc in 8th st for the next 2 lps and continue as before; if 3, sc in 8th st for the next 3 lps; if 6, sc in 6th st on your next lp and continue as before; if 5, sc in 6th st for the next 2 lps and continue as before; if 4, for the next 3 lps. This process will ensure that your last ch-7 will contain 7 sts on your cast-on hem. End first rnd with ch-7.

Round 2 Sl st in first ch sp of your first lp of ch-7s (to connect first rnd) and sl st for the next 2 chs (3 sl sts in total), sc in 4th ch sp, which is the center of your first lp of ch-7s. * Ch 7, sc in 4th ch sp. Repeat from * until end of rnd, ending with ch-7.

Round 3 Sl st in first ch sp of 2nd lp of ch-7s (to connect 2nd rnd) and sl st for the next 2 chs (3 sl sts in total), sc in 4th ch sp, which is the center of your first lp of ch-7s. * Ch 5, sc in 4th ch sp. Repeat from * until end of rnd, ending with ch-5.

Round 4 Sl st into first ch sp of first lp of ch-5s (to connect 3rd round) and sl st for 1 more ch, sc in 3rd ch of your first lp of ch-5s. * Ch 3, sc in 3rd ch of lp of ch-5s. Repeat from * until end of rnd, ending with ch-3.

Round 5 Sl st in first ch sp of your first lp of ch-3s (to connect 4th rnd) and sc in 2nd ch. * Ch 1, sc in 2nd ch of lp of ch-3s. Repeat from * until end of rnd, ending with ch-1.

Round 6 Sl st to st before first ch of 5th rnd (to connect 5th rnd) and sc in ch-1 sp, but do not chain any more. * Sc in each ch-1. Repeat from * until end of rnd. Sl st to first sc to join.

Round 7 * Sk 1 sc and sc in next sc, turning garment as necessary. Repeat from *, decreasing to the end as the circle closes. Knot and cut yarn, leaving an end not less than 12" long.

Finishing Using yarn needle or No. 13 hook, bring beg and end of yarn to wrong side of shirt. Using yarn needle, travel finishing end through crocheted sts, taking shortest path in direction of hem. Knot gently to first available st under hem, being sure that thread has a minimum of tension behind the knot. Hide end further by running it beyond the knot for approximately 12 sts under hem; then cut. Hide beg thread in a similar manner, traveling it for approximately 12 sts in opposite direction to end thread.

Long-Sleeved Net Topping

The upper part of the T-shirt that is removed to make this pullover may be saved and used to make the Teens' Bolero Top (page 63).

Materials

long-sleeved T-shirt in color and size of your choice, preferably 100% cotton knit, ribbed
1 ball (53 yds.) of No. 5 pearl cotton yarn in matching or contrasting color to T-shirt
1 No. 13 crochet hook (steel)
1 size B crochet hook
1 size D crochet hook
tape measure
felt-tipped pen or chalk
ruler
yardstick
straight pins
sewing scissors
sewing needle and thread
yarn needle

Preparation

1. Lay out T-shirt on flat surface with both side seams lying at extreme edges.

2. Using tape measure, measure length of the seam where sleeve joins the body from top seam juncture to side seam juncture (Figure II-7). If this measurement is 7" or less, place a reference mark with felt-tipped pen or chalk at a point on this seam 1¼" above underarm juncture. If the measurement lies between 7" and 8", place reference mark 1½" above underarm juncture; if more than 8", 1¾". Repeat for other side.

3. Now place an additional reference mark on top edge of each sleeve at a distance of 4" down from juncture of top seam and top of sleeve seam (Figure II-7).

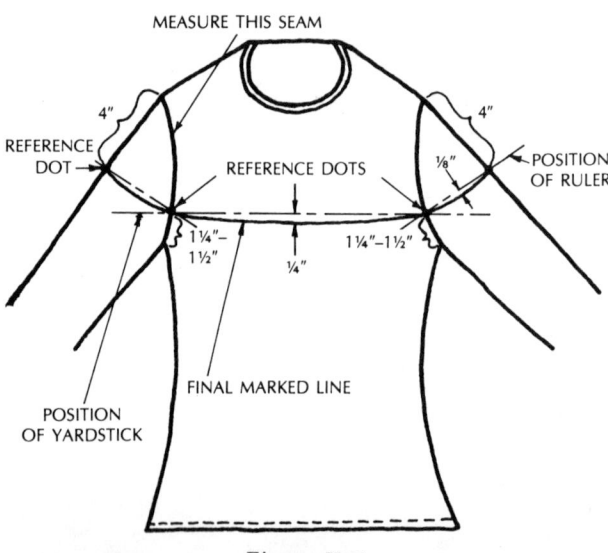

Figure II-7

4. Lay the bottom edge of a ruler across upper part of sleeve to connect the reference marks. Using this edge as a guide, draw a gentle arc between the reference marks, dipping below the ruler's edge about ⅛" at center of the sleeve. If you lack confidence to draw this arc freehand, you may connect the reference marks with a straight line, using the bottom edge of the ruler as a guide. Repeat for other sleeve.

5. Now lay the bottom edge of the yardstick across the front of the shirt, connecting the reference marks of the sleeve seams. Draw a gentle arc connecting these marks, using the yardstick edge as a guide and dipping below the edge of the yardstick about ¼" at the center of the shirt. Again, if you feel you cannot draw this arc freehand, you may connect the marks with a straight line, using the bottom edge of the yardstick as a guide.

6. To aid in cutting, you may want to place a row of straight pins about 1" above and/or below the marked line on the body and sleeves of the T-shirt, pinning the front of the fabric to the back.

7. Cut off entire top of T-shirt with sewing scissors just below marked line, cutting front and back simultaneously. Remove pins.

8. Turn T-shirt inside out and fold back raw edge to form a hem of ⅜" to ½". Pin in place, working your way around top of shirt, carefully lining up ribs in hem with ribs in body of shirt.

9. Baste hem with sewing thread, leaving a 2" to 3" thread at beg and end for easy thread removal later. Use minimal tension during basting. Remove pins.

Crochet

Starting anywhere except at center of Front or Back and using a No. 13 crochet hook and pearl cotton yarn, cast 7 sts per inch into material, following directions set out in Casting into Fabric in Part I. After casting all around top and sleeves, sl st in first sc.

Round 1 Using size D hook, * ch 9, sk 8 sts on your cast-on hem, and sc in 9th st. Repeat from * until you are three-fourths of the way around. Count remaining sts on your cast-on hem and divide this number by 9. You will then have a quotient and be left with a remainder of 1, 2, 3, etc., up to 8, or 0, if the number of remaining sts on your hem is exactly divisible by 9. If your remainder is 0, continue as before. If your remainder is other than 0, sc in 8th st for the number of lps shown in the table below, and then continue as before.

Remainder	Number of Loops
1	1
2	2
3	3
4	4
5	5
6	6
7	7
8	8

This process ensures that your last ch-9 will contain 9 sts on your cast-on hem. End first rnd with ch-9.

Round 2 Sl st in first ch sp of your first lp of first rnd. Sl st for 3 more chs (4 sl sts in total), sc in 5th ch sp, which is the center of your first lp. * Ch 7, sc in 5th st of your next lp. Repeat from * until end of rnd, ending with ch-7.

Round 3 Sl st in first ch sp of your first lp of ch-7s. Sl st for 2 more chs (3 sl sts in total), sc in 4th ch sp of your first lp of 2nd rnd. * Ch 7, sc in 4th ch sp of your next lp. Repeat from * until end of rnd, ending with ch-7.

Round 4 Repeat 3rd rnd.

Round 5 Repeat 3rd rnd.

Round 6 Sl st in first ch sp of your first lp of ch-7s of fifth rnd. Sl st for 2 more chs (3 sl sts in total) and sc in 4th ch sp, which is the center of your first lp of 5th rnd. * Ch 5, sc in 4th ch sp of your next lp. Repeat from * until end of rnd, ending with ch-5.

Round 7 Sl st in first ch sp of your first lp of ch-5s of 6th rnd. Sl st for 1 more ch (2 sl sts in total) and sc in 3rd ch sp, which is the center of your first lp of ch-5s. * Ch 5, sc in 3rd ch sp of your next lp. Repeat from * until end of rnd, ending with ch-5.

Round 8 Repeat 7th rnd.

Round 9 Sl st in first ch sp of your first lp of ch-5s of 8th rnd. Sl st for 1 more ch (2 sl sts in total), sc in 3rd ch sp, which is the center of your first lp of ch-5s of 8th rnd. * Ch 3, sc in 3rd ch sp of your next lp. Repeat from * until end of rnd, ending with ch-3.

Round 10 Hdc in first ch sp of your first lp of ch-3s of 9th rnd. Sc in 2nd ch sp of this lp and hdc in 3rd ch sp. * Hdc in first ch sp of your next lp of ch-3s. Sc in 2nd ch sp of this lp and hdc in 3rd ch sp. Repeat from * until end of rnd. Sl st to first hdc.

Round 11 Change to size B hook. Sc in every st of 10th rnd. Sl st to first sc of rnd. Knot gently and cut yarn, leaving an end of not less than 12".

Finishing Bring beg end to wrong side of fabric, using yarn needle or No. 13 hook. Using yarn or tapestry needle, travel finishing end through crocheted sts, taking shortest path in the direction of the hem. Knot gently to first available st under hem, leaving minimal tension behind knot. Hide end further by traveling it approximately 12 sts under hem; then cut. Hide beg end in a similar manner by knotting gently to first available st under hem and then traveling it for approximately 12 sts in opposite direction to the finishing end; then cut.

Sleeveless Tank Top Dress

This dress can be sewn quickly by hand or machine with just two side seams and one sewn hem. The lacy, net crocheted top gives it just the right touch, making it suitable for formal wear, especially in black.

Materials

- 1½ yds. (60" wide) of a light-ribbed or interlock-woven dress material, such as Qiana®, Nyestra®, or any polyester-cotton blend, in color of your choice
- 1 ball (53 yds.) of No. 5 pearl cotton yarn in matching or contrasting color to dress material
- 1 No. 13 crochet hook (steel)
- 1 size D crochet hook
- 1 piece of stiff wrapping paper, 5' x 3', for pattern
- yardstick
- felt-tipped pen or chalk
- right angle or square
- pencil
- scissors
- straight pins
- sewing scissors
- sewing needle and thread
- yarn needle

Preparation

Figures II-11, II-12 and II-13 present dimensions for dress patterns in Small, Medium and Large sizes, respectively. The seam allowance may be varied during the sewing operation, so that the Small can accommodate dress sizes 8–10, the Medium, 12–14, and the Large, 16–18. The patterns allow sufficient material for floor-length hems or shorter.

1. Lay out paper to be used for pattern on floor or large table and smooth, so that it is wrinkle-free.
2. Using the yardstick and felt-tipped pen, mark the centerline, as shown in Figure II-8, starting a few inches below the top short edge of the paper and running it down the center to within a few inches of the bottom of the paper. Now place a reference dot at the beginning of this line at the top. Find the top-to-bottom distance of the dress pattern in Figures II-11, II-12, or II-13, depending on your size (e.g., 50¾" for Small), and measure down this distance from your first reference dot. Place another reference dot on the centerline at this distance, near the bottom of the paper (Figure II-8.)

SLEEVELESS TANK TOP DRESS 37

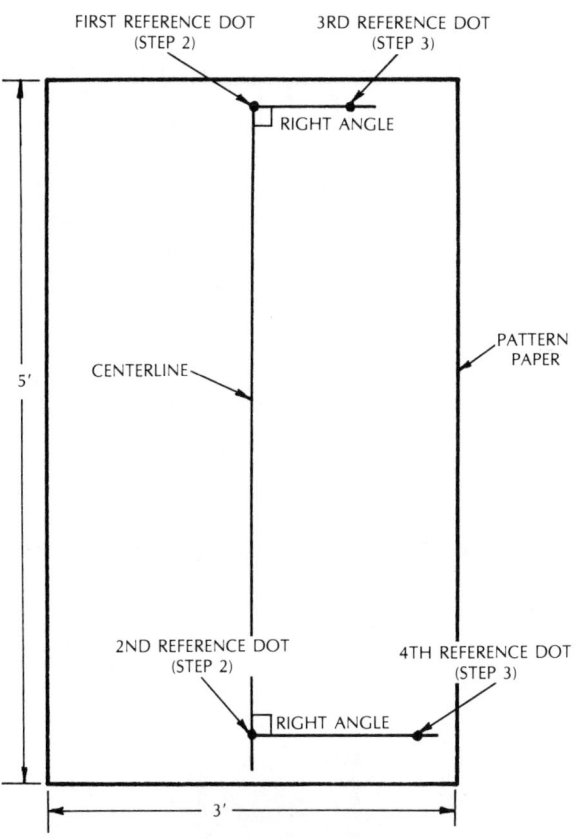

Figure II-8

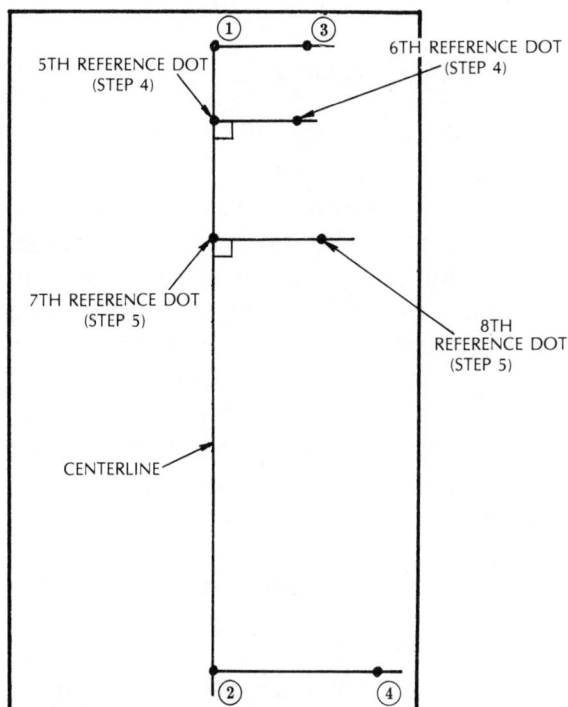

Figure II-9

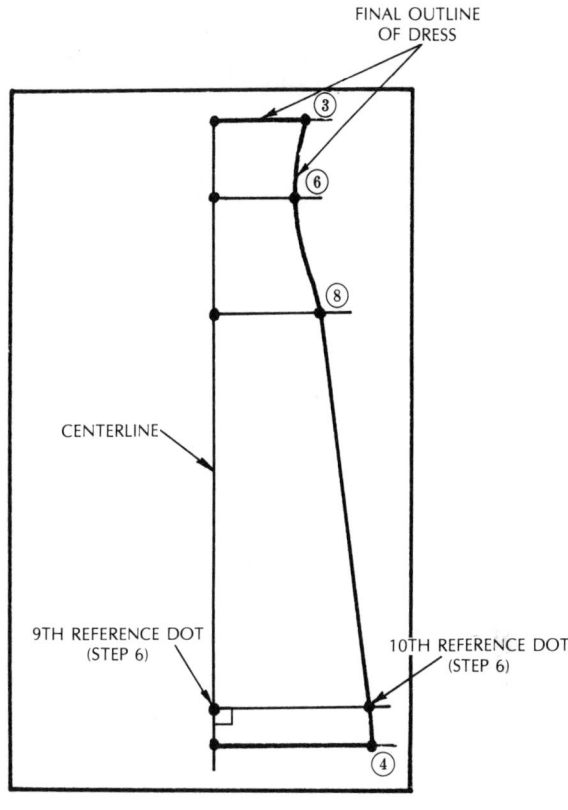

Figure II-10

3. Using a right angle guide, such as a draftsman's triangle or the hard cover of a large book, draw a line at right angles to the centerline at the first (upper) reference dot; draw the line off to the right and about 12" long. Now do the same at the second (lower) reference dot, making it about 18" long (Figure II-8). Consult the proper figure for your size and find the dimension across the top of the dress. Divide this measurement by 2. Measure off the resultant distance (e.g., 7⅞" for Small) from the top centerline dot across the top line and place your third reference dot there. Now find the width across the bottom for your size (e.g., 28" for Small), divide by 2, and place your fourth reference dot at this distance along bottom line (Figure II-8).

4. Again consult your size figure and find the dimension that gives the distance from the top of the dress to the line that connects the narrowest part of the waist (e.g., 6" for Small). Measure down this distance from your first reference dot and place your fifth

SMALL

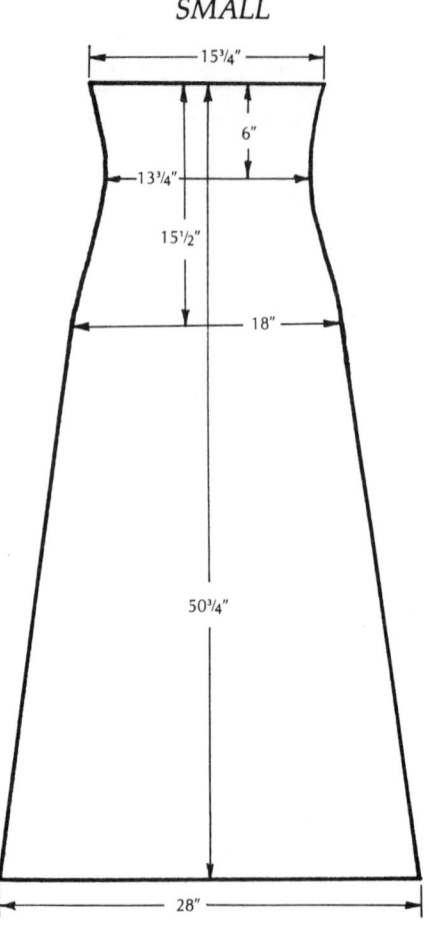

Figure II-11

MEDIUM

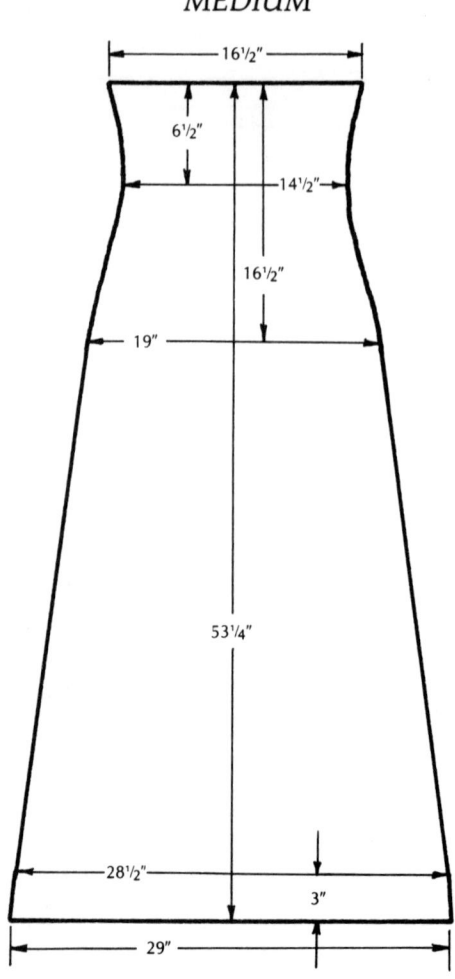

Figure II-12

reference dot at this distance (Figure II-9). Using right angle guide, draw a line off to the right, about 8" long, from dot 5. Consulting the proper figure, find the distance across the narrowest part of the waist, divide by 2, and mark your sixth reference dot on the line you have just drawn at this distance from dot 5.

5. Consult your figure and find the dimension from the dress top to the line connecting the widest part of the hipline (e.g., 15½" for Small), and measure this distance down the centerline from dot 1, placing your seventh reference dot at this point. Using the right angle, extend a line off to the right from this dot for about 12". Find the distance across hipline from the proper figure, divide by 2 (e.g., 9" for Small), and place eighth reference dot at this distance from dot 7 along line you have just drawn (Figure II-9).

6. If your size is Small, skip this step. If Medium or Large, consult proper figure for distance from bottom of dress to the next line up, which joins the final points of taper. Measure this distance up the centerline from dot 2 (e.g., 3" for Medium) and place your ninth reference dot on centerline (Figure II-10). Use the right angle to extend a line about 15" from this dot. Find your dimension of length of line joining end of taper points, divide by 2 (e.g., 14¼" for Medium), and place your last reference dot at this distance from centerline.

7. Using the felt-tipped pen and yardstick, connect dot 8 to dot 10 with a straight line, if you are a Medium or a Large; if Small, connect dot 8 to dot 4. For Medium and Large, connect dot 4 to dot 10 with a straight line (Figure II-10).

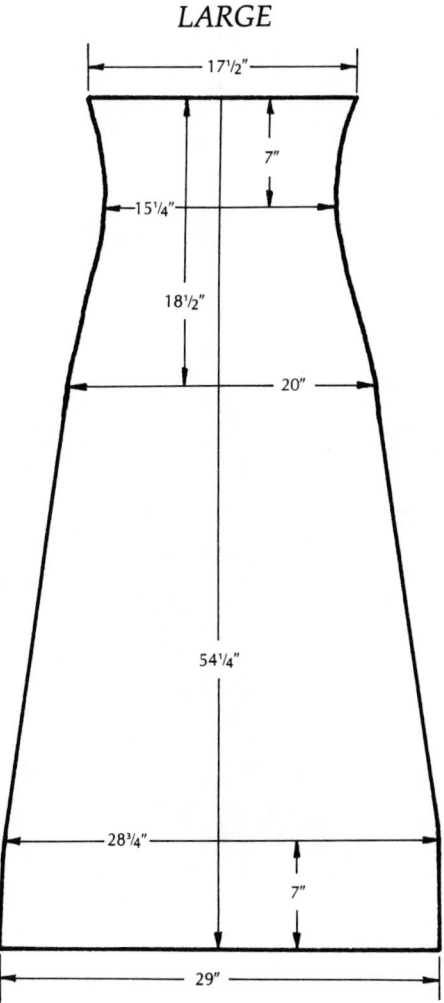

Figure II-13

8. Using a pencil, draw a gentle arc from dot 3 through dot 6 and joining dot 8. You may have to erase and redo this line until it appears as shown in Figure II-10, with a smooth transition into the straight line at dot 8. Once you have it right, go over it with felt-tipped pen.

9. Fold the pattern paper along centerline with marked side up. Using paper scissors, cut both sheets along top, side and bottom marked lines. Open pattern.

10. Fold dress material exactly in half, lengthwise, with wrong sides facing outward. Lay material on flat surface, smoothing out wrinkles. Place paper pattern over material, with centerline running lengthwise at fold line, and trace outline of pattern on material with felt-tipped pen or tailor's chalk. Remove pattern and pin fabric front to back, about 1" in from marked lines all around.

11. Using sewing scissors, cut front and back of material simultaneously, just inside marked lines.

12. Baste both side seams with sewing thread, leaving a seam allowance of $\frac{1}{4}$" to $\frac{3}{4}$", depending on whether your size is on the low or high end of the Small, Medium or Large size ranges. Remove pins, turn dress right side out, and try on. The dress should cling at the waist and then flare slightly just below the hipline. You may want to rebaste to make the desired adjustments.

13. After making the necessary corrections, turn dress wrong side out and sew final seams with matching thread by hand or machine. Do not sew the top or bottom hems.

14. From this point prepare the top hem by following the instructions given in steps 7 and 8 for the Sleeveless Tank Top (page 29), and follow the crochet instructions for the top. After completing the crochet, try dress on, pin the bottom hem to desired length, baste, and sew.

Long-Sleeved Net-Topped Evening Gown

This design is a combination of the Sleeveless Tank Top Dress (page 36) with a full net topping and completely seamless long sleeves. The result is a ravishing evening gown that can be worn to the most formal of affairs.

Materials

Same as for Sleeveless Tank Top Dress, except: 4 balls (53 yds. each) of No. 5 pearl cotton yarn

Preparation

1–12. Same as for Sleeveless Tank Top Dress.

13. After making the necessary corrections, turn dress wrong side out and sew final seams with matching thread by hand or machine. Do not sew top or bottom hems.

14. Fold back raw edge at top of dress to form a 3/8" to 1/2" hem and pin in place, working your way around the top of the dress and lining up the ribbing or grain of weave. Baste hem with sewing thread; remove pins.

Crochet

NOTE: Instructions are given for size Small; Medium and Large sizes are in parentheses.

First Side   Make a sl kn on size D hook with No. 5 yarn, leaving a 36" end, and ch 126. Change to No. 13 hook and sc into top hem where it meets side seam, according to directions in Casting into Fabric in Part I. Cast 7 sts per inch across hem to opposite seam. Change back to size D hook and ch 133; turn.

Row 1   Sc in 14th ch from hook, * ch 7, sk 6 chs and sc in 7th ch sp. Repeat from * up ch, across top, counting cast sts instead of chs, and down next ch until you reach a point 12" from the end, as shown in Figure II-14. Count the remaining chs and divide this number by 7. Disregard the quotient and you will be left with a remainder of 1, 2, etc., up to 6, or 0, if the number of your remaining chs is exactly divisible by 7. If your remainder is 0, continue as before. If it is other than 0, sc in 8th ch sp for the number of lps equal to your remainder, then continue as before. This process ensures that your last sc of your last ch-7 lp will end in your last ch sp. After sc in this ch sp, ch 7; turn.

Row 2   Sc in 4th ch sp, which is the center of the lp, * ch 7, sc in 4th ch sp of the next lp. Repeat from * all across sleeves and top, ending with sc in 7th ch sp of last lp. Ch 7; turn.

Rows 3–8 Repeat 2nd row. End 8th row by knotting yarn in 4th ch sp of last lp and cutting, leaving a 36″ end.

Second Side Repeat cast-on and first through 8th rows as for First Side, entering the other hem from the opposite seam to the one you entered in First Side.

Row 9 Repeat 3rd row; do not ch 7 at end.

Row 10 (closing row) With hook in 4th ch sp of last lp of 9th row, ch 3, sl st in first ch sp of corresponding first lp of 8th row of First Side. Sl st for 2 more chs, sc in 4th ch sp of this lp. * Ch 3, sc in 4th ch sp of next corresponding lp of 9th row of Second Side. At this point, place 4 or 5 small safety pins up the length of the sleeve, joining the proper corresponding lps to aid in the sleeve closure. Repeat from *, zig-zagging until you have completed 22 (21, 20) lps. Place 4 or 5 safety pins along the length at the top of the other sleeve to connect corresponding lps, using your last pin as shown in Figure II-15. This pin should connect First Side to Second Side at the point where neckline is to meet top of the other sleeve, corresponding to the point at which you have stopped crochet. Its position may be further checked by counting the number of lps from the wristline up to it, which should equal the 22 (21, 20) lps of the first sleeve.

When pinned properly, * ch 7, sc in 4th ch sp of next lp of 8th row of First Side. Repeat from * until you reach the safety pin at the other end of the neckline. Then, with hook in 4th ch sp of last lp, ch 3, sc in 4th ch sp of corresponding lp of Second Side. Repeat from * at beg of 10th row, zig-zagging to close the top of the second sleeve. End with sc in 4th ch sp of last lp of Second Side; knot yarn and cut, leaving a 36″ end.

Row 11 (closing row) Make a sl kn on hook, leaving a 36″ end. Sl st to first ch sp of ch-126 that began First Side. Sl st for 2 more chs, sc in 4th ch sp. * Ch 3, sc in 4th ch sp in first lp of Second Side. Pin sleeve in 4 or 5 places to aid in remainder of sleeve closure, then repeat from *, as in 10th row, zig-zagging up bottom of sleeve to underarm seam at top hem. Knot yarn and cut, leaving a 6″ end.

Repeat this procedure for other sleeve, slip-stitching to 7th-from-last ch sp of the ch-133 to begin.

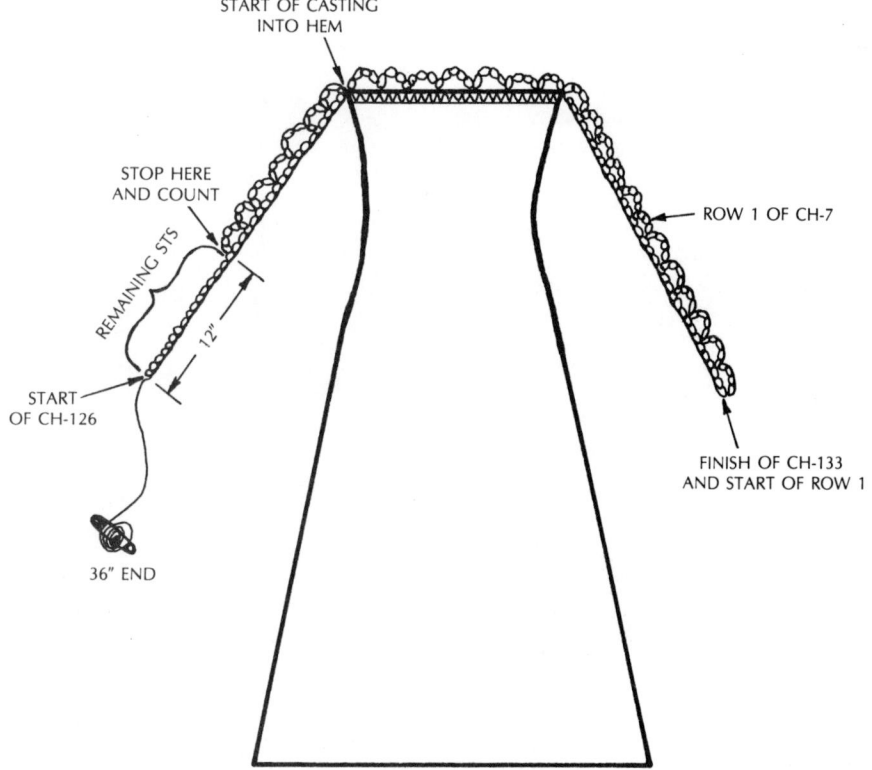

Figure II-14

Finishing Hide 6" ends at top hem by traveling them under hem with a yarn needle for approximately 12 sts on hem; then cut. Hide 36" ends at wristline by traveling them up sleeves with yarn needle, taking shortest path through the crocheted lp toward the top hem. Knot gently to the first available st under hem and then travel further for approximately 12 sts under hem; then cut.

Try gown on, pin bottom hem to desired length, baste, and sew.

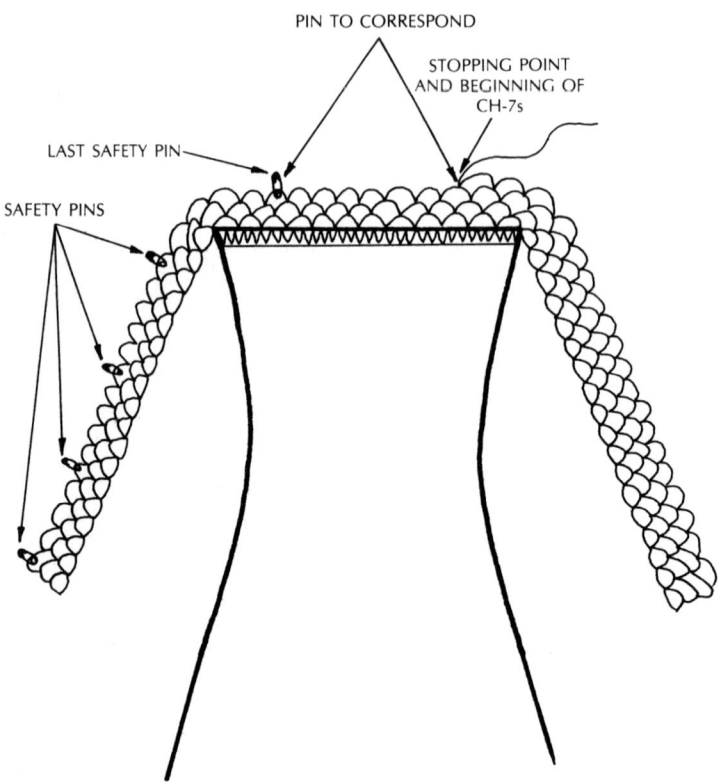

Figure II-15

Tricolor Rosette Leotard/Tights

This flowery rosette enlivens the usual single-colored dancer's leotard and/or tights. The leotard can then double as a bathing suit, or you may want to crochet the rosette into your own bathing suit.

Materials

leotard and/or tights, or bathing suit in your choice of color and size
2 balls (53 yds. each) of No. 5 pearl cotton yarn in main contrasting color (color A) for each rosette
1 ball (53 yds.) of No. 5 pearl cotton yarn in *each* of the 2 secondary contrasting colors (colors B and C) for each rosette
½ ball (26½ yds.) of No. 5 pearl cotton yarn in color matching fabric for each rosette
1 No. 5 crochet hook (steel)
1 No. 13 crochet hook (steel)
1 size B crochet hook
stiff cardboard or oaktag for template
compass
scissors
pencil
felt-tipped pen or chalk
sewing scissors
straight pins
sewing needle and thread
yarn needle

Leotard Preparation

NOTE: The variation in stretchability of weave for different manufacturers of leotards and bathing suits precludes the ability to give exact dimensional instruction as to the placement of templates. The following instruction

guarantees the correct placement, however, since it allows the garment to be marked while on the body.

1. Using compass and stiff cardboard, scribe a circle 3" in diameter for Small, 3$\frac{3}{16}$" in diameter for Medium, or 3$\frac{7}{16}$" in diameter for Large. Mark centerpoint of circle with dot.
2. Cut out template on scribed line. Stab the compass point through the centerpoint dot; then enlarge this hole slightly with a sharp pencil point.
3. Put leotard on and place or have someone place the template on the midriff, as shown in Figure II-16, midway between the bottom of the bustline and the navel. When in place, mark centerpoint of template on fabric by pushing the tip of the felt-tipped pen through the center hole of the template.
4. Take off leotard and place on a flat surface, front side up. Place template over

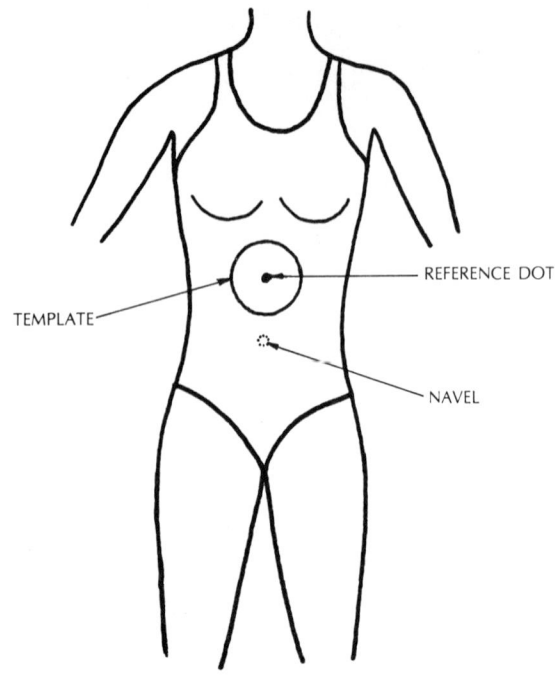

Figure II-16

reference mark so that it shows through the center hole. Trace around template with the pen and cut out the circle of fabric just outside the marked line.

5. Turn garment wrong side out and fold back raw edge of circular cutout to form a ⅜" to ½" hem. Start at top of circle (nearest bustline) and place a straight pin in the hem, being sure to line up weave lines in hem with those in the body of the fabric. Repeat for bottom of the circle. Now add a few more pins, as needed, around circumference of circle, being sure hem lies flat against the body fabric.

6. Baste hem with sewing thread, leaving a 2" to 3" end of basting thread at start and finish. Remove pins.

Tights Preparation

1. Using compass and stiff cardboard, scribe a circle 2¾" in diameter for Small, 3" in diameter for Medium, or 3¼" in diameter for Large. Cut out template on scribed line.

2. Lay tights out on a flat surface with front facing up. Be sure leg seam at the back surface runs down exact center of the leg. Place template on left (or right) leg surface, as shown in Figure II-17, with top edge of template 11" below top of waistband elastic. Center template by adjusting distances from either edge of template to right and left edges of leg until equal (Figure II-17).

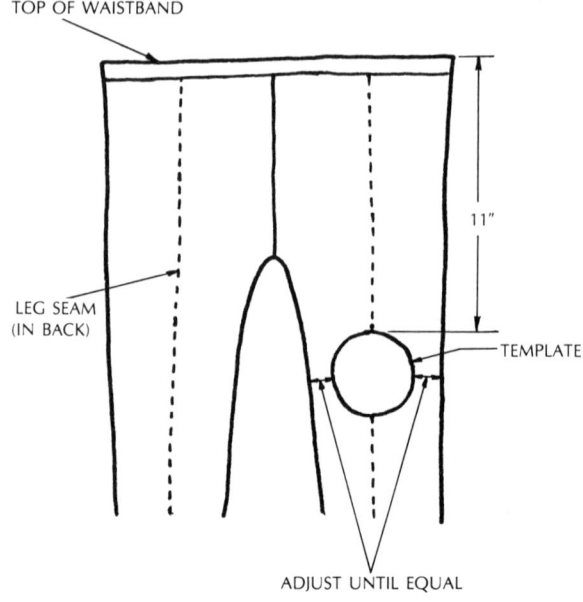

Figure II-17

3. When in place, trace around template with felt-tipped pen; then cut out circle of fabric just outside the marked line.
4. Repeat step 5 of Leotard Preparation.
5. Repeat step 6 of Leotard Preparation.

Leotard/Tights Crochet

Using No. 13 hook and yarn in fabric-matching color, make a sl kn and cast into circular hem, according to directions set out in Casting into Fabric in Part I. Remove basting thread, replace hook with size B hook, and insert into first cast st. Yarn-over-hook with color A yarn and complete sl st with color A yarn. Cut original yarn, leaving a 5" end.

Round 1 Work hazelnut st in same st with 7 strands on hook to close, work hazelnut in every cast st around hem. End with sl st to first hazelnut.

Round 2 Replace with No. 5 hook, sc in every hazelnut around, sl st to first sc to join.

Round 3 Replace with size B hook, dec 1 sc in first 2 sc (see Decreasing in Part I), dec 1 sc in each of next pair of sc around, ending with sl st to first sc to join.

Round 4 *Sc in next st, ch 8, sc in same st, ch 8, sl st in same st, sc in each of next 2 sc. Repeat from * around, ending with sl st to first sc.

Round 5 Replace with No. 5 hook, sl st to first ch-8 sp, ch 3, sl st to next ch-8 sp, * sl st to next ch-8 sp, ch 3, sl st to next ch-8 sp. Repeat from * around, ending with sl st in last ch-8 sp.

Round 6 Sl st in first ch-8 sp, insert hook into first ch-3 sp, yoh, pull through sp, yoh, and finish sc with color B yarn. Cut color A yarn, leaving a 5" end. Ch 1, work hazelnut st in same ch-3 sp with 16 strands to close. * Sl st to next inverted "V" space, which is between the st you are in and the next ch-3 sp. Hazelnut in next ch-3 sp. Repeat from * around, ending with sl st in last inverted "V" space.

Round 7 Replace with size B hook, insert in first hazelnut st, complete 1 sc with fabric-matching color yarn. Cut color B yarn, leaving a 5" end. Sc in every hazelnut around; change to color C in last hazelnut. Cut fabric-matching color yarn, leaving a 5" end.

Round 8 Sl st to first sc, ch 1, * hazelnut with 11 strands to close in same st, sl st to next sc, ch 1. Repeat from * around, until hazelnuts close rosette. Knot yarn and cut, leaving a 5" end.

Finishing Bring all ends to wrong side, using a yarn needle or No. 13 hook. Knot each end gently in place, making sure that sts are even on right side. Using a yarn needle, travel each end through the crocheted sts of its corresponding color, gently pulling on the end until all hazelnuts are closed. When end is firmly in place, knot again and cut.

Poncho Dress Ensemble

Modifying the basic dress described in Sleeveless Tank Top Dress (page 36) to a strapless style and topping it with a mini-poncho fashioned from the same dress material leaves you with a distinctively fashioned ensemble. You may also use the poncho in combination with other dresses or tops in your wardrobe.

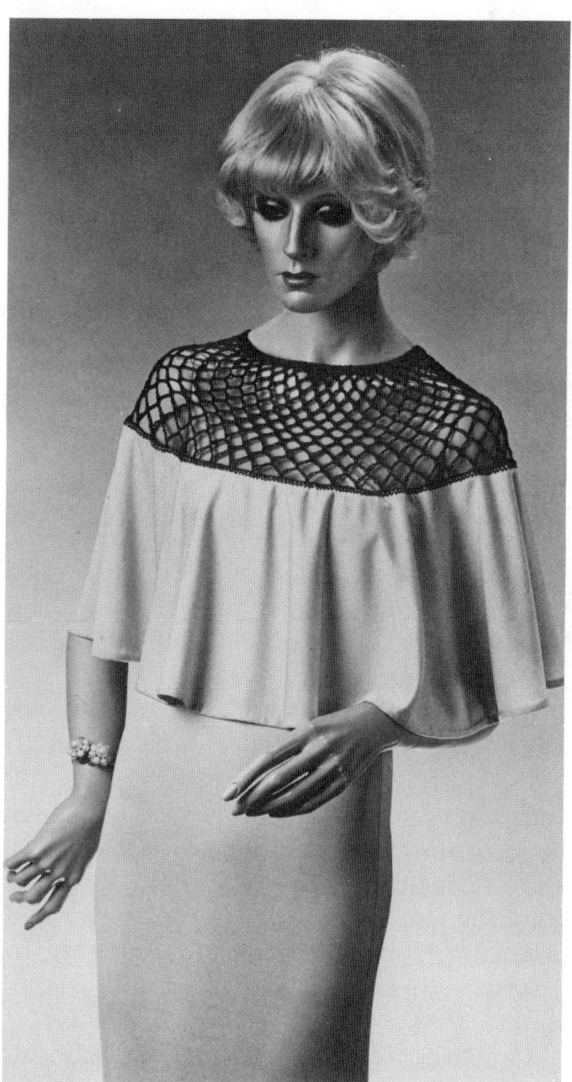

Materials

Dress

Same as for Sleeveless Tank Top Dress (page 36), except:
1 yd. (¼" wide) of oval, cross-sectioned elastic
safety pin

Poncho

1 yd. of same material used in dress
2 balls (53 yds. each) of No. 5 pearl cotton yarn in matching or contrasting color to dress material
1 No. 13 crochet hook (steel)
1 size B crochet hook
1 size D crochet hook
1 piece of stiff wrapping paper, 3' x 3', for pattern
1 piece of stiff cardboard, 18" x 2", for compass
thumbtack
pencil
felt-tipped pen or chalk
sewing scissors
sewing needle and thread
straight pins
yarn needle

Dress Preparation

1–13. Follow steps 1–13 in Sleeveless Tank Top Dress (page 36).

14. To determine proper length of the elastic closure, wrap the piece of elastic around your body at the top of the bustline with the ends in front. Stretch the elastic until the tension feels proper against your chest. The tension may be further tested by inhaling and exhaling a few times. Allowing for a ½" to 1" overlap, cut the end of the elastic once you have determined the proper stretched length.

15. With dress still wrong side out, fold back raw edge at top to form a hem which will be ⅜" from top to stitchline when sewn (to allow elastic to slip through). Pin hem carefully in place and baste. Sew with matching thread, leaving a 2" opening for insertion of elastic. Remove pins and basting thread.

16. Pin a 1" safety pin to end of elastic and thread it through the hem, making sure the opposite end remains visible for final closure. Overlap elastic ends for a distance of ½" to 1" and sew closed with a fine sewing needle. Close last 2" of hem over elastic.

17. Turn dress right side out and try on. Pin bottom hem to desired length, baste, and sew.

Poncho Preparation

1. Mark a reference dot at the center of your 3' x 3' piece of pattern paper. To construct a simple compass, push a thumbtack through a piece of 18" x 2" stiff cardboard, about 1" from end, as shown in Figure II-18. Remove thumbtack and measure down 15¼" from tack hole, placing a dot at this point. Then push the tack through this dot.

2. Scribe a circle 30½" in diameter on the pattern paper by placing thumbtack at end of compass through center dot of the pattern paper and pushing a sharp pencil point through the tack hole at the other end (Figure II-18). Hold tack in place at the center and swing compass around the full circle, using the pencil as a handle.

3. Make another thumbtack hole on your compass at a distance of 7¾" from original hole. In the same manner as step 2, scribe a circle 15½" in diameter around the same center dot. Cut out both circles with paper scissors and you will be left with a doughnut-shaped template.

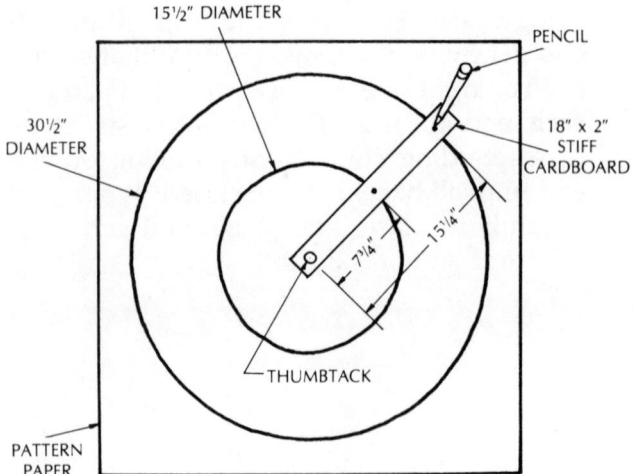

Figure II-18

4. Transfer the template pattern to the wrong side of the poncho material by tracing both circular outlines with felt-tipped pen or tailor's chalk.

5. Using sewing scissors, cut outer circle out of fabric, just inside the marked line. Now cut out inner circle just outside the marked line.

6. Fold back raw edge of outer circle to form a ¼" hem and pin in place all around. Baste; then sew final hem with matching thread.

7. Fold back raw edge of inner circle to form a hem ⅜" to ½" deep and pin in place all around circle. Baste hem, leaving 2" ends at start and finish. Remove pins.

Poncho Crochet

Using No. 13 hook and pearl cotton yarn, cast 6 sts per inch into inner hem, according to directions set out in Casting into Fabric in Part I.

Round 1 Using size D hook, * ch 9, sk 6 sts on hem and sc in 7th st on hem. Repeat from * until three-fourths of the way back to beg. Count remaining sts on hem and divide this number by 7. Disregard the quotient and you will be left with a remainder of 1, 2, 3, etc., up to 6, or 0, if the number of remaining sts on hem is exactly divisible by 7. If your remainder is 0, continue as before. If your remainder is other than 0, sc in 8th st for the number of lps shown in the table below, and then continue as before.

Remainder	Number of Loops
1	1
2	2
3	3
4	4
5	5
6	6

This process ensures that your last ch-9 will contain 7 sts on your cast-on hem. End first rnd with ch-9.

Round 2 Sl st in first ch sp of your first ch-9 lp. Sl st for 3 more chs, sc in 5th ch sp, which is the center of your first lp of ch-9s. * Ch 7, sc in 5th ch sp of your next lp of ch-9s. Repeat from * , ending rnd with ch-7.

Round 3 Sl st in first ch sp of your first ch-7 lp. Sl st for 2 more chs, sc in 4th ch sp, which is the center of the first lp of ch-7s. * Ch 7, sc in 4th ch sp of your next lp of ch-7s. Repeat from *, ending with ch-7.

Round 4 Sl st in first ch sp of your 2nd rnd of ch-7s, sl st for 2 more chs, sc in 4th ch sp, which is the center of your first lp of ch-7s of 3rd rnd. * Ch 5, sc in 4th ch sp of your next lp of ch-7s. Repeat from *, ending with ch-5.

Rounds 5–11 Sl st in first ch sp of your first lp of ch-5s of pr rnd. Sl st for 1 more ch, sc in 3rd ch sp, which is the center of your first lp of ch-5s of pr rnd. * Ch 5, sc in 3rd ch sp of your next lp. Repeat from *, ending with ch-5.

Round 12 Sl st in first ch of first lp of ch-5s. Sl st for 1 more ch, sc in 3rd ch sp of this lp. * Ch 3, sc in 3rd ch sp of next lp. Repeat from *, ending with ch-3.

Round 13 Sl st in first ch of first lp of ch-3s, sc in 2nd ch sp, * ch 1, sc in 2nd ch sp of next lp. Repeat from *, ending with ch-1.

Rounds 14, 15 Sl st to sc before first ch-1 lp, sc in ch-1, * ch 1, sc in next ch-1. Repeat from *, ending with ch-1.

Round 16 Change to size B hook and repeat 14th rnd. End by knotting yarn and cutting, leave a 24" end.

Finishing Using a yarn needle, travel the loose end through the crocheted lps, taking shortest path to hem. Knot gently to first st under hem; hide further by traveling for about 12 more sts under hem; then cut.

Net Hat

By using a commercial brim material in a color to match a particular outfit in your wardrobe, you can transform this easy-to-make hat into a fashionable accessory, or it can become a floppy, casual style when made from denim, duck or canvas.

Materials

1 16" × 20" or 32" × 10" piece of semistiff hat brim material. Stiff felt or nylon window-screening material may also be used. If denim or canvas is used, two layers, each right side out, should sandwich a layer of stiff interfacing between, so twice the amount of material as shown above will be required for brim material, plus the amount for interfacing.
1 ball (53 yds.) of No. 5 pearl cotton yarn in matching or contrasting color to brim material
2 yds. (¾" wide) of bias binding in color matching brim material or yarn
1 No. 13 crochet hook (steel), if using denim or canvas
1 No. 8–13 crochet hook (steel) (Use the largest size that will pass easily through holes in commercial brim material or screening.)
1 size B crochet hook
pencil
1 piece of stiff cardboard or oaktag, 18" x 12"
right angle or square
yardstick
felt-tipped pen or chalk
scissors
sewing scissors
sewing needle and thread
yarn needle

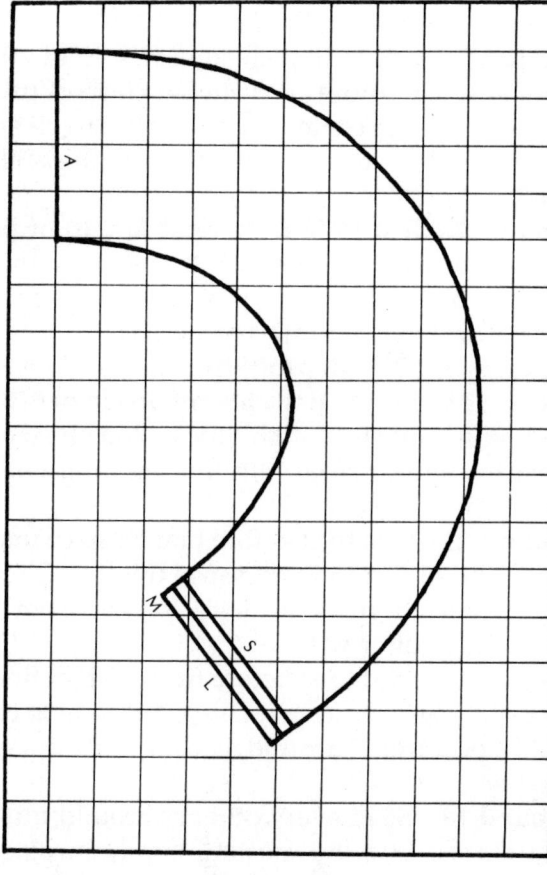

EACH SQUARE = 1" x 1"

Figure II-19

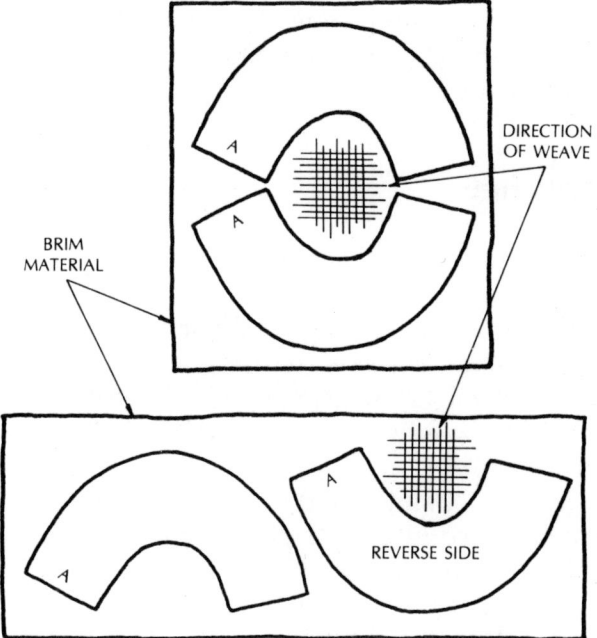

Figure II-20

Preparation

1. Using pencil, construct an 18" x 12" rectangle on cardboard or oaktag, using a right angle, square, or hard cover of a large book to ensure right angles at all corners. With yardstick, mark off all edges of your rectangle with small dots at 1" intervals. Connect corresponding dots with pencil lines so that you end up with the background grid shown in Figure II-19.

2. Still with pencil, darken line A (Figure II-19) on your grid. Then transfer curved lines to your grid by noting where and at what general angle they intersect grid lines, making short pencil strokes to correspond. When completed, check over curved lines to see that they are similar to the curves in Figure II-19 and make necessary corrections. Note that the S, M and L of Figure II-19 are alternate ending lines for Small, Medium and Large sizes, respectively. Connect pencil strokes with a smooth pencil line and recheck appearance, correcting with pencil where necessary. When correct, trace over pencil line with felt-tipped pen.

3. Using paper scissors, cut template out of cardboard right on the scribed line. Consult Figure II-20 for best alternate layout to suit your brim material. Using felt-tipped pen, trace the template once, right side up; then turn over and trace again. Note the relationship of the brim material weave to A edges. If you are using 2 layers of fabric sandwiching an interface layer as your brim material, you must trace each template position twice for fabric and once for interfacing.

4. Cut patterns out of brim material just inside lines. Using thread in color matching brim material, sew A edges together with 3 lines of stitching, allowing an overlap of ¼" to ⅜". Repeat for other edges. If you are using 3 layers of brim material, sew edges of each layer separately. Then, making sure that right side of fabric is out for top and bottom layer, sew an oval lp joining all layers; start about ¾" from outside edge of the brim and go all the way around, conforming to outside curvature of the brim. Repeat this operation with a series of oval lps, about ⅜" apart, until you reach a distance of about ¾" from inner edge.

5. Finish outer edge by sandwiching it with ¾" bias binding, pinned all around and sewn with 2 lines of stitching.

Crochet

Cast onto inner edge with pearl cotton yarn, following directions set out in Casting into Fabric in Part I. If using denim or canvas, cast with a No. 13 hook. If using screening or commercial brim material, use largest size hook that passes easily through the holes. Sl st to connect.

Round 1 Using size B hook, * ch 7, sk 6 sts on hem, sc in 7th. Repeat from * around, ending with ch-7.

Round 2 Sl st in first ch sp of first lp of pr rnd, sl st for 2 more chs, sc in 4th ch sp of this lp, which is the center, * ch 7, sc in 4th ch sp of next lp. Repeat from * around, ending with ch-7.

Rounds 3, 4 Repeat 2nd rnd.

Round 5 Sl st to first ch sp of first lp of 4th rnd, sl st for 2 more chs, sc in 4th ch sp, which is the center of this lp. * Ch 5, sc in 4th ch sp of next lp. Repeat from * around, ending with ch-5.

Round 6 Sl st to first ch sp of first lp of pr rnd, sl st for 1 more ch, sc in 3rd ch sp, which is the center of this lp. * Ch 5, sc in 3rd ch sp of next lp. Repeat from * around, ending with ch-5.

Round 7 Repeat 6th rnd.

Round 8 Sl st to first ch sp of first lp of 7th rnd, sl st for 1 more ch, sc in 3rd ch sp of this lp, which is the center. * Ch 3, sc in 3rd ch sp of next lp. Repeat from * around, ending with ch-3.

Round 9 Sl st to first ch sp of first lp of pr rnd, sc in 2nd ch sp, which is the center of this lp, * ch 3, sc in 2nd ch sp of next lp. Repeat from * around, ending with ch-3.

Rounds 10, 11 Repeat 9th rnd.

Round 12 Sl st to first ch sp of first lp of 11th rnd, sc in 2nd ch sp, * ch 1, sc in 2nd ch sp of next lp. Repeat from * around, ending with ch-1.

Round 13 Sl st to st before first ch sp of first lp of 12th rnd, sc in first ch sp of this lp. * Ch 1, sc in first ch sp of next lp. Repeat from * around, ending with ch-1.

Round 14 Sl st to st before first ch sp of first lp of 13th rnd, sc in first ch sp, * sc in next ch sp. Repeat from * around, ending with sl st to first sc.

Round 15 Sc in every other sc around until pat closes. End by knotting gently in place and cutting yarn, leaving an 18" end.

Finishing Hide loose end by traveling it with yarn or tapestry needle through the crocheted lps in the direction of inner edge of brim. Knot gently to first available st at underside of brim; hide further by traveling it through approximately 12 sts on underside of brim hem; then cut.

Evening Purse Bag

A chic accessory to the various dress styles previously presented, this bag can be made from a leftover scrap of the original dress material. For an embellished version of this purse see Evening Shoulder Bag on page 65.

Materials

1 piece of dress material, 8" x 12"
½ ball (26½ yds.) of No. 5 pearl cotton yarn in matching or contrasting color to dress material
1 No. 13 crochet hook (steel)
1 size B crochet hook
pencil
right angle or square
ruler
1 piece of stiff cardboard or oaktag, 8½" x 8"
felt-tipped pen or chalk
scissors
straight pins
sewing scissors
sewing needle and thread
yarn or tapestry needle

Preparation

1. Using pencil and right angle (or hard cover of a large book), construct a rectangle measuring 8½" x 8" on cardboard or oaktag. Mark each edge of rectangle with small dots spaced at ½" intervals. Connect corresponding dots with pencil lines to form background grid, as shown in Figure II-21. Transfer bag pattern to your grid by noting where outline crosses each grid line and at what general angle. Duplicate, using short pencil strokes. When complete, check for errors and connect pencil strokes with a continuous pencil line. Recheck and correct with pencil, smoothing out curves. Finally, trace over pencil line with felt-tipped pen.

2. Using paper scissors, cut pattern out on line. Fold 12" edge of dress material in half, with both wrong sides out. Place template over material with straight top edge in line with material weave. Trace outline on material with felt-tipped pen or tailor's chalk.

3. To aid in cutting and seaming, pin material front to back at intervals about ½" inside outline. Cut both layers out of fabric simultaneously, just inside marked line.

4. Using thread of matching color, seam with 2 lines of stitching about ¼" from edges, leaving top edge of bag raw. Turn bag right side out and fold back top edge to form a hem slightly deeper than ¼". Pin in place all around top.

Crochet

Using No. 13 hook and pearl cotton yarn, cast into top pinned hem, starting at a side seam and following the directions set out in Casting into Fabric in Part I. Pass other side seam and continue back to start.

Round 1   Using size B hook, sl st to first sc (at first side seam). * Ch 5, sk 4 sts on hem, sc in 5th st. Repeat from * around, ending with ch-5.

Round 2   Sl st to first ch sp of first lp of ch-5s, sl st 1 more ch, sc in 3rd ch sp, which is the center of this lp. * Ch 5, sc in 3rd ch sp of next lp. Repeat from * around, ending with ch-5.

Round 3   Repeat 2nd rnd.

Round 4   Sl st to first ch sp of first lp of 3rd rnd, sl st 1 more ch, sc in 3rd ch sp of this lp. * Ch 3, sc in 3rd ch sp of next lp. Repeat from * around, ending with ch-3.

Round 5   Hdc in first ch of first lp of ch-3s, sc in next ch, hdc in 3rd ch. * Hdc in first ch of next lp, sc in next ch, hdc in next ch. Repeat from * around, ending with approximately 5 loose sl sts to the st *before* the st which is directly in line with and above the side seam. Sc in this st, then sc for 2 more sts, keeping these 3 sts centered above the side seam.

Strap   Ch 3; turn; hdc in first sc long enough to equal the length of the 3 chs you have just made. Hdc in 2nd sc with the same length, hdc in 3rd sc with the same length. Ch 3; turn. Continue in this fashion to total 15 rows of 3 hdc, or desired strap length. Making sure that strap is not twisted, end with sl st to st *just before* st which is directly in line with and above other side seam. Sl st to this st, then sl st to next st. Knot gently and cut yarn, leaving a 6" end.

Finishing   Using a yarn or tapestry needle, travel loose end through the crocheted lps, taking shortest path in direction of hem. Knot gently to first available st under hem; then hide the end further by traveling it under approximately 10 sts on hem; then cut.

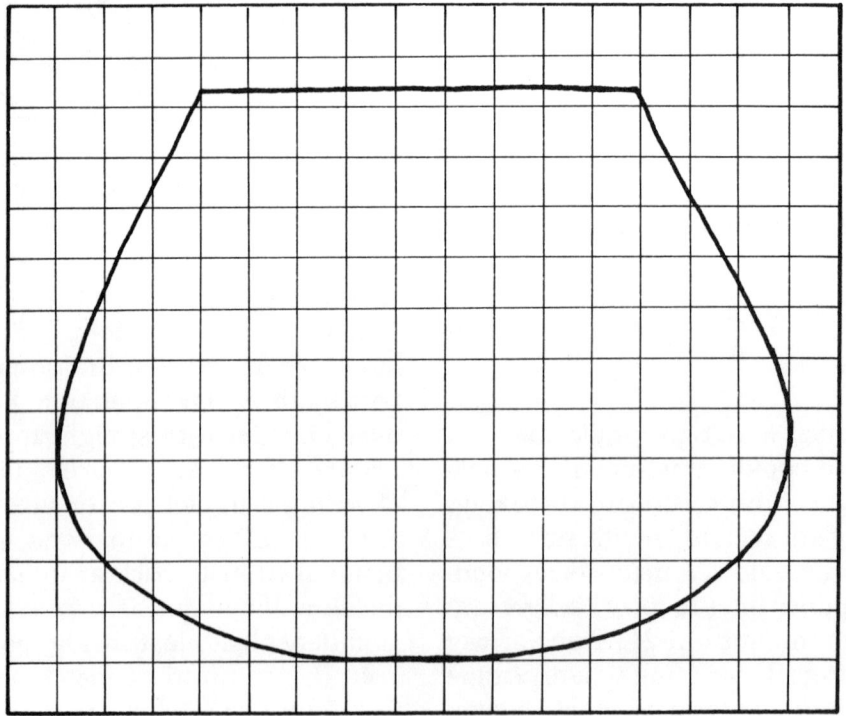

EACH SQUARE = ½" x ½"

Figure II-21

Sturdy Tote Bag

Materials

1 yd. (36" wide) of canvas in dark shade of your choice
125 yds. (about $\frac{1}{16}$" thick) of cord or heavy twine in light, neutral shade
crochet hooks in sizes B, C, E, J and K
china marker
ruler
right angle or square
compass
scissors
sewing scissors
straight pins
sewing needle and button/carpet sewing thread
18 ($\frac{3}{16}$") silver eyelets and eyeletting tool
safety pins

Preparation

1. Using china marker, construct a rectangle measuring 36" x 10" on wrong side of canvas. Make sure corners are correct by using right angle or cover of a large book. Scribe a circle 12" in diameter alongside the rectangle. Cut rectangle and circle out of canvas.
2. Fold rectangle in half, wrong sides out, and seam 10" edges tog with 2 rows of stitching, about $\frac{1}{4}$" deep, using button/carpet thread.
3. Open rectangle, still wrong side out, to form a cylinder, and pin circular piece to end, about $\frac{3}{8}$" from each raw edge, all the way around. Sew securely about $\frac{1}{4}$" in from raw edge.
4. Fold back other edge of the cylinder to form a hem $\frac{1}{2}$" deep and pin in place all around. Using china marker, place a dot about 1" from side seam at center of hem; then

place dots all around hem at just a hair less than 2" intervals, so that you will have 18 evenly spaced dots.
5. Puncture dots with eyeletting tool and insert eyelets, using tool and being sure that finished side of eyelet faces right side of bag. Turn bag right side out.

Crochet

Round 1 Using size C hook and facing hem on inside of bag, make sl kn, sc in eyelet nearest side seam. * Ch 7, sc in next eyelet.

Repeat from * around, ending with sl st to first ch sp of your first ch-7. Sl st for 1 more ch.
Round 2 Sl st through loophole in ch-7 lp you are working. Ch 1. With size K hook, do hazelnut st in same loophole with 6 strands on hook to close. * Ch 3, do hazelnut st in next lp, as before. Repeat from * around, ending with ch-3.
Round 3 Using size J hook, sl st to first hazelnut of pr rnd, ch 1. * Sc in each ch sp of ch-3 and in each hazelnut. Repeat from * around.
Round 4 Sl st to first sc of pr rnd, sc in every sc of pr rnd.
Round 5 Using size B hook, sl st to first sc of pr rnd, * ch 7, sk 4 sc and sc in 5th sc. Repeat from * around, ending with ch-7.
Round 6 Using size K hook, sl st for 2 chs and do hazelnut st in same loophole you are working, with 6 strands on hook to close. * Ch 3, do hazelnut st the same way in next loophole. Repeat from * around, ending with ch-3.
Round 7 Repeat 3rd rnd.
Round 8 Repeat 4th rnd.
Round 9 Repeat 5th rnd.
Round 10 Repeat 6th rnd.
Round 11 Repeat 3rd rnd.
Round 12 Repeat 4th rnd, ending with sc in first sc.
Round 13 Using size E hook, * ch 5, sk 1 sc and sc in 2nd sc. Repeat from * around, ending with ch-5.
Round 14 Sl st to first sc of pr rnd, * ch 5, sc in next sc. Repeat from * around, ending with ch-5.
Round 15 Using size B hook, repeat 14th rnd, ending with sc in last sc and knotting gently in place. Cut yarn, leaving a 12" end.
Strap Press bag down on a flat surface with side seam at exact center, facing you. Place 2 small safety pins in the eyelets at extreme right and left edges of bag. There should be 8 eyelets between these 2 eyelets. Now locate the 2 adjacent ch-5 lps of the 15th rnd that are directly above and in line with one of the pinned eyelets and mark them for reference with 2 small safety pins.
Row 1 Using size B hook, sc in first sc of the first of these pinned lps. Ch 5, sc in last sc of this lp. Ch 5, sc in last sc of 2nd pinned lp.
Row 2 Ch 5; turn; sc in center sc of these 2 lps, ch 5, sc in last sc.
Rows 3, 4 Repeat 2nd row.
Row 5 Ch 3; turn; sc in center sc of lps, ch 3, sc in last sc of lp; turn.
Rows 6–105 Repeat 5th row.
Rows 106–109 Repeat 2nd row.
Row 110 (joining row) Mark 2 ch-5 lps of 15th rnd with safety pins by following line of other pinned eyelet at hem of bag. Making sure strap is not twisted, use size B hook and sl st in first sc of proper pinned lp securely, sl st through 4 chs of your last lp of ch-5s of 109th row, sc in 5th ch and center of 2 pinned lps. Sl st 4 chs of last lp of ch-5s on strap, sc securely in last ch of 2nd lp on bag. Knot yarn and cut, leaving a 12" end.
Finishing Using a yarn needle, bring all loose ends to inside of bag. Travel them through the sts of the crocheted lps for their entire lengths so that they will remain secure.

Window Sunburst

This beautiful window decoration is designed to hook onto the lower sash of a 26" x 26" (or larger) window frame. Without obstructing the light or the view, it greatly enhances the character of any room with the distinctive qualities of hand crochet.

Materials

1 piece of light nylon with length and width 8" greater than the dimensions of canvas stretchers (see below)
½ ball (26½ yds.) of No. 5 pearl cotton yarn in color to match nylon fabric (color A)
½ ball (26½ yds.) of No. 5 pearl cotton yarn in each of 5 other colors in pattern (colors B, C, D, E and F) (Suggestion: pattern works best if color C is black.)
1 No. 13 crochet hook (steel)
1 size E crochet hook
1 piece of stiff cardboard, 14" x 2", for compass
thumbtack
yardstick
pencil
1 piece of stiff wrapping paper or light cardboard, 2' x 2', for template
scissors
felt-tipped pen or chalk
sewing scissors
straight pins
sewing needle and thread
2 prs. of canvas stretchers in largest size possible to fit within your window frame (They should not be smaller than 26" x 26".)
stapling gun
awl
1 roll (1½" wide) of adhesive-backed fabric tape in color to match nylon fabric
2 (¾") screweyes
2 (¾") brass cup hooks

Preparation

1. To construct a simple compass in order to make template, push a thumbtack through the 14" x 2" piece of cardboard, about 1" from the end of the short side. Remove tack and measure 11" from the tackhole, placing a reference dot there. Push thumbtack through dot and enlarge first tackhole slightly with the point of a sharp pencil.

2. Push tack at end of compass through the center of the 2' x 2' piece of stiff pattern. Holding center tack firmly, push a sharp pencil through the other tackhole and, using the pencil as a handle, swing the compass completely around to mark a circle on the template paper. Cut circle out of paper directly on marked line.

3. Lay out nylon fabric on a flat surface and place circular template over it so that it is centered. Trace around circle with felt-tipped pen and cut circle out of fabric just outside marked line.

4. Fold back raw edge of circular cutout to form a hem ⅜" to ½" deep; pin in place all around, making sure hem is flat and not pulling or stretching. Baste hem with sewing thread and remove pins.

Crochet

Using No. 13 hook and color A yarn, cast around hem, following directions set out in Casting into Fabric in Part I. End with sl st to first sc, knot and cut color A yarn, leaving a 4" end.

Round 1 Using size E hook and color B yarn, make a sl kn, leaving an 8" end, sc in next st on hem, * ch 9, sk 8 sts on hem, sc in 9th st. Repeat from * until you are three-fourths of the way around. Now count the remaining sts on your cast-on hem and divide this number by 9. Disregard the quotient; this will leave you with a remainder of 1, 2, 3, etc., up to 8, or 0, if the number of remaining sts on your hem is exactly divisible by 9. If your remainder is 0, continue as before. If your remainder is other than 0, sc in 10th st on your hem for the number of lps shown in the table below, and then continue as before.

Remainder	Number of Loops
1	1
2	2
3	3
4	4
5	5
6	6
7	7
8	8

This process ensures that your last ch-9 will contain exactly 9 sts on your cast-on hem. End first rnd with ch-9.

Round 2 Sl st to first ch sp of first lp of first rnd, sl st for 4 more chs, sc in 5th ch sp, which is the center of this lp. * Ch 9, sc in 5th ch sp of next lp. Repeat from * around, ending with sl st to first ch sp of first lp of 2nd rnd, sl st for 3 more chs, insert hook in 5th ch sp, yoh, ptl; finish sc with color C. Cut color B yarn, leaving an 8" end.

Round 3 Ch 9, sc in 5th ch sp of 2nd lp of 2nd rnd, * ch 9, sc in 5th ch sp of next lp. Repeat from * around, ending with sl st to first ch sp of first lp of 3rd rnd, sl st for 3 more chs, insert hook in 5th ch sp, yoh, ptl; finish sc with color D in 5th ch sp of this lp. Cut color C yarn, leaving an 8" end.

Round 4 * Ch 7, sc in 5th ch sp of next lp of 3rd rnd. Repeat from * around, ending with ch-7.

Round 5 Sl st in first ch sp of first lp of 4th rnd, sl st for 2 more chs, sc in 4th ch sp, which is the center of this lp. * Ch 7, sc in 4th ch sp of next lp. Repeat from * around, ending with sl st to first ch sp of first lp of 5th rnd, sl st for 2 more chs, insert hook in 4th ch sp, yoh, ptl; finish sc in 4th ch sp with color C. Cut color D, leaving an 8" end.

Round 6 * Ch 7, sc in 4th ch sp of next lp of 5th rnd. Repeat from * around, ending with sl st to first ch sp of first lp of 6th rnd, sl st for 2 more chs, insert hook in 4th ch sp, yoh, ptl; finish sc in 4th ch sp of this lp with color E. Cut color C yarn, leaving an 8" end.

Round 7 * Ch 7, sc in 4th ch sp of next lp of 6th rnd. Repeat from * around, ending with ch-5.

Round 8 Sl st to first ch sp of first lp of 7th rnd, sl st for 2 more chs, sc in 4th ch sp of this lp. * Ch 5, sc in 4th ch sp of next lp of 7th rnd. Repeat from * around, ending with sl st to first ch sp of first lp of 8th rnd, sl st for 1 more ch, insert hook in 3rd ch sp, yoh, ptl; finish sc in 3rd ch sp with color C. Cut color E, leaving an 8" end.

Round 9 * Ch 5, sc in 3rd ch sp of next lp of 8th rnd. Repeat from * around, ending with sl st to first ch sp of first lp of 9th rnd, sl st for 1 more ch, insert hook in 3rd ch sp, yoh, ptl; finish sc in 3rd ch sp of this lp with color F. Cut color C, leaving an 8" end.

Round 10 * Ch 5, sc in 3rd ch sp of next lp of 9th rnd. Repeat from * around, ending with sl st to first ch sp of first lp of 10th rnd, sl st for 1 more ch, sc in 3rd ch sp of this lp.

Round 11 Repeat 10th rnd, ending with sl st to first ch sp of first lp of 10th rnd, sl st for 1 more ch, insert hook, yoh, ptl; finish sc with color C. Cut color F, leaving an 8" end.

Round 12 * Ch 5, sc in 3rd ch sp of next lp of 11th rnd. Repeat from * around, ending with sl st to first ch sp of first lp of 12th rnd, sl st for 1 more ch, insert hook, yoh, ptl; finish sc with color B. Cut color C, leaving an 8" end.

Round 13 * Ch 3, sc in 3rd ch sp of next lp of 12th rnd. Repeat from * around, ending with sl st to first ch sp of first lp, sl st for 1 more ch, sc in 3rd ch sp of this lp.

Round 14 * Ch 3, sc in 2nd ch sp of next lp of 13th rnd. Repeat from * around, ending with sl st to first ch sp of first lp of 14th rnd, insert hook, yoh, ptl; finish sc with color C. Cut color B, leaving an 8" end.
Round 15 * Ch 3, sc in 2nd ch sp of next lp of 14th rnd. Repeat from * around, ending with sl st to first ch sp of first lp of 15th rnd, insert hook, yoh, ptl; finish sc with color D in 2nd ch sp of this lp. Cut color C, leaving an 8" end.
Round 16 * Ch 3, sc in 2nd ch sp of next lp of 15th rnd. Repeat from * around, ending with sl st to first ch sp of first lp of 16th rnd, sc in 2nd ch sp of this lp.
Round 17 * Ch 3, sc in 2nd ch sp of next lp of 16th rnd. Repeat from * around, ending with sl st to first ch sp of first lp of 17th rnd, insert hook, yoh, ptl; finish sc in 2nd ch sp with color C. Cut color D, leaving an 8" end.
Round 18 * Ch 1, sc in 2nd ch sp of next lp of 17th rnd. Repeat from * around, ending with sl st to st *before* ch-1 sp of first lp of 18th rnd, insert hook in ch-1 sp, yoh, ptl; finish sc with color E. Cut Color C, leaving an 8" end.
Round 19 * Ch 1, sc in ch-1 sp of next lp of 18th rnd. Repeat from * around, ending with sl st to st before first ch-1 sp, sc in ch-1 sp.
Round 20 * Ch 1, sc in ch-1 sp of next lp of 19th rnd. Repeat from * around, ending with sl st to st before first ch-1 sp, insert hook in ch-1 sp, yoh, ptl; finish sc in ch-1 sp with color C. Cut color E, leaving an 8" end.
Round 21 * Ch 1, sc in ch-1 sp of next lp of 20th rnd. Repeat from * around, ending with sl st to st before first ch-1 sp, insert hook in ch-1 sp, yoh, ptl; finish sc in ch-1 sp with color F. Cut color C, leaving an 8" end.
Round 22 * Ch 1, sc in ch-1 sp of next lp of 21st rnd. Repeat from * around, ending with sl st to st before first ch-1 sp of first lp, sc in ch-1 sp.
Round 23 * Sc in next ch-1 sp. Repeat from * around, ending with sl st to first sc.
Round 24 Insert hook in first sc, yoh, ptl; finish first sc with color C. Cut color F, leaving an 8" end. Sc in every sc around, ending with sl st to first sc, insert hook in first sc, yoh, ptl; finish next sc with color B. Cut color C, leaving an 8" end.
Round 25 Sc in every sc around, ending with sl st to first sc.
Round 26 Repeat 25th rnd, ending with sl st to first sc, insert hook in first sc, yoh, ptl; finish next sc with color C. Cut color B, leaving an 8" end.
Round 27 Sc in every sc, ending with sl st to first sc, insert hook, yoh, ptl; finish next sc with color D. Cut color C, leaving an 8" end.
Round 28 Sc in every sc, ending with sl st to first sc.
Round 29 Sc in every *other* sc, ending with sl st to first sc, insert hook, yoh, ptl; finish next sc with color C. Cut color D, leaving an 8" end.
Round 30 Sc in every other sc, ending with sl st to first sc, insert hook, yoh, ptl; finish sc with color E. Cut color C, leaving an 8" end.
Round 31 Sc in every other sc, ending with sl st to first sc.
Round 32 Repeat 31st rnd, ending with sl st to first sc, insert hook, yoh, ptl; finish next sc with color C. Cut color E, leaving an 8" end.
Round 33 Sc in every other sc, ending with sl st to first sc, yoh, finish next sc with color F. Cut color C, leaving an 8" end.
Round 34 Sc in every other sc to close. Knot gently and cut yarn, leaving a 6" end.
Finishing Using No. 13 hook, bring all ends to wrong side. Knot each end gently. Using yarn needle, travel each end through approximately 15 sts of corresponding color and knot gently. Travel for approximately 6 sts more; then cut yarn. Travel end at hem for approximately 12 sts under hem; knot gently; travel for about 6 more sts; cut yarn.

Assembly

1. Assemble canvas stretcher frame by interlocking joints. Lay out crocheted sunburst on a flat surface with wrong side facing you. Place frame over design so that it is centered, being sure that the longer dimension of the fabric corresponds with the longer canvas stretcher.

2. Starting with this longer dimension and making sure that you do not uncenter the design, gently bring the fabric over the frame and fold it back just before it reaches the inside frame edge, as shown in Figure II-22.

Then fold it again just before it reaches the outside edge (Figure II-22). Using staple gun, place a staple at the center of the frame (position 1 of Figure II-23).

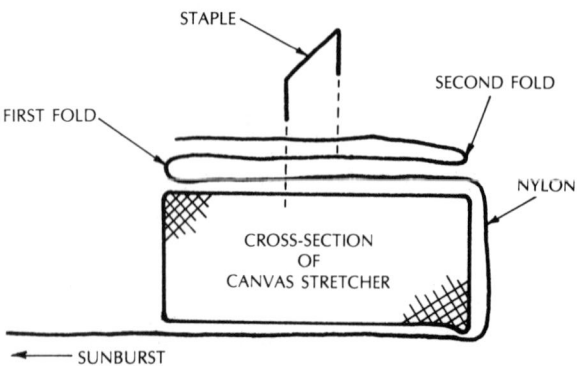

Figure II-22

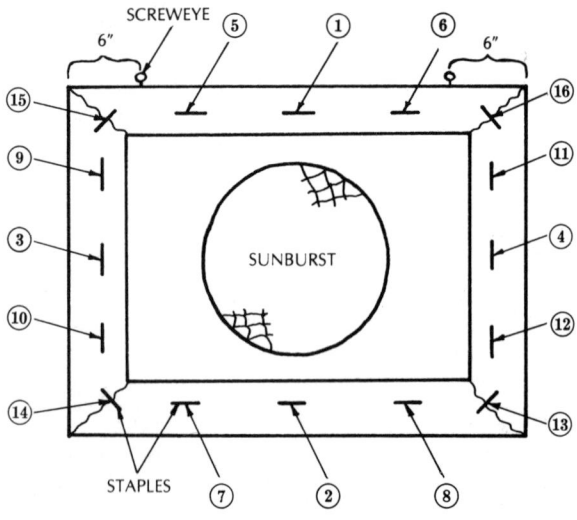

Figure II-23

3. Now do the same for the opposite side (position 2 of Figure II-23), this time pulling fabric slightly so that the tension across the center of the design is firm but not tight.

4. Repeat this procedure for the shorter leg (position 3 of Figure II-23), keeping outline of design circular while gently pulling fabric.

5. Positions 4 through 12 should then be stapled in a similar manner to step 4, gently pulling fabric while watching out for circularity of design outline.

6. Excess fabric at corners should be neatly overlapped and folded so that they lie as flat as possible against frame, and should be stapled down as shown (positions 13 through 16).

7. Cover staples and fabric folds by framing with 1½" wide adhesive-backed fabric tape in available color that best matches fabric.

8. Attach 2 (¾") screweyes to top edge of frame by starting holes 6" from either end (Figure II-23) with awl, making sure that you do not tear fabric when screwing eyes down.

9. Place completed frame in proper position in window and make 2 reference marks on window sash frame by pushing the awl through the screweye lps. Deepen these holes with the awl and screw in 2 (¾") brass cup hooks to sash frame, with hooks pointing upward. The sunburst can now be attached by holding it horizontally, engaging the hooks with the eyes, and letting the entire frame drop gently into a vertical position.

Scallop Ruffle Kerchief

Materials

½ yd. (45" wide) of silky kerchief material, such as rayon; or cotton, if preferred
1 ball (53 yds.) of No. 5 pearl cotton yarn (color B)
2 balls (95 yds. each) of No. 8 pearl cotton yarn, 1 for color A, 1 for color C
1 No. 13 crochet hook (steel)
1 No. 14 crochet hook (steel), if kerchief material is of fine weave
1 piece of stiff wrapping paper, 42" x 20", for pattern
felt-tipped pen or chalk
yardstick
right angle or square
scissors
sewing scissors
straight pins
sewing needle and thread
yarn needle

Preparation

1. Lay out pattern shown in Figure II-24 on stiff wrapping paper by drawing a 40" line about 1" from the 42" edge. Find the center of this line by measuring in 20" from end and place a dot there.
2. Using a right angle or cover of a large book, draw a perpendicular line at the center dot. Measure up 17" from the dot and place another dot. Now connect this dot to the ends of the 40" line forming the triangle shown in Figure II-24. With paper scissors, cut out triangle directly on marked lines.
3. Transfer triangular pattern to wrong side of kerchief material by tracing around outline with felt-tipped pen. Cut triangle out of fabric with sewing scissors just inside marked lines.
4. Fold back raw edge of triangle about ¼" or less; then fold again to form a double-layered hem. Pin in place all the way around, baste with sewing thread, and remove pins.

Crochet

Using No. 13 hook (or No. 14 for very finely woven material) and color A (No. 8) yarn, start casting into hem at a point 9" from end on base of triangle (Figure II-24). Cast according to instructions given in Casting into Fabric in Part I. End cast with sl st to first sc.

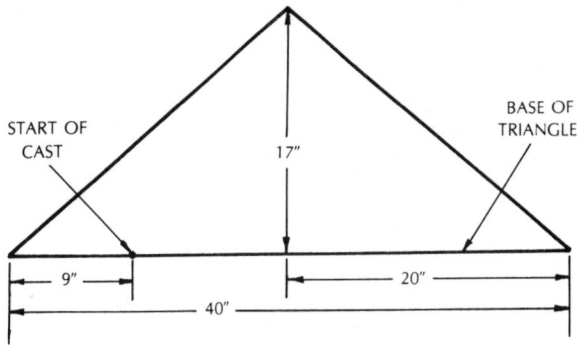

Figure II-24

Row 1 Using No. 13 hook, sc in next sc on hem, sc for 2 more sc. * (Sc, hdc, dc, hdc, sc) in next sc, sc in next 3 sc (cluster made). Repeat from * around triangle, ending with sl st to st *before* first cluster, yoh, complete sc in first st of cluster with color B (No. 5) yarn. Cut color A yarn, leaving an 8" end.

Base of triangle/Row 2 Sc in every st across base of triangle until you reach a point 9" from the other end (Figure II-25), ending with sc in last st of cluster, sl st to next sc on hem; turn.

Row 3 Yoh, sc in first st of cluster with color C. Cut color B, leaving an 8" end. Sc across to start of 2nd row (Figure II-25). Knot gently; then cut yarn, leaving an 8" end.

Remainder of triangle/Row 2 Make a sl kn with color B yarn, sc in first st of first cluster that is 9" from point of triangle (Figure II-25). Sc in every sc across until you reach a point 9" from the other end (Figure II-25), end with sc in last sc of cluster, sl st to next sc on hem; turn.

Row 3 Repeat row 3 as for Base of triangle.

Finishing Knot each end gently in place. Using a yarn or tapestry needle, bring ends under hem and travel for a few inches. Then bring out, knotting again to nearest st. Bring under again and travel for a few more inches; then cut.

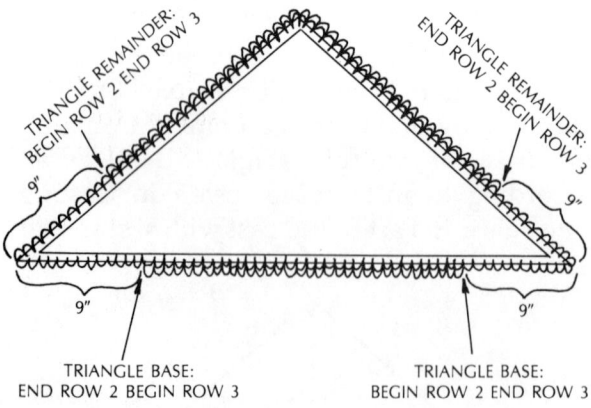

Figure II-25

Rosette-Bordered Skirt

Transform a plain skirt into a richly decorated peasant style with these ten hand-crocheted rosettes.

Materials

1 skirt, unpleated, slightly flared (maximum dimension X of Figure II-26: 23"), preferably 1 color
8 balls (95 yds. each) of No. 8 pearl cotton yarn in variegated shades to match color of skirt
1 No. 14 crochet hook (steel)
small piece of stiff cardboard or oaktag for template
ruler
cloth tape measure
compass
felt-tipped pen or chalk
scissors
sewing scissors
straight pins
sewing needle and thread
yarn needle

Preparation

1. Scribe a circle 3" in diameter on stiff cardboard or oaktag with compass and cut out directly on scribed line.

2. Lay out skirt on a flat surface with side seams at extreme edges. Using cloth tape measure to conform to curvature of hemline, measure dimension X of Figure II-26, at a distance of 4½" above bottom of hemline.

3. Divide dimension X by 10, giving you dimension Y for your skirt. This dimension will be the distance between circles, as shown in Figure II-27. Starting near the left-hand seam, place the circular template on the skirt

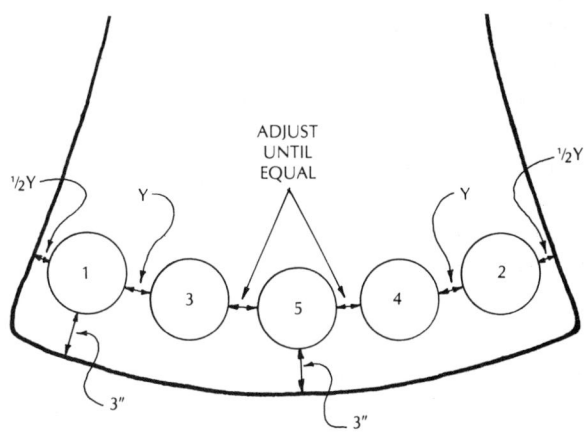

Figure II-27

so that the left edge of the circle is *half* of dimension Y from the left side seam and the bottom edge is 3" from bottom of hemline. When in position, trace around template with felt-tipped pen.

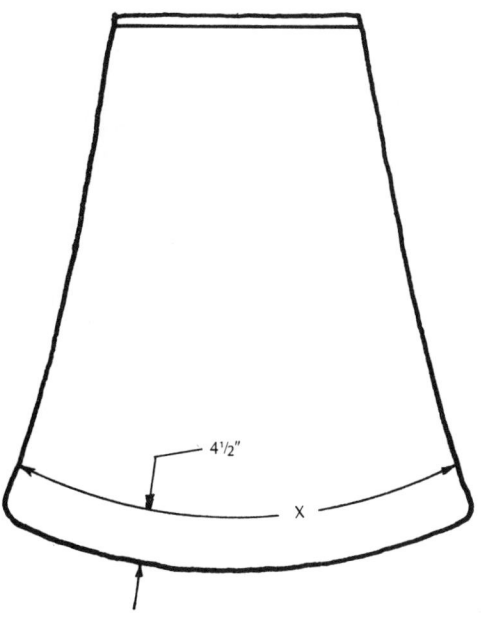

Figure II-26

4. Repeat step 3 for right side, this time adjusting template so that right edge is half of dimension Y from right side seam.

5. Now mark the second-from-the-left circle (circle 3 in Figure II-27) with the left edge of the template, using the distance *equal* to dimension Y from the right edge of the first circle.

6. Repeat step 5 for the second-from-the-right circle (circle 4), this time keeping the length of dimension Y between the right edge of the template and the left edge of circle 2.

7. For the fifth and central circle, you may have to compensate slightly for small errors made during previous measurements. Place the circular template between circles 3 and 4, making sure that the bottom edge is 3" from bottom of hemline, and adjust it so that the distances from the left and right edges to circles 3 and 4 are equal. If these distances are the same as dimension Y, your previous measurements were perfect. If not, a fraction of an inch difference will not spoil the visual symmetry in the final product. Trace around circle 5 with felt-tipped pen.

8. Turn skirt over and repeat the marking procedure for the 5 circles on the other side.

9. Using the sewing scissors, cut out all 10 circles just outside the marked lines. Turn skirt wrong side out. Fold back the raw edge at the top of one of the circles to form a hem about 3/8" deep and pin in place, making sure that the weave lines in the hem match up to the weave lines in the body of the skirt fabric.

Repeat for bottom of circle. Now pin remainder of hem, making sure that it lies flat, without pulling or stretching. Baste hem with sewing thread, leaving a 2" end at beg and end for easy thread removal later; remove pins. Repeat procedure for remaining 9 circles.

NOTE: Two sets of crochet instructions for the skirt border are presented. The first will produce a full and firm rosette pattern. As an alternate, you may prefer to choose the second set, which will give you a more delicate and spacious pattern.

Crochet

Make a sl kn on No. 14 hook with 2 strands of No. 8 yarn. Cast into the hem of one of the circles according to directions set out in Treble Crochet Casting into Fabric in Part I, chaining 5. End with sl st to first trc.

Round 1 With No. 14 hook and 2 strands of yarn, ch 1, 2 hdc in same trc. * Sk 3 trc on hem, 3 hdc in 4th trc. Repeat from * until three-fourths of the way around, then count the remaining trc on your cast-on hem. Divide this number by 3, disregarding the quotient, leaving you with a remainder of 1, 2 or 0. If your remainder is 0, continue as before. If it is 1, hdc in 5th trc for your next step; then continue as before. If your remainder is 2, hdc in 5th trc for your next 2 steps; then continue as before. End with sl st to ch-1 sp that began rnd.

Round 2 Ch 5, 2 trc in same ch-1 sp. * Sk 3 hdc of pr rnd, 3 trc in 4th hdc, keeping the length of the trc equal to the ch-5 length. Repeat from * until three-fourths of the way around, then count the remaining hdc of first rnd. Divide this number by 3, leaving you with a remainder of 1, 2 or 0. If your remainder is 0, continue as before. If 1, trc in 5th hdc for your next step; then continue as before. If 2, for the next 2 steps; then continue as before. End with sl st to top of ch-5 sp that began rnd.

Round 3 * Sk 3 trc, sc in 4th trc. Repeat from * until pat is closed. Knot yarn and cut, leaving a 9" end.

Repeat all of the above steps for remaining 9 circles.

Finishing Using No. 14 hook, bring ends to wrong side. With yarn needle, travel center end through sc and trc toward hem. Bring under hem, knotting to first available st under hem. Then travel further for approximately 12 sts under hem and cut yarn. Knot other end to first available st under hem, then travel further for approximately 12 more sts before cutting.

Alternate rosette pattern

Make a sl kn on No. 14 hook with 2 strands of No. 8 pearl cotton yarn. Cast into the hem of one of the circles, following instructions set out in Treble Crochet Casting into Fabric in Part I of this book, chaining 5. End with sl st to first trc.

Round 1 Ch 1, make 2 hdc in sp of sl st which ended cast-on. Sk 3 trc and * make 3 hdc in 4th st, sk 3 sts. Repeat from * until three-fourths of the way around, then count the remaining trc on your cast-on hem and divide this number by 3. This will leave you with a quotient and a remainder of 1, 2 or 0, if the number of remaining sts is exactly divisible by 3. If your remainder is 0, continue as before. If your remainder is 1, sk 4 sts and hdc in 5th for your next step; then continue as before. If your remainder is 2, sk 4 sts and hdc in 5th for your next 2 steps; then continue as before. End with sl st to ch-1. Now cut one of the 2 strands you are working with, leaving a 6" end, and continue crochet with remaining strand.

Round 2 Ch 3, 2 trc in same sl st sp as in beg of first rnd. * Sk 3 hdc of first rnd, 3 trc in 4th hdc. Repeat from * until three-fourths of the way around, then count the remaining hdc of first rnd and divide this number by 3. This will leave you with a quotient and a remainder of 1, 2 or 0. If your remainder is 0, continue as before. If your remainder is 1, sk 4 hdc and trc 3 times in 5th hdc for your next step; then continue as before. If your remainder is 2, sk 4 hdc and trc 3 times in 5th hdc for your next 2 steps; then continue as before. End with sl st to top of ch-5.

Round 3 Ch 5, * sk 1 hdc of 2nd rnd and trc once in next hdc. Repeat from * until end of rnd, ending with sl st to top of ch-5.

Round 4 Sc in every *other* trc of 3rd rnd until pat is closed. Knot gently in place and cut yarn, leaving a 12" end.

Repeat all steps for remaining 9 circles.

Finishing Using No. 14 hook, bring all ends to wrong side. With yarn or tapestry needle, travel each end at the center through sc, long trc, and hdc toward hem. Bring under hem, knotting gently to first available st under hem. Then travel further for approximately 12 sts under hem and cut yarn. Knot 6" end left at end of first rnd gently in place, travel toward hem, and finish in a similar manner to center ends. Knot hem ends to first available st under hem, travel for approximately 12 sts under hem, then cut yarn.

Teens' Bolero Top

In the interest of conservation, this stylish top can be made from the remainder of the T-shirt left over from cutting the Long-Sleeved Net Topping (page 33).

Materials

Same as for Long-Sleeved Net Topping (page 33) except:

long- or short-sleeved T-shirt (or top thereof) in color of your choice, preferably 100% cotton knit, ribbed

8 balls (53 yds. each) of No. 5 pearl cotton yarn, 4 in color to match T-shirt top (color A), 4 in contrasting color to T-shirt

Preparation

1–7. Follow the instructions in steps 1 through 7 for Long-Sleeved Net Topping.

8. Turn top of T-shirt inside out and fold back raw edge to form a ⅜" to ½" hem. Pin in place, working around front of shirt, sleeve bottom, back of shirt, and other sleeve bottom, carefully lining up ribs in hem with ribs in body of shirt.

9. Baste hem with sewing thread, leaving 3" ends for easy thread removal later. Remove pins.

Crochet

Using No. 13 hook and color A yarn, cast into basted hem of T-shirt top, including sleeve bottoms, according to directions set out in Casting into Fabric in Part I, starting at either sleeve seam at back of shirt. End by inserting hook into first cast st, yoh with color B yarn, and complete sl st with color B yarn. Cut color A yarn, leaving a 5" end. Remove No. 13 hook from lp and replace with size B hook.

Round 1 Sc in sl st, * sk next cast st, ch 1, sc in next cast st. Repeat from * across back and then front, *excluding* both sleeve bottoms.

Round 2 Sc in first sc of first rnd, * ch 1, sk next ch-1 sp, sc in next sc. Repeat from * all around, ending with ch-1.

Round 3, etc. Repeat 2nd rnd to achieve a length of 6". Complete last sc of last rnd with color A yarn (see instructions for changing colors set out in Part I.) Work rnds of same 2nd rnd pat for length of 2" more; then knot yarn and cut, leaving a 5" end.

Ruffled Edging With right side of back facing you, make a sl kn on size B hook with color B yarn and sl st to any st in cast row at center of back.

Round 1 Ch 4, trc in next cast-on st and in every st in cast-on hem all around, including sleeve bottoms, ending with sl st to top of ch-4 first made.

Round 2 * Ch 6, sk 3 trc, sc in 4th trc. Repeat from * all around. End with insertion of hook into first sc made, yoh with color A yarn, and complete sl st with color A. Knot color B yarn and cut, leaving a 5" end.

Round 3 Work (sc, dc, trc, dc, sc, dc, trc, dc, sc) cluster into first ch-6 lp of 2nd rnd and in every ch-6 lp around, ending with sl st to first sc in first cluster made. Knot yarn and cut, leaving a 5" end.

Finishing Hide all loose ends according to instructions set out in Finishing in Part I.

Evening Shoulder Bag

A fancy embellishment to the Evening Purse Bag previously described (page 51), this bag, if fashioned from a scrap of leftover dress material, can provide the perfect accessory to one of the formal dress styles.

Materials

Same as for Evening Purse Bag (page 51) except:
2 balls (53 yds. each) of No. 5 pearl cotton yarn
2 (½" diameter) costume jewelry pearls

Preparation

Follow instructions in steps 1 through 4 of Evening Purse Bag.

Crochet

Follow instructions for Evening Purse Bag up to and including end of 4th rnd.
Strap Sc in 3rd ch sp of last ch-5 lp of 3rd rnd, ch 3, sl st to first ch sp of first lp of ch-3s of 4th rnd, ch 5, turn, sc in last sc of 4th rnd. * Ch 5, turn, sc in first sc. Repeat from * until shoulder strap is desired length (generally about 38"); then, making sure that strap is not twisted, sc to 2nd ch sp of the ch-3 lp that is directly above and in line with the other side seam. This sp will either be to the left or right of the seam, depending on which side of the strap your last ch-5 ended. Ch 3, sc in 2nd ch sp of next ch-3 lp which is on opposite side of seam. Knot gently in place and cut yarn, leaving a 12" end.

Festoons Count the number of sts on your cast-on hem between seams on one side of bag. Divide this number by 12, which will leave you with a quotient and a remainder. If your quotient is 2, you will be skipping 1 st on your hem and crocheting your ch-9 lps in every other st. If your quotient is 3, you will be skipping 2 sts and crocheting in every 3rd st; if 4, every 4th st.

Your remainder will tell you how many sts to sk from left (or right, if you prefer) seam before starting first lp. Divide the remainder by 2, discard the fraction if your remainder is an odd number, and start this number of sts from the left (or right) seam. For example, if your remainder is 8, divide by 2 and sk 4 sts from seam, sl st in 5th. If your remainder is 5, divide by 2, discard the one-half, and sk 2 sts, etc.

Row 1 Make a sl kn, leaving a 3" end, sl st to proper starting st as determined above, * ch 9, sl st to next proper st as determined above. Repeat from * until 12 lps are formed, ending with sl st to last appropriate st on hem; turn.

Row 2 Sl st to first ch sp of last ch-9 lp of pr r, sl st for 3 more chs, sc in 5th ch sp. * Ch 9, sc in 5th ch sp of next lp of pr r. Repeat from * across row, ending with sc in 5th ch sp of first lp of pr r.

Rows 3–10 Repeat 2nd row.

Row 11 Sl st to first ch sp of last lp of 10th row, sl st for 4 more chs, sl hook into 5th ch sp of adjacent ch-9 lp and again into 5th ch sp of last lp of 10th row; then complete sl st. Knot yarn gently in place and cut, leaving an 8" end.

Repeat for other festoon.

Finishing Bring all hem ends to wrong side of bag with yarn needle. Knot each end to first available st under hem; travel further with yarn needle for approximately 12 more sts under hem; then cut yarn. Using yarn needle, travel 12" strap end through crocheted sts in shortest path toward hem. Knot to first available st under hem; travel further for approximately 12 more sts under hem; then cut. Slip costume jewelry pearl over each festoon end and draw up firmly to tip of festoon; then triple-knot yarn under pearl and cut.

Bridesmaids' Trailing Coverlet

An enchanting bridesmaid's ensemble can be created by making the Sleeveless Tank Top Dress (page 36) or Long-Sleeved Net-Topped Evening Gown (page 40) and this coverlet from the same dress material.

Materials

Same as for Poncho under Poncho Dress Ensemble (page 45), except:
2 yds. (60" wide) of a light-ribbed or interlock-woven dress material, such as Qiana®, Nyestra®, or other polyester-cotton blend, in color of your choice

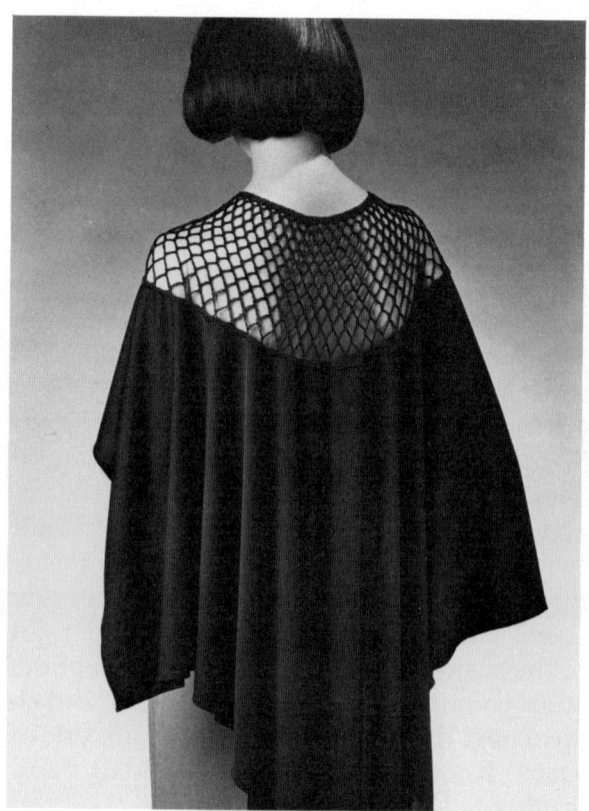

Preparation

1–3. Follow steps 1 through 3 for Poncho Preparation under Poncho Dress Ensemble.

4. In same manner as step 2, scribe a circle 15½" in diameter, with the same center dot. Using a yardstick, draw a diameter line anywhere on the template, connecting one edge of the circle which is 30½" in diameter to the other edge, passing through center dot (Figure II-28).

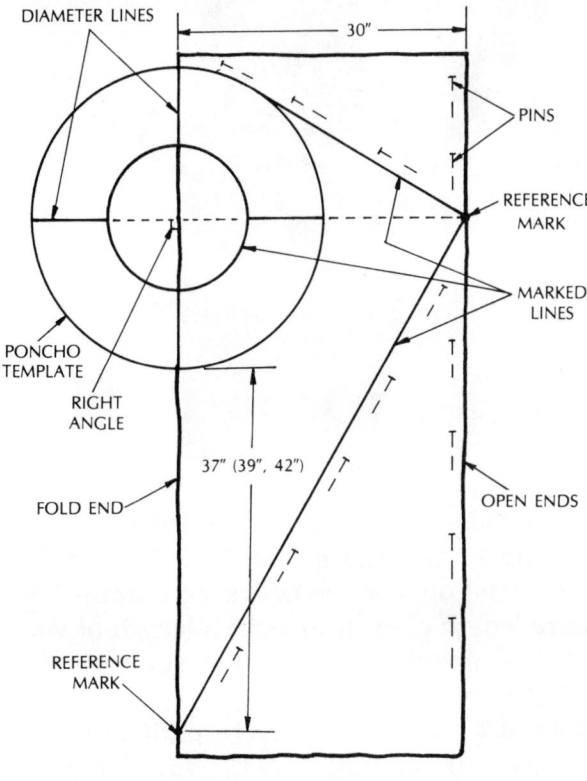

Figure II-28

5. Using right angle, draw a line perpendicular to the diameter line you have just made, passing through the center dot. Extend this line with the yardstick, marking it to both edges of outer circle. Now cut out both circles with paper scissors, leaving a doughnut-shaped template.

6. Fold dress material in half lengthwise, with wrong sides out, and lay flat on your work surface. Place a row of straight pins along the edge, pinning both open ends tog so that they line up. Smooth out all wrinkles, so that the material lies in a perfect rectangle.

7. Place poncho template over folded edge with one of its diameter lines directly in line with this edge, as shown in Figure II-28. Be sure top edge of template is close to top raw edge of material so none will be wasted. Using the yardstick, extend the other diameter line in the direction of the open end, marking *only* a small reference mark at edge with felt-tipped pen.

8. Using the yardstick, connect this reference mark to outer template circle by adjusting until yardstick edge is just tangent (touching) to circle at top end of material. Mark a line along this edge with felt-tipped pen, continuing it along circular edge of template up to fold line of material.

9. Using tape measure, measure down from lower edge of poncho template along fold line, a distance of 37" for Small, 39" for Medium, or 42" for Large; place a second reference mark at fold line with the pen.

10. Connect this reference mark with first one with a marked line, using 2 yardsticks, a steel tape measure, or other long straightedge as a guide.

11. Place rows of straight pins outside the 2 marked lines to aid in cutting. Trace the inner semicircle of poncho template with the felt-tipped pen. Using sewing scissors, cut this semicircle out of both layers of material, just outside marked line. Now cut out remainder of pat just inside marked lines.

12. Fold back the material of the circular cutout to wrong side to form a hem ⅜" deep. Pin carefully in place, making sure hem lies flat; then baste with sewing thread. Remove pins.

13. Baste and hem all other raw edges to a hem depth of ¼" with thread in matching color.

Crochet

Follow directions for Poncho under Poncho Dress Ensemble (page 45).

Costume Leotard

Transform an ordinary leotard into a glittering show costume with this metallic crochet topping. Or use it as an alternate pattern for the Long-Sleeved Net Topping (page 33) on a T-shirt for formal wear.

Materials

dancer's leotard in color and size of your choice (Suggestion: black.)
2 (20-gram) (approximately 260 yds.) balls of polyester-nylon metallic yarn (Suggestion: silver.)
1 ball (53 yds.) of No. 5 pearl cotton yarn in color matching leotard
1 No. 11 crochet hook (steel)
1 size B crochet hook
1 size D crochet hook
tape measure
felt-tipped pen or chalk
ruler
yardstick
straight pins
sewing scissors
sewing needle and thread
yarn needle

Preparation

Follow steps 1 through 9 set out in Long-Sleeved Net Topping, substituting "leotard" for "T-shirt."

Crochet

Using No. 11 hook and metallic yarn, start cast into any point on back hem, following directions in Treble Crochet Casting into Fabric in Part I, chaining 9. End cast with sl st to 9th ch of first ch-9.

Round 1 Using size D hook, ch 7, trc in first trc of cast-on row and in every trc around. Be sure length of your trc equals length of your ch-7. End with sl st to 7th ch of your first ch-7 of this rnd.
Round 2 Ch 5, trc in first trc of first rnd and in every trc around, making sure length of your trc equals length of your ch-5. End with sl st to 5th ch of ch-5 which began rnd.
Round 3 Ch 3, trc in first trc of pr rnd and in every trc around, making sure length of your trc equals length of your ch-3. End with sl st to top of first ch-3.
Round 4 Ch 2, trc in first trc of pr rnd and in every trc around, keeping your trc length consistent with ch-2 length. End with sl st to 2nd ch of first ch-2.
Round 5 Ch 9, trc in every *other* trc of 4th rnd, keeping proper length of your trc. End by inserting hook into 9th ch of your last ch-9, yoh, ptl; complete sc with No. 5 pearl cotton yarn, leaving a 5" end. Cut metallic yarn, leaving an 18" end.

Edging
Round 1 Change to size B hook; turn garment and work with right side facing you. Ch 1, sc 2 times in sc you have just made to bring in the new yarn. Sc 3 times in first trc of 5th rnd and 3 times in every trc around. End with sl st to ch-1 which began rnd.
Round 2 Hdc in first sc and in every sc around. End with sl st to first hdc.
Round 3 Sl st loosely in first hdc of Edging 2nd rnd and in every hdc around. Knot yarn gently and cut, leaving a 3" end.
Finishing Grasp the 18" metallic yarn end with one hand and the 5" pearl cotton yarn end with the other. Pulling gently, bring the sc into line with the other sts. Using No. 11 hook or yarn needle, knot each end to the nearest available st of its corresponding color. Using yarn needle, travel metallic yarn through crocheted sts, taking shortest path in direction of leotard hem. Knot gently to first available st under hem. Travel further for approximately 12 sts under hem, then cut yarn.

Using yarn needle, travel pearl cotton yarn through approximately 10 sts of its same color, knot gently in place, travel further for approximately 10 more sts, then cut yarn. Finish other end of pearl cotton yarn in similar manner.

Knot metallic yarn end at hem to first available st under hem, travel for approximately 12 more sts under hem, and cut yarn.

Part III
Ladies', Men's and Children's Wear

Whirlpool-Motif Overblouse

This is a loose, lacy-patterned garment to be worn over a contrasting dress or gown.

Materials

28 balls (53 yds. each) No. 5 pearl cotton yarn in color of your choice
1 size H crochet hook (for Small or Medium)
1 size J crochet hook (for Large)
yarn needle
Gauge Each square should measure about 5½" x 5½" for Small and Medium and about 6" x 6" for Large.

Crochet

This overblouse is made by crocheting 28 individual whirlpool-motif squares, which are joined in the manner shown in Figure III-1.
   Ch 6, sl st to first ch sp to form lp.
Round 1   * Ch 7, sc in lp. Repeat from * 3 more times.
Round 2   * Ch 6, sc 3 times in next lp. Repeat from * 3 more times.
Round 3   Ch 6, sc 3 times in first lp of 2nd rnd, sc in next 2 sc, inserting hook in back lp of sc only, as directed in Ribbed Crochet in Part I. * Repeat from * around.
Round 4   * Ch 6, sc 3 times in next ch-6 lp and sc in back lps of next 2 sc. Repeat from * around.
Rounds 5–8   Repeat 4th rnd.
Round 9   * Ch 6, sc in ch-6 lp of 8th rnd, ch 6, sk first sc of group and sc in back lps of each of the next 13 sc. Repeat from * around.
Round 10   * Ch 6, sc in first ch-6 lp of 9th rnd, ch 6, sc in next lp, ch 6, sk first sc of group, sc in each sc up to next-to-last sc of the same group. Repeat from * around.
Round 11   * Ch 6, sc in first ch-6 lp of 10th rnd, ch 6, dc 4 times in center ch-6 lp, ch 6, sc in next ch-6 lp, ch 6, sk first sc, sc in each next sc until next-to-last sc. Repeat from * around.
Round 12   * Ch 6, sc in ch-6 lp, ch 6, sc 3 times in same lp, ch 3, sk 4-dc group, sc 3 times in next lp, ch 6, sc in next lp, ch 6, sk first sc and sc in each next sc up to next-to-last sc. Repeat from * around.
Round 13   * Ch 6, sc in lp, ch 6, sc 3 times in next lp, ch 10, sk 3-sc group, the ch-3, and the next 3-sc group, sc 3 times in next lp, ch 6, sc in next lp, ch 6, sk first sc and sc in each next sc, skipping last sc in group. Repeat from * around.
Round 14   * Ch 6, sc in next lp, ch 6, sc 3 times in next lp, ch 6, dc 4 times in ch-10 lp, ch 6, sc 3 times in next lp, ch 6, sc in next lp, ch 6, sk first sc and sc in next 3 sc. Repeat from * around.
Round 15   Ch 6, sc in next lp, * ch 6, sc 3

times in next lp, ch 6, dc 4 times in next lp, ch 14, dc 4 times in next lp, ch 6, sc 3 times in next lp, ch 6, sc in next lp, ch 3, sc in next lp. Repeat from * around.

Round 16 Ch 5, sc in next lp, ch 10, sc in next lp, ch 10, sc in 5th ch sp of corner lp, ch 10, sc in 10th ch sp of same lp. Repeat this pat, making ch-10 lps and skipping the ch-3 at top of sc groupings to form corners. End by joining last ch-10 with sl st to the sc after the first ch-5 of 15th rnd. Knot gently and cut yarn, leaving a 4″ end.

Joining Squares Start your next square in the same manner as the first, up to and including 15th rnd.

Round 16 Ch 5, sc in next lp, ch 10, sc in next lp, ch 10, sc in 5th ch sp of corner lp, ch 5, sc in corner lp of first square, ch 5, sk 4 chs of the square you are working on, sc in 5th ch sp, ch 5, sc in corresponding lp of first square, ch 5, sc in next lp of square you are working; continue in this manner, joining next 5 lps.

Most squares on the front of the overblouse are to be joined this way. Note that on the back some squares require sc in the center lp of one side to start, rather than the corner lp (Figure III-1). Also note that squares X on the front join squares Y for only three-fourths of the way along their common border, the remainder joining squares Z on back to close underarm.

Border for Sleeves and Overblouse Bottom After joining squares to form overblouse, make the border.

Round 1 Make sl kn, sc to center ch sp of any corner lp (on sleeve or bottom), ch 7, dc in same ch sp, ch 5, * sc in next sc, ch 8, dc in next sc, ch 6, dc in same sc, ch 8. Repeat from * around sleeve or bottom, considering the joining point of 2 squares as a sc. End with ch-5, sl st to 3rd ch sp of original ch-7.

Round 2 Ch 7, dc 4 times in lp, ch 3, dc in same lp, ch 6, * sc twice in next sc, ch 8, dc in next ch-6 lp, ch 3, dc 4 times in same lp, ch 3, dc in same lp, ch 8. Repeat from * around, ending with ch-6, sl st in 3rd ch sp of original ch-7.

Round 3 Sl st in lp, ch 3, dc 3 times in same lp, * ch 5, sk the 4-dc grouping, dc 4 times in next lp, ch 9, sc in next sc, ch 9, dc in lp preceding next 4-dc grouping. Repeat from * around, ending with ch-9, sl st to 3rd ch sp of original ch-3. Knot gently and cut yarn, leaving a 4″ end. Repeat for other sleeve or bottom.

Neckline Edging Make a sl kn, sc in any lp at neckline, * ch 8, sc in next lp. Repeat from * until you reach a sharp corner where 2 squares join. At corner, ch 4 instead of ch 8; then continue. End with sc in first sc. Knot gently and cut yarn, leaving a 4″ end.

Finishing Hide all loose ends as instructed in Finishing in Part I.

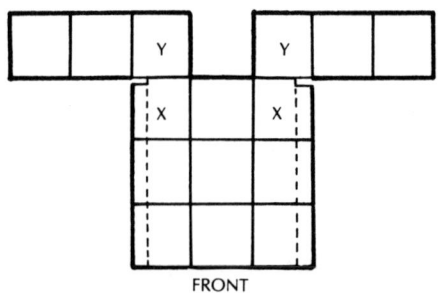

FRONT

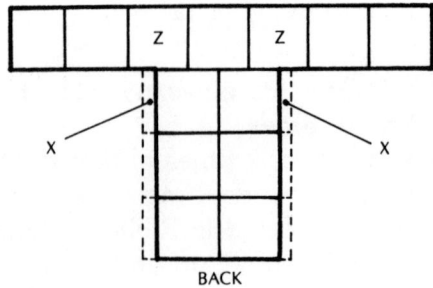

BACK

Figure III-1

Barbary Coast Halter

Reminiscent of an old San Francisco saloon girl's corset, this top can be worn with jeans or on the beach with a contrasting bathing suit bottom.

Materials

2 balls (95 yds. each) of No. 8 pearl cotton yarn in each of 4 colors: A, B, C and D (Suggestion: A—black, B—green, C—violet, D—red.)
1 No. 13 crochet hook (steel)
1 size B crochet hook
yarn needle
Gauge 7 sts = 1"; 4 rows = 1"; 2 strands of yarn; size B hook.

Crochet

This pat is worked with 1 row hdc, 1 row dc, 1 row hdc, etc., throughout, forming a tube of 27" in circumference (for Small or Medium) or 28" (for Large). See Figure III-2. To achieve the thin stripe effect for the black (color A) rows, always start and finish these with hdc.

Using size B hook and 2 strands of No. 8 pearl cotton yarn, make a sl kn with color A, leaving a 5" end. Ch 38 (45 for Large). Turn.
Row 1 Hdc in 3rd ch from hook and in each ch across, ch 3, turn.
Row 2 Dc in first hdc of 1st row and in each hdc across, ch 2, turn.
Row 3 Hdc in first dc of 2nd row, hdc in each dc across, completing next-to-last dc. In last dc of 2nd row, yoh, enter hook in last dc, ptl, yoh with color B, pull through all 3 lps. Cut color A yarn, leaving a 5" end, ch 3, turn.
Row 4 Dc in first hdc and in each hdc across, ch 2, turn.

Repeat this pat of hdc, dc, hdc until you have a band of color B 1¾" wide, ending on a dc row; then change back to color A according to the instructions at end of 3rd row. Complete the thin row of color A again, change to color C for a 3" band, etc., until you have completed all the color bands shown in Figure III-2. Then knot color C gently and cut yarn, leaving a 24" end.

Join the tube by threading the 24" end through a yarn needle and following the instructions set out in Joining in Part I.

Edging Make a sl kn with color A, leaving a 5" end; sc into any row sp on top edge of back that is *not* in color A. Sc across in every row sp until you reach band of color A. Then * ch 3, sl st to first ch sp of ch-3, and sc in next row sp of color A. Repeat from * 2 more times, then continue to sc along edge until you reach next band of color A. Repeat again from * 3 times, etc., all the way around the top edge. End with sl st to first sc. Knot gently and cut yarn, leaving a 6" end.

Straps Try halter on and place 4 small safety pins where shoulder straps should begin and end on front and back.

Make a sl kn with color A on No. 13 hook and sl st to st at one of the safety pins on back. Ch 80, try halter on, place strap over shoulder, and check to see how much longer the strap should be. Ch this additional amount, then sl st to st under safety pin on front. Knot gently in place and cut yarn, leaving a 6" end. Repeat for other strap.

Tassel-tie With No. 13 hook and color A yarn, make a sl kn; then ch until you have a 40" length (42" for Large). Knot yarn and cut, leaving a 1½" end. Thread ch through yarn needle and enter needle in color A band at point X in Figure III-2. Sew chain through bottom edge with running stitches, as shown in Figure III-2, passing in and out of crocheted sts. Bring the other end out through point X.

Make tassels at each end of tie ch according to instructions set out in Tassels and Fringes in Part I, using 5 turns of double-strand yarn and a 1¾" template length. Cut final tassel length to 1¼".

Finishing Finish all ends according to instructions set out in Finishing in Part I, leading all color A ends into color A bands.

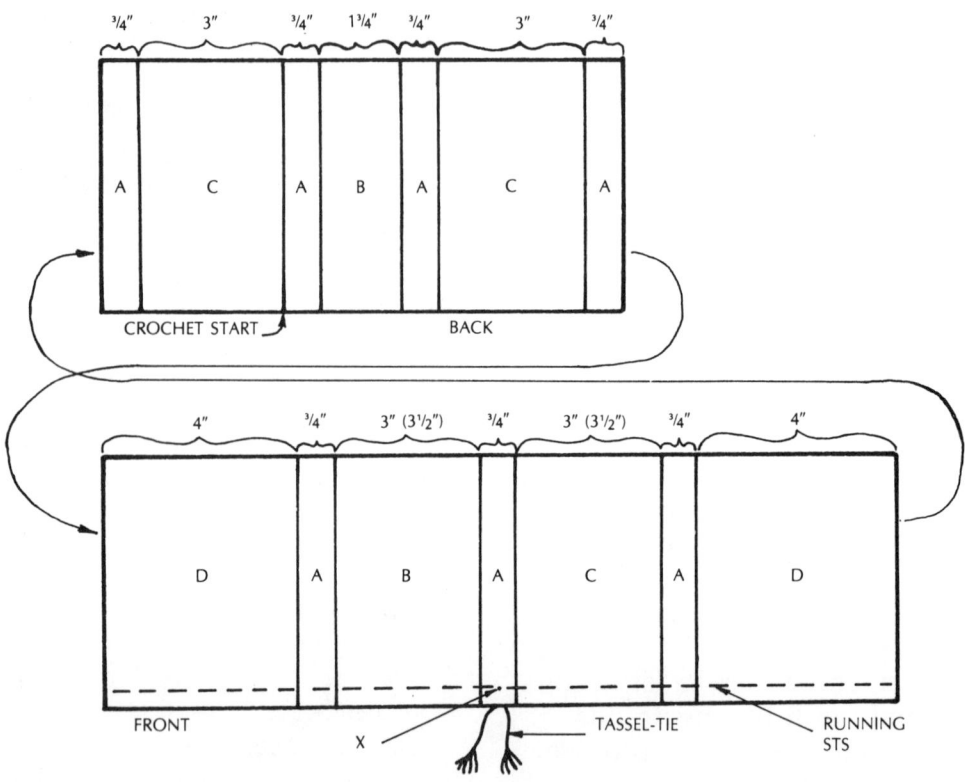

Figure III-2

Cotton Mini-Poncho

Materials

20 balls (50 yds. each), of No. 5 pearl cotton yarn in color A (Suggestion: black.)
8 balls (50 yds. each) in each of 2 colors: B and C (Suggestion: B—lavender, C—turquoise.)
1 size K crochet hook
yarn needle
Gauge   7 sc = 2"; 6 rows = 2"; 3 strands of yarn; size K hook.

Crochet

This mini-poncho is composed of 2 crocheted rectangles that are sewn together along the lines shown in Figure III-3. The pat is worked with 3 strands of yarn throughout.

Make a sl kn with 3 strands of color A yarn on size K hook, leaving 4" ends. Ch 51 loosely to measure 14" (for Small and Medium; ch 58 to measure 16" for Large).

Row 1   Sc in 2nd ch sp from hook and in each ch sp across. End with ch-1; turn.
Row 2   Sk ch, sc in first sc of pr r, sc across, ch 1; turn.
Rows 3–8   Repeat 2nd row. After next-to-last sc of 8th row, insert hook into last sc, yoh, ptl; complete sc by yarning over hook with a 3-strand mix of colors A, B and C. Cut color A yarn, leaving 5" ends. Ch 1; turn.

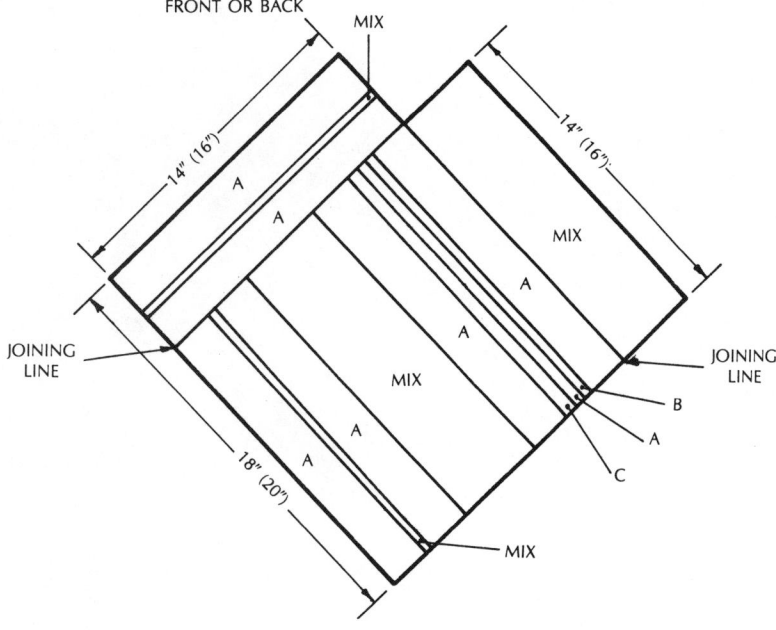

Figure III-3

Row 9 Sc in first sc of 8th row, sc in every sc across. After completing next-to-last sc, insert hook into last sc, yoh, ptl; complete sc by yarning over hook with color A. Cut yarn of mixed colors, leaving 5" ends. Ch 1; turn.

Rows 10–18 Repeat 2nd row. At last sc of 18th row, change to mixed colors as described above.

Rows 19–34 Repeat 2nd row. At last sc of 34th row, change to color A.

Rows 35–42 Repeat 2nd row. Change to color B at end of 42nd row.

Rows 43, 44 Repeat 2nd row. Change to color A.

Row 45 Repeat 2nd row. Change to color C.

Rows 46, 47 Repeat 2nd row. Change to color A.

Rows 48–55 Repeat 2nd row. Change to mixed colors.

Rows 56–71 Repeat 2nd row. Change to color A.

Rows 72–79 Repeat 2nd row. Change to mixed colors.

Row 80 Repeat 2nd row. Change to color A.

Rows 81–88 Repeat 2nd row. End by knotting yarn gently in place and cut, leaving 5" ends.

Repeat all the above for the other rectangle.

Joining Using yarn needle, sew end of one rectangle to side of the other with 3 strands of color A yarn, as shown by joining lines in Figure III-3, and following directions set out in Joining in Part I. Repeat for the other joining connection.

Fringe Using a 6½" template length and 4 turns of triple-strand yarn, make fringe according to directions set out in Tassels and Fringes in Part I. Cut to a 6" length. Use colors corresponding to colored bands along the side of the rectangle; then repeat this pat along the color A end.

Finishing Finish all ends according to instructions set out in Finishing in Part I.

Striped Demi-Cloche

Materials

1 skein (4 oz.) of 4-ply wool or acrylic yarn (color A)
1 length (40') of same type yarn in contrasting color (color B)
1 size I crochet hook
1 size J crochet hook
yarn needle
safety pin
Gauge 3 sts = 1"; 5 rows = 2"; 2 strands of yarn; size J hook.

Crochet

This pat is worked with 2 strands of yarn throughout and all sc are worked into the *back*

loop only of each st, according to instructions set out in Ribbed Crochet in Part I.

Using 2 strands of color A yarn and size J hook, make a sl kn, leaving a 5" end. Ch 4, sl st to back lp of first ch, ch 1 (counts as 1 sc), sc in same sp, 2 sc in back lps of each sc, until the outside circumference of your ring contains 24 sts. Place a small safety pin in last (24th) sc. This pin will be moved to the last st of each rnd hereafter.

Round 1   Sc in every sc up to and including sc with safety pin. Move safety pin to last sc made.

Round 2   2 sc in first sc of 1st rnd, * sc in next sc, 2 sc in next sc. Repeat from * around. Move safety pin.

Round 3   Sc in every sc around (even rnd).

Round 4   2 sc in first sc of 3rd rnd, * 1 sc in each of the next 2 sc, 2 sc in next sc. Repeat from * around.

Round 5   Repeat 3rd rnd.

Round 6   2 sc in first sc of 5th rnd. * 1 sc in each of the next 3 sc, 2 sc in next sc. Repeat from * around.

Rounds 7–10   Repeat 3rd rnd. For last sc of 10th rnd, insert hook into back lp, yoh, ptl; finish sc by yarning over hook with color B yarn. Cut color A yarn, leaving a 5" end.

Rounds 11, 12   Change to size I hook and sc in every sc. For last sc of 12th rnd, change back to color A as directed in 10th rnd.

Round 13   Sc in every sc. Change back to color B for last sc.

Rounds 14, 15   Repeat 11th and 12th rnds.

Rounds 16–18   Sc in every sc. End 18th rnd with sl st to first sc.

Finishing   Do reverse st (see Part I for instructions) around bottom of hat, entering hook in center of sts and taking *both* lps instead of just the back lp. End with sl st to first reverse st. Knot yarn gently in place and cut, leaving a 5" end. Hide all ends according to instructions set out in Finishing in Part I.

Three-Pouch Belt

Keep your hands free by storing your purse articles in this useful and fashionable outerwear accessory.

Materials

1 skein (4 oz.) of 4-ply wool or acrylic yarn in each of 3 colors: A, E and F (Suggestion: A—blue, E—brown, F—red.)
1 skein (2 oz.) of same type yarn in each of 3 complementary colors: B, C and D (Suggestion: B—tan, C—orange, D—gold.)
1 size J crochet hook
yarn needle
safety pin

Crochet

Make a sl kn on size J hook with color A yarn, leaving a 21" end. Wind end into a small ball and keep it intact with a safety pin for later use. Ch 24; turn.

Row 1   Sc in 2nd ch from hook and in each ch across. Ch 1; turn.

Row 2   Sc in first sc and in every sc across. Ch 1; turn.

Rows 3–29   Repeat 2nd row. For last sc of 29th row, insert hook into last sc, yoh, ptl, yoh with color B yarn, and complete sc. Cut color A yarn, leaving a 6" end. Ch 1; turn.

Row 30 Sc in each of first 2 sc, hazelnut st in next sc (6 strands on hook when closing st), * sc in each of next 2 sc of pr r, hazelnut st in next sc (6 strands on hook for st closure). Repeat from * across, ending with sc in 2 sc. Change to color A in last sc, according to instructions for 29th row. Ch 1; turn.

Rows 31–33 Repeat 2nd row, ending last sc of 33rd row with color C. Ch 1; turn.

Row 34 Repeat 30th row. Complete last sc with color A. Ch 1; turn.

Rows 35–37 Repeat 2nd row, ending with a change to color D in last sc of 37th row. Ch 1; turn.

Row 38 Repeat 30th row, ending last sc with color A. Ch 1; turn.

Rows 39–42 Repeat 2nd row, ending last sc of 42nd row with color E. Ch 1; turn.

Row 43 Repeat 30th row, ending last sc with color A. Ch 1; turn.

Rows 44–47 Repeat 2nd row, ending last sc of 47th row with color F. Ch 1; turn.

Row 48 Repeat 30th row. Change to color A. Ch 1; turn.

Rows 49–52 Repeat 2nd row, ending last sc of 52nd row with *same color*. Knot yarn gently and cut, leaving a 21" end.

Hide all ends except 21" ends according to directions set out in Finishing in Part I. Fold the longer dimension of finished piece in half to form pouch with wrong sides out. Join the sides tog using a yarn needle and the 21" ends, according to instructions set out in Joining in Part I. Turn pouch right side out.

Repeat all of the above instructions for the 2nd pouch, substituting colors as follows: A for F, B for E, C for A, D for C, E for B, F for D.

Repeat again for the 3rd pouch, substituting colors as follows: A for E, B for F, C for B, D for D (same), E for A, F for C.

Belt Make a sl kn with color F yarn, leaving a 5" end. Ch 76; turn.

Row 1 Sk 1 ch, sc in every ch across, ch 1, turn.

Row 2 Sk 1 ch, sc in each of next 2 sc of pr r, hazelnut st in next sc (6 strands on hook to close), sc in each of next 2 sc, hazelnut st in next sc, sc in next sc; complete next sc with color A. * Hazelnut in next sc, sc in next 2 sc. Repeat from * 4 more times, changing to color C in last sc.

Repeat from * 5 times, changing to color E in last sc. Repeat from * 5 times, changing to color D in last sc. Repeat from * 5 times, changing to color B. Repeat from * *twice*, changing to color F. Ch 1; turn.

Row 3 Sk 1 ch, sc in every st across, ch 1, turn.

Row 4 Sk 1 ch, sc in next 2 sc, hazelnut, sc in next 2 sc, hazelnut in next sc, sc in next sc; complete next sc with color B. * Hazelnut in next sc, sc in next 2 sc. Repeat from * 4 more times, changing to color C in last sc.

Repeat from * 5 times, changing to color E in last sc. Repeat from * 5 times, changing to color D in last sc. Repeat from * 5 times, changing to color B. Repeat from * *twice*, changing to color F. Ch 1; turn.

Row 5 Sk 1 ch, sc in each of next 3 sc. With back of first pouch facing you, sl st to first st of both front and back at top corner of pouch to 4th sc of this row. Continue to sl st across top of *back* of first pouch for 21 more sts along the belt. For last sc (23rd st), include both back and front sts of pouch to 26th st of belt. For next st on belt (27th), sl st to front and back top corner sts of 2nd pouch, and repeat as for first pouch, making sure to include both front and back of 2nd pouch for last sl st. For 50th st on belt, sl st to top corner of front and back of third pouch; then repeat procedure. After 2nd top corner of 3rd pouch, sc in last 3 sc of 4th row of belt. Knot yarn gently and cut, leaving a 5" end.

Tie Closure Cut 6 38" lengths of yarn, 1 in each color. Fold in half and insert into end of belt at 3rd row, according to instructions set out in Tassels and Fringes in Part I. Keeping all 12 strands tog, knot at a distance of $2\frac{1}{2}$" from bottom of fringe. Repeat at other belt end.

Fringes Using 7" lengths of each of the 6 colors, attach fringes to the bottom of each pouch directly under each of the 7 hazelnut sts, according to the directions set out in Tassels and Fringes in Part I.

Finishing Hide all loose ends according to Finishing instructions in Part I.

Medieval Belt and Choker

Deco Clutch

Victorian Blouse

Men's Ski Sweater

Costume Leotard

Glitter Coverlet

Disco Scarf

Sleeveless Tank Top Dress

Two-Piece Bikini

Three-Pouch Belt

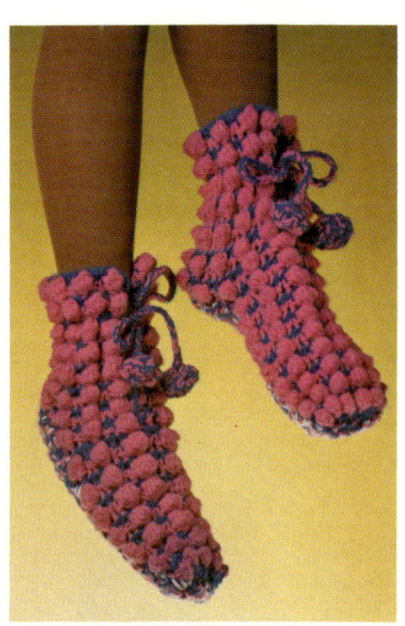
Winter Booties

Fan Shawl

Multicolor Full Poncho

Rainbow Hooded Cape

One-Piece Sunsuit

Barbary Coast Halter

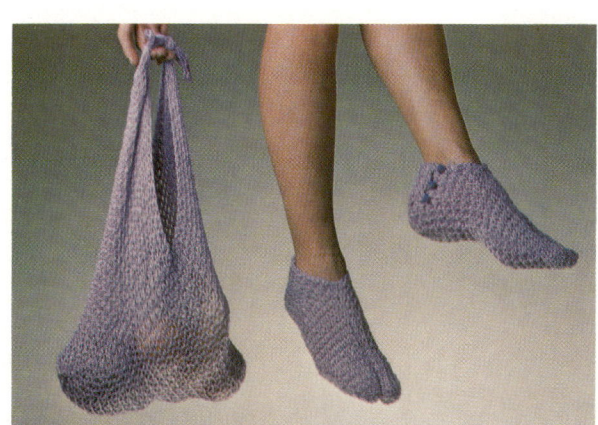
Oriental Tote and Slippers

Teens' Bolero Top

Cotton Mini-Poncho

Patchwork-Motif Sweater

Jute Planter

Window Sunburst

New York Skyline Wall Hanging

Interwoven Tablecloth

Show Kitchen Towel

Oval Floor Mat

Scintillating Blanket/Wall Hanging

One-Piece Sunsuit

Patterned after a bathing suit of the twenties, this sunsuit provides the comfort of cotton on a hot summer day.

Materials

12 balls (175 yds. each) of mercerized crochet cotton in each of 3 colors: A, B and C (Suggestion: A—lavender, B—turquoise, C—green.)
1 size H crochet hook (for Small and Medium)
1 size I crochet hook (for Large)
yarn needle
safety pins
straight pins
Gauge 5 sc=1"; 5 rows=1"; 2 strands of yarn; size I hook.

Crochet

NOTE: The body of this sunsuit is formed from a basic tube; crochet is done with 2 strands of yarn throughout.

Make a sl kn on size I hook (all sizes) with 2 strands of color A yarn, leaving 4" ends. Ch 118 (for Small or Medium) to measure 28", or ch 123 (for Large) to measure 29". Sl st to first ch, being careful not to twist ch.

Round 1 Sc in 2nd ch. Place a small safety pin in sc just made and sc in every ch around. This safety pin will be moved to first sc of each rnd hereafter to indicate beg of rnds.

Rounds 2–6 Sc in first sc and in every sc around, moving pin. For last sc of 6th rnd, insert hook into last sc of 5th rnd, yoh, ptl, and complete sc by yarning over hook with 2 strands of color B yarn. Cut color A yarn, leaving 5" ends.

Rounds 7–13 Repeat 2nd rnd. Complete last sc of 13th rnd with 2 strands of color C yarn, as described above. Cut color B yarn, leaving 5" ends.

Rounds 14–20 Repeat 2nd rnd. Change to color B for last sc of 20th rnd.

Rounds 21–26 Repeat 2nd rnd. Change to color A.

Rounds 27–37 Repeat 2nd rnd. Change to color B.

If you are a Small or Medium, try tube on at this point. If a tighter waist is desired, change to size H hook for next 7 rnds; then change back to size I hook.

Rounds 38–43 Repeat 2nd rnd. Change to color C.

Rounds 44–49 Repeat 2nd rnd. Change to color B.

Rounds 50–56 Repeat 2nd rnd. Change to color A.

Rounds 57–67 Repeat 2nd rnd. Change to color B.

Rounds 68–73 Repeat 2nd rnd. Change to color C.

Rounds 74–79 Repeat 2nd rnd. Change to color B.

Rounds 80–86 Repeat 2nd rnd. Change to color A.

Rounds 87–97 Repeat 2nd rnd. Change to color B.

Rounds 98–104 Repeat 2nd rnd. Complete 104th rnd with same color B. Knot yarn and cut, leaving a 4" end.

Place tube on a flat surface in such a position that the loose ends of color-changing rnds form a centerline, as shown in Figure III-4. Pin the front to the back with straight pins at extreme right and left edges of tube at the bottom. Turn tube over so that the ends are facing away from you. The part now facing you will be the front of the sunsuit. Place a safety-pin marker in exact center st of the front at the bottom row.

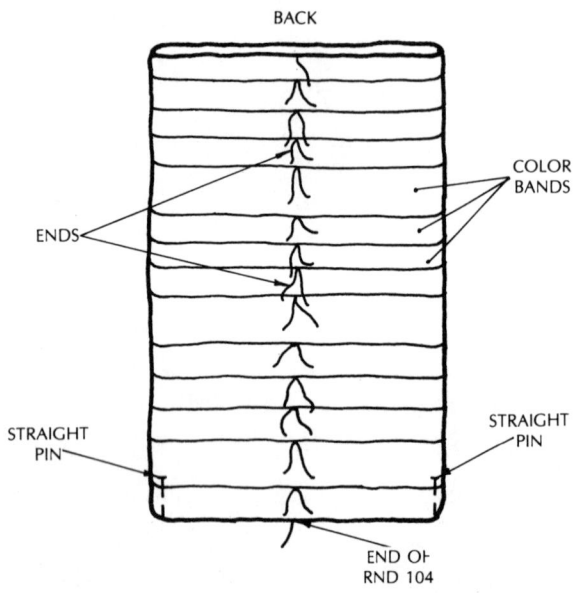

Figure III-4

Crotch Make a sl kn with 2 strands of color C yarn, leaving 4" ends.

Row 1 Starting with 8th sc away from central safety-pin marker, sc 15 sts in direction toward the marker and past it, so that these 15 sts are centered by the pin. Ch 1; turn.

Row 2 Sc in first sc and in each of the 15 sc across. Ch 1; turn.

Rows 3–17 Repeat 2nd row.

Rows 18–21 Repeat 2nd row, increasing 1 sc at beg and end of row (see instructions set out in Increasing in Part I), so that the 21st row will contain 23 sc. Turn garment over.

Using color B ends of 104th rnd as a guide, start single-crocheting to 12th sc from center st (color B ends), working toward it so that the 23 sts of the 21st row join the corresponding sts of 104th rnd. Remove straight pins.

First Leg

Round 1 Sc to next sc of 104th rnd after crotch joining. Place a safety pin in sc just made. This safety pin will be moved to the first sc of each rnd hereafter. Sc in every sc around to start, including side of crotch.

Round 2 Sc in first sc of first rnd, move safety pin, and sc in every sc around.

Rounds 3–6 Sc in first sc, move pin, and sc around. Complete last sc of 6th rnd with 2 strands of color B yarn.

Rounds 7–12 Repeat 2nd rnd. Change to color A at end of 12th rnd.

Rounds 13–23 Repeat 2nd rnd, finishing with *same* color A. Knot yarn and cut, leaving a 4" end.

Second Leg Make a sl kn with color C yarn, leaving a 4" end, and sc to st on crotch where it joins 104th rnd at other leg. Place a safety pin in this sc. Sc in every sc around, repeating procedure for First Leg.

Shoulder Straps Lay garment on a flat surface with front facing you, properly centered. Measure in 3" from either side at top to the st which will designate beg of the shoulder strap joining. Place a safety pin in this st and in the 3 other corresponding sts on front and back of the garment.

Row 1 Make a sl kn with 2 strands of color A, leaving a 4" end. Starting on the front of the garment and working toward the center (away from the armhole), with the wrong side facing you, sc in safety-pinned st and sc in next 10 sts. Ch 1; turn.

Row 2 Sk 1 ch, sc in every sc (11 sc in all), ch 1, turn.

Row 3 Sk 1 ch, dec 1 sc at beg and end of row (see instructions set out in Decreasing in Part I), single-crocheting across (9 sc made), ch 1, turn.

Row 4 Repeat 3rd row (7 sc made).

Row 5 Sk 1 ch, sc in every sc across. Complete last sc of row with color B, ch 1, turn.

Rows 6–11 Sk 1 ch, sc in every sc across. Change to color C at end of 11th row.

Rows 12–17 Repeat 6th row. Change to color B at end of 17th row.

Rows 18–23 Repeat 6th row. Change to color C.
Rows 24–29 Repeat 6th row. Change to color B.
Rows 30–35 Repeat 6th row. Change to color A.
Row 36 Sk 1 ch, sc in every sc across, ch 1, turn.
Row 37 Sk 1 ch, inc 1 sc at beg and end of row, single-crocheting across (9 sc made), ch 1, turn.
Row 38 Repeat 37th row (11 sc made).
Row 39 Sk 1 ch, sc in every sc across. Knot yarn and cut, leaving a 5" end.

Using a yarn needle, connect end of strap according to instructions set out in Joining in Part I, using safety-pin marker on back of garment as a guide.

Repeat above for other shoulder strap.

Finishing Hide all loose ends according to instructions set out in Finishing in Part I.

Basic Brimmed Hat

Materials

2 skeins (3 oz. each) of 4-ply wool or acrylic in variegated colors (color A)
2 skeins (2 oz. each) of 4-ply wool or acrylic in complementary solid color (color B)
1 size E crochet hook
1 size J crochet hook
yarn needle
safety pins
Gauge 3 sc = 1"; 5 rows = 2"; 2 strands of yarn; size J hook.

Crochet

NOTE: Two strands of yarn are to be used throughout all of the following instructions.

Crown Make a sl kn on size J hook with 2 strands of color A yarn, leaving a 5" end. Ch 4, sl st to first ch, ch 1, sc in same sp, 2 sc in each of the next 3 chs. Continue to make 2 sc in each sc until you have 24 sts on the circumference of your ring. Place safety-pin marker in your 24th st just made. This safety pin will be moved hereafter to indicate the last st of each rnd.

Round 1 Sc in every sc up to and including the pinned sc. Move safety pin to last sc made.

Round 2 2 sc in first sc of first rnd. * Sc in next sc, 2 sc in next sc. Repeat from * around. Move pin.

Round 3 Sc in every sc around (even rnd).

Round 4 2 sc in first sc, * sc in each of next 2 sc, 2 sc in next sc. Repeat from * around.

Round 5 Repeat 3rd rnd.

Round 6 2 sc in first sc, * sc in each of next 3 sc, 2 sc in next sc. Repeat from * around.

Round 7 Repeat 3rd rnd.

Round 8 2 sc in first sc, * sc in each of next 4 sc, 2 sc in next sc. Repeat from * around.

For Large size only–Round 8A Repeat 3rd rnd.

For Large size only–Round 8B 2 sc in 1st sc, * sc in each of next 5 sc, 2 sc in next sc. Repeat from * around.

Rounds 9–21 Repeat 3rd rnd. For last sc of 21st rnd, insert hook into last sc of 20th rnd, yoh, ptl; complete sc by yarning over hook with color B yarn. Cut color A yarn, leaving 4" ends.

Brim

Round 1 Change to size E hook. Sc in every sc around.

Round 2 2 sc in first sc, * sc in next sc, 2 sc in next sc. Repeat from * around.

Round 3 2 sc in first sc, * sc in each of next 6 sc, 2 sc in next sc. Repeat from * around.

Round 4 Repeat first rnd.

Round 5 2 sc in first sc, * sc in each of next 7 sc, 2 sc in next sc. Repeat from * around.

Rounds 6–9 Repeat first rnd.

Round 10 2 sc in first sc, * sc in each of next 10 sc, 2 sc in next sc. Repeat from * around. For last sc of 10th rnd, change back to color A according to instructions of 21st rnd for Crown. Cut color B yarn, leaving 4" ends.

Round 11 Change back to size J hook, do reverse st around brim edge (see instructions set out in Reverse Stitch in Part I), end with sl st to first reverse st. Knot yarn and cut, leaving 7" ends.

Finishing Hide all ends according to instructions set out in Finishing in Part I.

Hand Warmer Muffler

This novel winter accessory protects both neck and hands from Jack Frost with a definite splash of style.

Materials

3 skeins (2 oz. each) of 4-ply wool or acrylic in variegated tones of same color, blending to pure white (color A)
1 skein (2 oz.) of same type yarn in solid color matching darkest tone of color A (color B)
1 skein (2 oz.) of same type yarn in white
1 size I crochet hook
1 size J crochet hook
yarn needle
straight pins

Crochet

Muffler Make a sl kn on size J hook with color A yarn, leaving a 5" end. Ch 295 to measure 70". If your ch is greater or smaller than 295 to obtain this measurement, be sure that it is an *odd* number. Ch 2; turn.
Row 1 Sk 2 ch, sc in next ch, * ch 1, sk 1 ch, sc in next ch. Repeat from * across. Ch 2; turn.
Row 2 Sk 2 ch and first sc, sc in first ch sp, * sk next sc, ch 1, sc in next ch sp. Repeat from * across. Ch 2; turn.
Rows 3–34 Repeat 2nd row. End 34th row with sc in last ch sp of 33rd row. Knot yarn and cut, leaving a 5" end.
Finishing Hide ends according to instructions set out in Finishing in Part I.
Pockets Make a sl kn on size I hook with color B yarn, leaving a 5" end. Ch 25, or the correct amount to measure 7½", ch 2, turn.
Row 1 Repeat first row for Muffler.
Rows 2–5 Repeat 2nd row for Muffler. For last sc of 5th row, insert hook into last ch sp of 4th row, yoh, ptl; complete sc by yarning over hook with white yarn. Cut color B yarn, leaving a 5" end. Ch 2; turn.
Rows 6–10 Repeat 2nd row for Muffler. For last sc of 10th row, change to color B yarn according to instructions of 5th row of Pockets, above. Ch 2; turn.
Rows 11–14 Repeat 2nd row for Muffler. Change to white at end of 14th row. Ch 2; turn.
Rows 15–17 Repeat 2nd row. Change to color B at end of 17th row.
Rows 18, 19 Repeat 2nd row. Change to white.
Row 20 Repeat 2nd row. Change to color A.
Rows 21–24 Repeat 2nd row. Change to white.
Row 25 Repeat 2nd row. Change to color B.
Rows 26, 27 Repeat 2nd row. Change to white.
Rows 28–30 Repeat 2nd row. Change to color B.

Row 31 Repeat 2nd row. *Do not change color.*

Carefully work a sc, ch 1, sk 1 st pat along edge, bottom and other edge of the rectangle you are working on to form a border in color B. Sl st to first sc of 31st row to complete border. Knot yarn and cut, leaving a 5" end. Repeat all of the above for the other pocket.

Finishing Hide ends of both pockets according to instructions set out in Finishing in Part I.

Using straight pins, pin both pockets to front of muffler, one at each end, with pocket fronts facing you. The starting chs of the pockets should line up with the extreme ends of the muffler, the edges of the pockets with the edges of the muffler.

Border and Pocket Joining Starting at either edge of the muffler about 18" from a pinned pocket, make a sl kn on size J hook with color B yarn, leaving a 5" end. Sc in a ch sp, then repeat from * of 2nd row for Muffler.

When reaching a pocket, continue pat, single-crocheting in ch sps of muffler and sts of pocket simultaneously, joining both. Work completely around muffler, joining the other pocket. End with sl st to first sc of this border. Knot yarn and cut, leaving a 5" end.

Finishing Remove pins and hide all ends according to instructions set out in Finishing in Part I.

Mini-Tank Halter

Materials

2 balls (175 yds. each) of mercerized crochet cotton in each of 3 colors: A, B and C (Suggestion: A—lavender, B—turquoise, C—green.)
1 size I crochet hook
yarn needle
safety pins
Gauge 5 sc=1"; 5 rows=1"; 2 strands of yarn; size I hook.

Crochet

NOTE: This halter consists of 2 crocheted pieces joined at the side seams. All crochet is done with 2 strands of yarn.

Make a sl kn on size I hook with 2 strands of color A yarn, leaving 10" ends. Ch 59 (for Small or Medium) to measure 14", or ch 64 (for Large) to measure 15". Ch 1; turn.

Row 1 Sk 1 ch, sc in next ch sp and across entire ch row. Ch 1; turn.

Row 2 Sk 1 ch, sc in first sc and across entire row. Ch 1; turn.

Rows 3–11 Repeat 2nd row. For last sc of 11th row, insert hook into last sc of 10th row, yoh, ptl; complete sc by yarning over hook with color B yarn, leaving 10" ends of color B. Cut color A yarn, leaving 4" ends.

Rows 12–22 Repeat 2nd row. At end of 22nd row, change to color C yarn as described above.

Rows 23–32 Repeat 2nd row. Change to color B at end of 32nd row.

Rows 33–43 Repeat 2nd row. Change to color A.

Rows 44–54 Repeat 2nd row. *Do not change color.* Knot yarn and cut, leaving 10" ends.

Repeat all of the above for Back. Using 10" ends and colors corresponding to proper

MINI-TANK HALTER 87

color bands, join Front to Back, wrong sides out, according to instructions set out in Joining in Part I.

Finishing Hide all excess ends according to instructions set out in Finishing in Part I. Turn inside out.

Lay garment out on a flat surface with side seams at extreme ends, first row at the bottom. Place 4 safety-pin markers on top row of Front and Back at a distance of 2¾" from each side seam. These markers will indicate beg of shoulder strap joinings.

Shoulder Straps Make a sl kn with 2 strands of color B yarn, leaving 5" ends.

Row 1 Sc directly in st under a safety-pin marker, sc in next 4 sts, heading toward center of garment. Ch 1; turn.

Row 2 Sk first ch, sc in first sc and next 4 sc. Ch 1; turn.

Rows 3–10 Repeat 2nd row, completing last sc of 10th row with color C and leaving 5" ends.

Rows 11–20 Repeat 2nd row. End 20th row with color B.

Rows 21–30 Repeat 2nd row. Change to color A.

Rows 31–40 Repeat 2nd row. Change to color B.

Rows 41–50 Repeat 2nd row. Change to color C.

Rows 51–60 Repeat 2nd row. Change to color B.

Rows 61–70 Repeat 2nd row. *Do not change color.* Knot yarn and cut, leaving 5" ends. Making sure not to twist strap, join end of strap just made to corresponding pin marker on other side of garment, using yarn needle as before.

Repeat the above for the other strap.

Finishing Hide all ends according to Finishing instructions in Part I.

Cotton Sweater-Blouse

Materials

40 balls (53 yds. each) of No. 5 pearl cotton yarn in pale pastel color of your choice
1 size E crochet hook
yarn needle
tape measure
safety pins
straight pins

Crochet

This sweater-blouse consists of 2 T-shaped crocheted pieces, as shown in Figure III-5, which are joined at the sides. Because of the flexible nature of the cluster stitches, 1 size fits all.

Make a sl kn on size E hook with pearl cotton yarn, leaving a 10" end. Ch 246 loosely, or ch the amount necessary to measure 55". Your number of chs must be a multiple of 3. Then ch 1; turn.

Row 1 Sk first ch, (1 sc, 1 ch, 1 sc) in 2nd ch sp from hook. * Sk 1 ch, (1 sc, 1 ch, 1 sc) in next ch sp. Repeat from * until end of row. Ch 1; turn.

Row 2 Sk 1 ch, (1 sc, 1 ch, 1 sc) in first sc of first 3-st cluster of pr r. * (1 sc, 1 ch, 1 sc) in first sc of next 3-st cluster. Repeat from * across row. End with ch-1; turn.

Row 3, etc. Repeat 2nd row until the width of your rectangle measures 6½". Knot yarn gently and cut, leaving a 10" end.

Lay out rectangle on a flat surface. Measure along bottom edge from extreme left end to point X in Figure III-5, a distance of 16½", and place a safety-pin marker at this point. The pin must be in a sc which begins a 3-st cluster

pat. Repeat for other side at point Y in Figure III-5.

Make a sl kn, leaving a 10" end, and (1 sc, 1 ch, 1 sc) in first cluster at safety-pinned point X. Repeat 2nd row, above, until you reach the other safety pin. At this point, finish a cluster, ch 1 and turn.

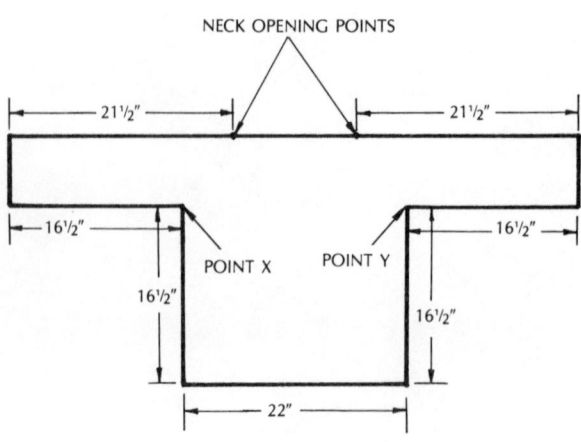

Figure III-5

Continue pat for as many rows as it takes to yield a 16½" height (Figure III-5). Knot yarn and cut, leaving a 10" end.

Repeat all of the above for the other side. After knotting yarn at the completion of the other side, measure off a 3-yard length of yarn before cutting.

Using straight pins, pin both sides tog, right sides out, along both side and sleeve seams. Starting with the 3-yard end, join both sides tog with yarn needle along side seam and corresponding sleeve seam, according to instructions set out in Joining in Part I. Then do the same for the other sleeve seams and side seams, using the 10" ends as far as they will go. Add new joining yarn where needed. Note from Figure III-5 that upper sleeve seams are joined for only 21½" from either wristline, which leaves a 12" neck opening.

Finishing Hide all unused ends according to instructions set out in Finishing in Part I.

Winter Booties

These expressively styled house slippers will provide plenty of warmth for feet and ankles.

Materials

2 skeins (4 oz. each) of 4-ply wool or acrylic yarn for color A (Suggestion: pink.)
2 skeins (2 oz. each) of same type yarn for color B (Suggestion: turquoise.)
1 ball (100 yds.) of heavy cotton kite twine in white
1 size G crochet hook
1 size K crochet hook
yarn needle
safety pins

Crochet

These slippers are made in 2 parts—a sole and a top—which are then joined together. The instructions are for women's Medium, so you may work them tightly for Small, loosely for Large.

Sole Make a sl kn on size K hook with 1 strand each of colors A and B, plus 1 strand of white twine, leaving 6" ends. Ch 7; turn.
Row 1 Sc in 2nd ch from hook and in each ch across. Ch 1; turn.
Row 2 Sc in each of the first 3 sc, 2 sc in 4th sc, 1 sc in each of remaining 2 sc. Ch 1; turn.
Row 3 Sc in each sc across. Ch 1; turn.
Rows 4–6 Repeat 3rd row.
Row 7 Sc in each of first 3 sc, insert hook in next sc, yoh, ptl, insert hook in next sc, yoh, ptl, yoh, pull through 3 lps on hook (dec made). Sc in each of the next 2 sc. Ch 1; turn.
Row 8 Repeat 3rd row.
Row 9 Repeat 2nd row.
Row 10 Repeat 3rd row.
Row 11 Sc in each of first 3 sc, 2 sc in 4th sc, 1 sc in each of next 3 sc. Ch 1; turn.
Rows 12, 13 Repeat 3rd row.
Row 14 Sc in each of next 4 sc, 2 sc in 5th sc, 1 sc in each of next 3 sc. Ch 1; turn.
Rows 15, 16 Repeat 3rd row.
Row 17 Sc in each of next 4 sc, 2 sc in 5th sc, 1 sc in each of next 4 sc. Ch 1; turn.
Row 18 Sc in each of next 4 sc, dec 1 sc as described in 7th row, 1 sc in each of last 4 sc. Ch 1; turn.
Rows 19, 20 Repeat 3rd row.
Row 21 Sc in each of first 3 sc, dec 1 sc as above, 1 sc in each of last 4 sc. Ch 1; turn.
Row 22 Sc in each of first 3 sc, dec 1 sc, 1 sc in each of last 3 sc. Ch 1; turn.
Row 23 Repeat 3rd row.
Row 24 Dec in first 2 sc, 1 sc in each of next 3 sc, dec again at end of row. Knot yarns and cut white twine, leaving a 4" end. Measure off 7 feet of yarn in colors A and B and cut.

Repeat all of the above for the other sole.

Slipper Top Make a sl kn with color B yarn and ch 32 to measure 10". Ch 1; turn.
Row 1 Sc in 2nd ch from hook and in each ch across. For last sc, insert hook in last ch sp, yoh, ptl; complete sc by yarning over hook with color A yarn. Cut color B yarn, leaving a 4" end. Ch 1; turn.
Row 2 Sc in each of first 2 sc, * do hazelnut st in next sc (see instructions for Hazelnut Stitch in Part I) with 6 total strands to close st. Sc in next 2 sc. Repeat from * until end of row (10 hazelnuts made). For last sc of row, change to color B as described in first row, above. Ch 1; turn.
Row 3 Sc in every sc across. Change to color A at end of row. Ch 1; turn.
Row 4 Repeat 2nd row.
Row 5 Repeat 3rd row.
Rows 6, 7 Repeat 2nd and 3rd rows.
Rows 8, 9 Repeat 2nd and 3rd rows.
Row 10 Repeat 2nd row.

You have thus far completed the top part of the anklet, which will have an opening for easy insertion of the foot. Now sl st with color A to first st of 10th row to close anklet.
Round 1 Repeat 2nd row. After changing to color B yarn, sl st to first sc of this rnd.
Round 2 Repeat 3rd row. After changing to color A, sl st to first sc of rnd.
Rounds 3, 4 Repeat first and 2nd rnds. Knot yarn and cut, leaving a 4" end.

Place 2 safety-pin markers in the 10th st from beg and 10th st from end of 4th rnd. Make a sl kn with color A yarn, leaving a 4" end, and work with right side of work facing you.
Row 1 Sc in right-hand pinned sc. Working toward center of slipper, do hazelnut st, repeating from * in 2nd row, above, until 6 hazelnuts are made, bringing you to sc in left-hand pinned sc. Change to color B. Ch 1; turn.
Row 2 Repeat 3rd row, above.
Rows 3, 4 Repeat 2nd and 3rd rows at beg of slipper top, making 6 more hazelnuts.
Rows 5, 6 Repeat 2nd and 3rd rows.
Rows 7, 8 Repeat 2nd and 3rd rows.
Rows 9, 10; 11, 12; 13, 14 Repeat 2nd and 3rd rows.
Rows 15, 16 Change to size G hook and repeat 2nd and 3rd rows.

Repeat all of the above for other slipper top.

Joining Thread 7' ends at toe end of sole through yarn needle and join sole to top as

instructed in Joining in Part I, working loosely at toe end. Repeat for other sole.
Finishing Hide all loose ends according to Finishing instructions in Part I.
Ties Make a sl kn on size K hook with 1 strand each of colors A and B yarn, leaving 5" ends. Ch tightly to measure 24". Knot yarn and cut, leaving 3" ends. Thread 5" ends into yarn needle and sew with a running st through top of anklet between 2nd and 3rd rows of hazelnuts, through sc row. Hide loose ends in ch. Repeat for other slipper.
Ball Ends for Ties Make a sl kn on size K hook with 1 strand each of colors A and B yarn, leaving 3" ends. Ch 2.
Round 1 6 sc in 2nd ch from hook.
Round 2 2 sc in each sc around.
Round 3 Dec 1 sc, as described in 7th row of Sole, 6 times around. Knot yarn and cut, leaving 6" ends. Stuff cup thus formed with scraps of yarn, then thread 6" ends through yarn needle and sew through sts of 3rd rnd. Pull tightly to close ball, and sew to end of tie ch.

Repeat for other end of tie ch, and twice more for other tie ch.

Multicolor Full Poncho

Materials

6 skeins (3½ oz. each) of 4-ply worsted wool or acrylic knitting yarn, 3 skeins in a combination of variegated colors (combination A), 3 in a complementary combination (combination B)
12 yds. of solid color contrasting yarn of same type
1 size I crochet hook
1 size K crochet hook
yarn needle
safety pins
Gauge 6 sc = 3"; 6 rows = 3"; 1 strand of yarn; size K hook.

Crochet

This pattern is worked loosely and will fit all sizes. It consists of 2 rectangles, each 27" x 33", joined tog as shown in Figure III-6, plus some finishing at the neckline and a lp fringe.

Make a sl kn with combination A yarn on size K hook, leaving a 6" end. Ch 65, or amount to produce a 33" length. Ch 1; turn.

Row 1 Sk 1 ch, sc in 2nd ch sp, sc in every ch sp across. End with ch-1; turn.

Row 2 Sk first ch, sc in every sc across. After next-to-last sc, insert hook in last sc of first row, yoh, ptl; complete sc by yarning over hook with combination B. Cut combination A yarn, leaving a 6" end. Ch 1; turn.

Rows 3, 4 Sk first ch, sc in every sc across. After next-to-last sc, insert hook in last sc of pr r, yoh, ptl; complete sc by yarning over hook with other combination. Cut original yarn, leaving a 6" end. Ch 1; turn.

Repeat 3rd and 4th rows alternately, changing colors at end of each row, until you have completed 54 rows, or 27" length. After last sc, knot yarn gently in place and cut, leaving a 6" end.

Now repeat all of the above for the other rectangle.

Joining Join 1 end of first rectangle to side of second, as shown by the joining lines of Figure III-6, following instructions set out in Joining in Part I. Join other side.

Neck Edging Make a sl kn on size I hook with the solid color yarn, leaving a 6" end. Ch 5, sc into neckline at point X of Figure III-6. Ch 5, trc in next sc of neckline and in every sc around. End by entering hook into top of first trc, yoh, ptl; complete sc with combination A yarn. Cut solid color yarn, leaving a 5" end.

Sc in every trc around, sl st to first sc. * Ch 5, sl st to 3rd ch sp of ch-5 just made, sc in next sc. Repeat from * around, ending with sc in last sc. Cut yarn, leaving a 6" end.

Fringe Using 2 strands of yarn, attach a 5½" lp fringe all around bottom of poncho, according to directions set out in Loop Fringe in Part I.

Finishing Hide all ends according to instructions set out in Finishing in Part I.

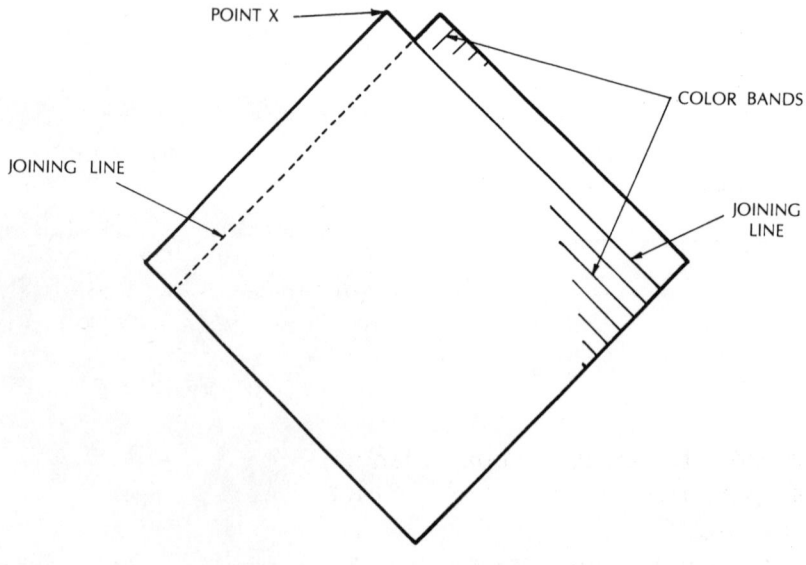

Figure III-6

Patchwork-Motif Sweater

"Patches" and borders that utilize an ambitious variety of crochet stitches and color combinations lend a sporty feeling to this attractive sweater.

Materials

2-ply wool or acrylic yarn in various textures of your choice in the following amounts:

Weight in Ounces	Color Identification	Recommended Color
3½	A	Maroon
1	B	White
1	C	Sky Blue
1	D	Mint Green
1	E	Rust
1	F	Red
10	G	Antique Gold
1	H	Navy
1	I	Light Gold

crochet hooks in sizes B, C, F and G (H for Large size only)
yarn needle
straight pins

Crochet

NOTE: Specific instructions for Small, Medium and Large sizes are given where necessary throughout the following.

The procedure for assembling the various parts that comprise this sweater will consist of the following basic steps:

1. Crochet the bordered frames of back and front, then join with 2 side seams. Picot-edge the bottom.

2. Crochet upper front and sleeve fronts tog, joining to bordered front.
3. Crochet upper back and sleeve backs tog, joining to bordered back and bottom of sleeve fronts. Join sleeve tops.
4. Add tapered portions to wrist ends of sleeves and neckline with picot edging.

Center Back Make a sl kn on size G hook with color A yarn, leaving a 5" end. Ch 77, or an odd number to measure 13". Turn.

Row 1 Sc in 3rd ch from hook, * ch 1, sk 1 ch, sc in next ch sp. Repeat from * across row, ending with ch-2; turn.

Row 2 Sk 2 chs and first sc of pr r, * sc in next ch sp, ch 1, sk 1 sc. Repeat from * across, ending with ch-2; turn.

Rows 3–64 (to measure 12½") Repeat 2nd row. For last sc of last row, insert hook in last ch sp of pr r, yoh, ptl; complete sc by yarning over hook with color B yarn. Cut color A yarn, leaving a 5" end. Ch 2 with new color; turn.

Back Border For this border use size F hook for Small, size G hook for Medium, or size H hook for Large.

Round 1 Repeat 2nd row of Center Back. At end of row, after single-crocheting in last ch sp, ch 1 and sc in same sp (to form corner). Do *not* turn. Ch 1, * sk 1 row sp along side of work, sc in next row sp, ch 1. Repeat from * all along edge. At end of edge, sc in last row sp, ch 1, sc in first ch sp of original ch row. * Ch 1, sk 1 ch of ch row, sc in next ch sp. Repeat from * across ch row. End with sc in last ch sp, ch 1, * sk 1 row sp along other edge, sc in next row sp, ch 1. Repeat from * along final edge. At end of edge, sc in last row sp, ch 1, sc in first ch sp of color B row that started this rnd.

Round 2 * Ch 1, sc in next ch sp, sk 1 sc. Repeat from * around the 4 sides as before to produce the 2nd row of color B, making sure to sc, ch 1, sc in same sp at each corner. When you reach the start, complete the last sc with color C yarn according to the color-change instructions in the 64th row of Center Back. Cut color B yarn, leaving a 5" end.

Rounds 3–10 Consult Figure III-7 to aid in keeping track of the following color bands. Repeat the same pat from * in 2nd rnd, above, for 1 row along each of the 4 sides for color C. When back to start, change to color D, breaking off color C yarn. Work 1 rnd of color D, then return to color C for 1 rnd. Next are 2 rnds of color B, 1 of color A, and, finally, 2 rnds of color B. Knot color B yarn and cut, leaving a 5" end.

Consult Figure III-8 to check the measurements and placement of motifs.

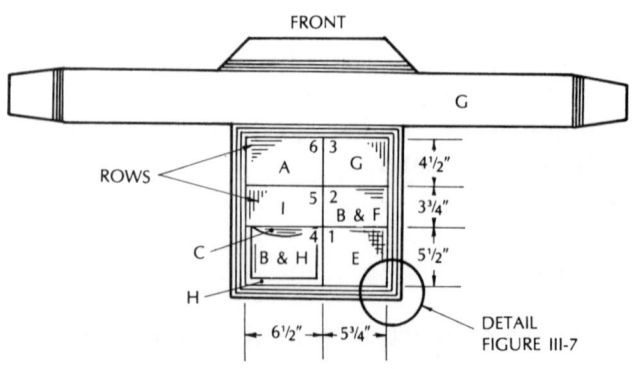

Figure III-8

Motif 1 Make a sl kn on size F hook with color E yarn, leaving a 5" end. Ch 33 to measure 5¾", then ch 1 more. Turn.

Row 1 Work (1 sc, 1 ch, 1 sc) in 2nd ch sp from hook. * Sk 1 ch, (1 sc, 1 ch, 1 sc) in next ch sp. Repeat from * until end of row, ending with ch-1; turn.

Row 2 Work (1 sc, 1 ch, 1 sc) in first sc of first 3-st cluster of pr r. * (1 sc, 1 ch, 1 sc) in first sc of next 3-st cluster. Repeat from * until end of row, ending with ch-1; turn.

Rows 3–31 (to measure 5½") Repeat 2nd row. Complete last sc of last row with color F, breaking off color E.

Motif 2

Row 1 Sc in every sc of your last row of Motif 1. Complete last sc with color B. Ch 1; turn.

Row 2 Sc in every sc across. Complete last sc with color F. Ch 1; turn.

Row 3 Sc in *back lp only* (see Ribbed Crochet in Part I) of every sc across. Complete last sc with color B. Ch 1; turn.

Rows 4 and 5, 6 and 7–18 and 19 (to measure 3¾") Repeat 2nd and 3rd rows alternately, ending with a color F row. Complete last sc of this row with color G instead of color B. Change to a size G hook and ch 2; turn.

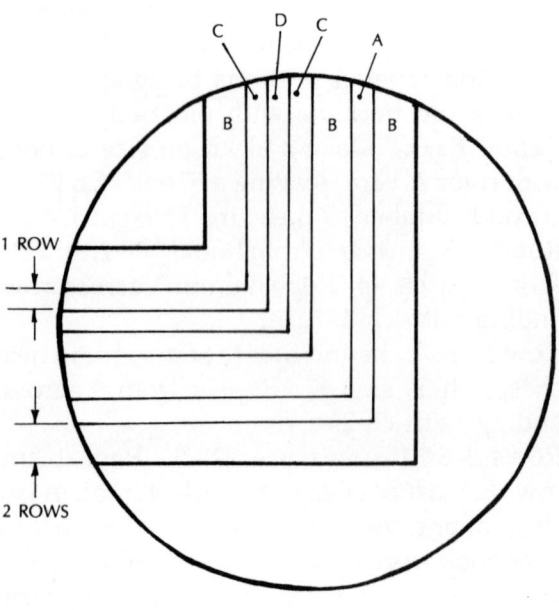

Figure III-7

Motif 3
Row 1 Sc in first sc of last row of Motif 2. * Ch 1, sk 1 sc, sc in next sc. Repeat from * across, ending with ch-2; turn.
Row 2 Sk 2 ch and first sc of pr r, sc in next ch sp, * ch 1, sk 1 sc, sc in next ch sp. Repeat from * across, ending with ch-2; turn.
Rows 3–23 (to measure 4½") Repeat 2nd row. End by knotting yarn and cutting, leaving a 5" end.

Motifs 4, 5 and 6 are all crocheted separately, then joined to the other motifs.
Motif 4 Make a sl kn on size F hook with color C yarn, leaving a 5" end. Ch 39 to measure 6½", then ch 2 more; turn.
Row 1 Dc in 3rd ch sp from hook and in every ch sp across row. End with ch-2 (counts as 1 dc); turn.
Row 2 Dc in 2nd dc and in every dc across. Ch 2; turn.
Rows 3–13 (to measure 5½") Repeat 2nd row. End by knotting yarn and cutting, leaving a 5" end.
Pocket for Motif 4 Make a sl kn with color B yarn, leaving a 4" end. Ch 16 to measure 3"; turn.
Row 1 Sc in 2nd ch sp and in every ch sp across, completing last sc with color H. Ch 1; turn.
Row 2 Sc in *back lps only* (see Ribbed Crochet in Part I) of every sc of pr r. Complete last sc with color B. Ch 1; turn.
Row 3 Sc in every sc of pr r across. Complete last sc with color H. Ch 1; turn.

Rows 4 and 5, 6 and 7–26 and 27 (to measure 5¾") Repeat 2nd and 3rd rows alternately, ending with a color B row. Complete last sc of last row with color H.

Ch 1, turn, sc in ch-1 sp and back lp of first sc of pr r. Sc in back lp of every sc across. After last sc on row, ch 1, sc in same sp (to form corner). *Do not turn,* but continue to sc in each row sp along edge. At end of edge, form corner again by ch 1, sc in same sp, then sc again in every sc across. At end of row, ch 1, and work back along the row you have just completed, single-crocheting in same ch-1 sp and across row. Turn next corner as before, sc in row sp of edge, turn last corner, and work back to beg of border. Knot yarn and cut, leaving a 1-yard end.

At this point, hide all loose ends of the pocket and all motifs made thus far, except the last 1-yard end just made, following directions set out in Finishing in Part I. Then thread your yarn needle with the 1-yard end of the pocket and sew the pocket to the front of Motif 4 with close running stitches, according to pat in Figure III-9. Cut yarn, leaving a 4" end.
Motif 5 Make a sl kn on size F hook with color I yarn, leaving a 24" end. Ch 22 to measure 3¾"; turn.
Row 1 Sc in 2nd ch from hook and in every ch across. Ch 1; turn.
Row 2 Sc in every sc across. Ch 1; turn.

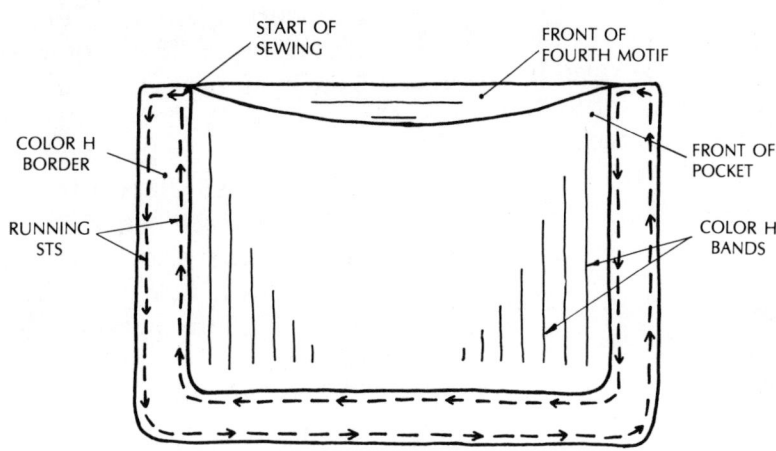

Figure III-9

Rows 3–34 (to measure 6½") Repeat 2nd row. Knot yarn and cut, leaving a 24" end.
Motif 6 Make a sl kn on size F hook with color A yarn, leaving a 24" end. Ch 40 to measure 6½"; turn.
Row 1 Hdc in 2nd ch from hook and in every ch across. End with ch-1; turn.
Row 2 Sc in *back lp* of every hdc across. Ch 1; turn.
Row 3 Hdc in first sc and in every sc across. Ch 1; turn.
Rows 4 and 5, 6 and 7–14 and 15 (to measure 4½") Repeat 2nd and 3rd rows alternately. End last row by knotting yarn and cutting, leaving a 24" end.

Join all unjoined motifs tog, using yarn needle and 24" ends and following Figure III-8. Hide all loose ends (see Joining and Finishing instructions in Part I).

Front Border Use same size hook for this border as was used for Back Border. Make a sl kn with color B yarn and, with right side facing you, sc in any sc in top row of motif 5. * Sk next sc, ch 1, sc in next sc. Repeat from * around the rows and edges of the 6 motifs as you did for the back border, chaining 1 and single-crocheting in the same sp to turn corners, for 2 complete rnds of color B. See Figure III-7 to check your work, which should be comprised of 1 rnd each of colors C, D and C again after the 2 rnds of color B, then 2 more of color B, 1 of color A, and finally 2 of color B. Knot yarn and cut, leaving a 5" end.

Using straight pins, pin front to back with wrong sides facing out, making sure that the rows of the center back are vertical and the pocket in the front is at the lower left (facing you) (Figure III-10). Join front to back along both side seams, using yarn needle and color B yarn; turn inside out.

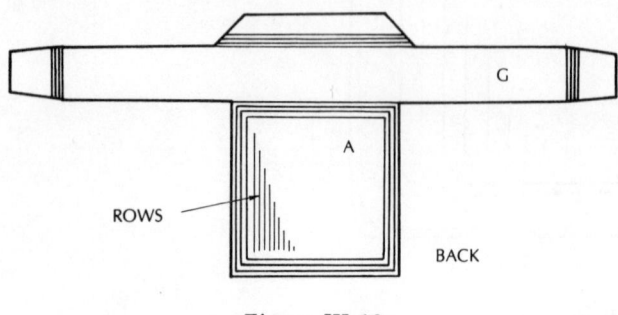

Figure III-10

Picot Edging Using same size hook as for border, make a sl kn with color B yarn, leaving a 5" end. With right side of back facing you, sc in any ch-1 sp at bottom, * ch 3, sl st in first ch sp of ch-3 just made, sk next sc, sc in next ch-1 sp. Repeat from * along entire bottom, past both side seams, ending with sl st to first sc made. Knot yarn and cut, leaving a 5" end.

Upper Front and Sleeve Fronts Make a sl kn on size G hook with color G yarn, leaving a 5" end.
Row 1 Ch 91 to measure 16". With right side of front facing you, sc in first ch-1 sp at top corner. * Ch 1, sk next sc, sc in next sc. Repeat from * across top of front. After last sc at opposite corner, ch 91, or the same amount you started with, then ch 2 more; turn.
Row 2 Sk 2 chs and sc in 3rd ch sp, * ch 1, sk 1 ch, sc in next ch. Repeat from * across ch row until you reach front. Then sk first sc, * sc in next ch sp, ch 1, sk next sc. Repeat from * until you reach ch row on other sleeve. Then repeat from * at beg of this row. End row with ch-2; turn.
Row 3 Sk 2 chs and first sc, sc in next ch-1 sp, * ch 1, sk next sc, sc in next ch-1 sp. Repeat from * across row, ending with ch-2; turn.
Rows 4–29 (to measure 5") Repeat 3rd row. End last row by knotting yarn and cutting, leaving a 4' end.

Upper Back and Sleeve Backs Make a sl kn on size G hook with color G yarn, leaving a 5" end.
Row 1 With right side of back facing you and working from end of sleeve inward, sc in first ch sp of ch row of *wrong* side of sleeve, * ch 1, sk next ch, sc in next ch sp. Repeat from * until you reach the back. Sc in first ch-1 sp of top row of the back, * ch 1, sk next sc, sc in next ch sp. Repeat from * across the back until you reach beg of other sleeve. Sc in first ch sp of other sleeve, then repeat from * at beg of this row, above. Ch 2; turn.
Rows 2–29 (to measure 5") Repeat 3rd row of Upper Front and Sleeve Fronts, above. Knot yarn and cut, leaving a 4' end.
Sleeve Joining Using yarn needle and 4' ends, join sleeve backs to sleeve fronts at top for a distance of 14½" in from either sleeve end to allow for neck opening.

Sleeve Borders Make a sl kn on size C hook with color B yarn, leaving a 5" end.
Round 1 With right side of back facing you, sc directly into a row sp at sleeve end. * Ch 1, sk 1 row sp, sc in next row sp. Repeat from * around, ending with ch-1.
Round 2 Sk 1 sc of pr rnd, sc in next ch-1 sp, * ch 1, sc in next ch-1 sp, sk next sc. Repeat from * around, completing last sc with color C. Ch 1.
Round 3 Repeat 2nd rnd, completing last sc with color D. Ch 1.
Round 4 Repeat 2nd rnd. Change to color C. Ch 1.
Round 5 Repeat 2nd rnd. Change to color B.
Rounds 6, 7 Repeat 2nd rnd. End 7th rnd with color A.
Round 8 Repeat 2nd rnd. Change to color B.
Rounds 9, 10 Repeat 2nd rnd. Change to color G.
Rounds 11–end Change to size B hook and repeat 2nd rnd for as many rnds as are required to measure 5" back to beg of first rnd for Small, 6" for Medium, or 7" for Large. Do not break off yarn at end of last rnd, but ch 1 instead.
Picot Edge for Sleeves Sk 1 sc and sc in next ch-1 sp, * ch 2, sl st to first ch sp of ch-2 just made, sk 1 sc, sc in next ch-1 sp. Repeat from * around, ending with sl st to first sc. Knot yarn and cut, leaving a 5" end.

Repeat Border and Picot Edge for other sleeve.

Neckline Border Make a sl kn on size G hook with color B yarn, leaving a 5" end.
Round 1 With right side of work facing you, sc in any ch-1 sp to the right of center on top of back. * Ch 1, sk next sc, sc in next ch-1 sp. Repeat from * around, ending with ch-1.
Round 2 Sk 1 ch and first sc, sc in next ch-1 sp, * ch 1, sk next sc, sc in next ch-1 sp. Repeat from * until you reach center of the back, at which point dec 1 st by inserting hook into ch-1 sp, yoh, ptl, sk next sc and enter hook in next ch sp, yoh again, pull through all 3 lps on hook. Then repeat from * around. Complete last sc of rnd with color C. Ch 1.
Round 3 Repeat 2nd rnd, again decreasing 1 st at center of the back. Complete last sc with color D. Ch 1.
Round 4 Repeat 2nd rnd, decreasing 1 st. Change to color C at end. Ch 1.
Round 5 Repeat 2nd rnd, this time decreasing 2 sts in the back, each about one-third the distance in from the points where the back meets the front (shoulder seams), *plus* 1 st at *each* of these points (4 dec made). End rnd with color B. Ch 1.
Round 6 Repeat 2nd rnd, decreasing 2 sts, each about 1" from shoulder seams on *front*. Keep color B. Ch 1.
Round 7 Repeat 2nd rnd, decreasing 1 st at center of back as in 2nd rnd. Change to color A. Ch 1.
Round 8 Repeat 2nd rnd with no dec. Change to color B. Ch 1.
Round 9 Repeat 2nd rnd with no dec. Keep color B. Ch 1.
Round 10 Repeat 2nd rnd with decreasing 5 sts—1 at center of back and 1 each at 1" from both shoulder seams in front and in back. End with change to color G. Ch 1.
Rounds 11–17 Try on sweater at this point. If neckline thus far fits easily over the head, use a size B hook for the following rnds. If neckline requires some stretching to fit over the head, use a size C hook. Repeat 2nd rnd, decreasing 1 st at each shoulder seam (2 dec made) for *each* rnd. End 17th rnd with ch-1.
Picot Edge for Neck Sk first sc, sc in next ch sp, * ch 3, sl st to first ch sp of ch-3 just made, sk next sc, sc in next ch-1 sp. Repeat from * all around neckline, ending with sl st to first sc. Knot yarn and cut, leaving a 5" end.
Finishing Hide all loose ends according to instructions in Finishing in Part I.

Glitter Coverlet

Materials

6 bobbins (1 oz. each) of metallic speckled nylon-acetate–blend yarn (Suggestion: black with gold and/or silver speckles.)
1 size J crochet hook
yarn needle

Crochet

Make a sl kn on size J hook, leaving a 5" end. Ch 1, pull lp on your hook out for a distance of 1¼", and make a lover's knot st (see Lover's Knot instructions in Part I). * Pull lp out to 1¼" and make lover's knot st. Repeat from * until you have 18 lps, or amount to measure 28". Turn.

Row 1 Pull lp out, make 2 lover's knots, and sc in 2nd knot part of cast row, as shown in Figure III-11. * Make 2 lover's knots and sc in next knot part of next lover's knot of cast row. Repeat from * until end of row. Make 3 lover's knots. Turn.

Row 2 Sc in first knot part of pr r, * make 2 lover's knots and sc in next knot part of pr r. Repeat from * until end of row. Make 3 lover's knots. Turn.

Rows 3–16 Repeat 2nd row. At end of 16th row, make 2 lover's knots. Turn.

Row 17 Sc in first unattached knot of 16th row, * make lover's knot, sc in next unattached knot of 16th row. Repeat from * until last unattached knot of 16th row, then make 2 lover's knots and sc to last (attached) knot of 16th row (Figure III-11). Knot yarn and cut, leaving a 5" end.

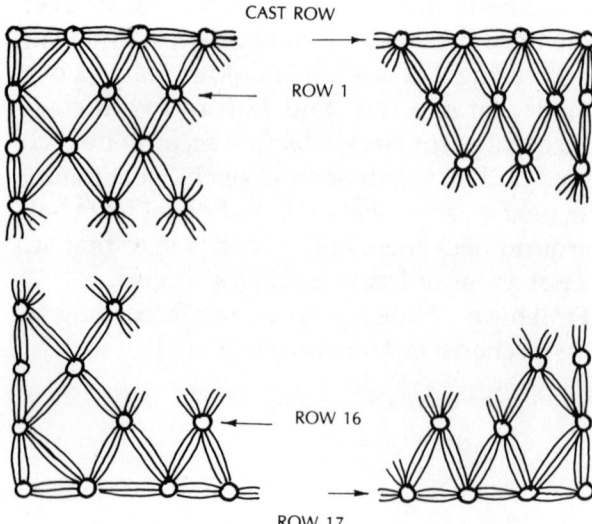

Figure III-11

Edging Make a sl kn, leaving a 5" end. With front of coverlet facing you, sc in knot at upper left corner, ch 3, 2 dc in sc, 2 sc in next lover's knot along left edge. * Ch 3, 2 dc in sc, 2 sc in next lover's knot. Repeat from * along left edge, bottom, and up right edge until you reach upper right-hand knot. In this knot work 3 sc, ch 3, sc in first ch sp of ch-3 just made (picot made). Sc in next knot along top, making the same picots in each knot. In the last knot (at upper left corner) work 2 sc, sl st to first sc that began edging. Knot yarn and cut, leaving a 5" end.

Ties Cut 2 lengths of yarn 60" each and fold in half. Make a sl kn on hook with 4 strands held tog, leaving 6" ends, and sc in upper left-hand corner knot. Ch the amount to measure 6", knot yarn, and cut, leaving 6" ends. Repeat for tie at other corner.

Tassels Attach 16-strand, 2" tassels to the ends of each tie according to instructions set out in Tassels and Fringes in Part I.

Finishing Hide all loose ends according to instructions set out in Finishing in Part I.

Fluffy House Slippers

Materials

3 skeins (3½ oz. each) of 4-ply knitting worsted or rug yarn in variegated tones of your choice
1 size K hook
safety pins
yarn needle

Gauge 5 sc = 2"; 5 rows = 2"; 3 strands of yarn; size K hook.

Crochet

NOTE: Three strands of yarn are used throughout. The instructions given are for ladies' Small size. Medium and Large are in parentheses.

Sole Make a sl kn with 3 strands on size K hook, leaving 4" ends. Ch 15 (18, 21) to measure 5" (6", 7"), or 2" less than the length of the foot to be fitted.

Round 1 2 sc in 2nd ch from hook. Place a small safety pin in first sc made. Sc in each ch until you reach next-to-last ch. In last ch, work 3 sc. Place another safety pin in center sc of 3-sc group just made. Working down other side of ch, sc in every ch sp, sl st to ch sp before sc with first safety pin.
Round 2 Ch 1, 3 sc in pinned sc. Remove pin and place it in center sc of the 3-sc group just made. Sc in each sc around until you reach the next pinned sc. Work 3 sc in pinned sc. Remove pin and place it in the center sc of the 3-sc group just made. Sc in each remaining sc across. Sl st to ch-1 made at beg of this rnd.
Round 3 Ch 1, sc in every sc until you reach 2nd safety pin. Work 3 sc in this sc, replace pin in center sc, and sc in every sc back to start. Sl st to ch-1 first made.
Round 4 Repeat 3rd rnd. Remove safety pins.
Sides and Top
Round 1 Ch 1. Make 1" long lp st (see Loop Stitch instructions in Part I) in first sc and in every sc around.
Rounds 2–7 Repeat lp st as in first rnd, all around. End 7th rnd by knotting yarn and cutting, leaving a 5" end.

Fold work in half with the *loopless* side out; locate the slipper front (toe end) by noticing where the sole widens due to inc of sc. Using yarn needle, join sides tog (according to Joining directions in Part I) to form instep, leaving a 4" to 5" opening for insertion of foot.

Make a sl kn with 2 strands of yarn and enter hook in any lp st near back of ankle opening. Make reverse st (see Reverse Stitch instructions in Part I) all around opening. End with sl st to first reverse st.

Repeat all of the above for the other slipper.
Finishing Hide all loose ends according to Finishing instructions in Part I.

Medieval Belt and Choker

Add a metallic spark to many outfits with this matched pair of versatile accessories.

Materials

2 balls (130 yds. each) of metallic polyester–nylon–blend yarn in gold or silver
1 size D crochet hook
2 size 1 snap fasteners
sewing thread in gold or silver
yarn needle

Crochet

Belt The belt is made of 2 identical pieces, joined at the center.

Make a sl kn, leaving a 5" end. Ch 8; turn.
Row 1 Sk 1 ch, sc in next ch sp and across. Ch 1; turn.
Rows 2–53 (to measure 10¼") Sc in every sc across. Ch 1; turn.
Rows 54–59 Sc in every sc up to center of the row, inc 1 sc at center (see Increasing instructions in Part I), and sc across. Ch 1; turn.
Rows 60–71 Repeat 2nd row (work even).
Row 72 Repeat 54th row (1 inc made).
Rows 73, 74 Repeat 2nd row.
Row 75 Repeat 54th row.
Row 76 Repeat 2nd row.
Rows 77–81 Repeat 54th row.
Rows 82–85 Repeat 2nd row.
Rows 86 and 87, 88 and 89–104 and 105 Repeat 2nd and 54th rows, alternating.
Row 106 Repeat 54th row.
Row 107 Sc across, inc 1 sc at 5th sc from beg, dec 1 sc at center (see instructions for increasing and decreasing in Part I), inc 1 sc at 5th st from end of row.
Rows 108, 109 Sc across, dec 1 sc at center.
Row 110 Sc across, dec 1 sc at 5th st from beg and end of row (2 dec made).
Rows 111, 112 Repeat 2nd row. Knot yarn and cut, leaving a 5" end.

Repeat all of the above for the other section, but leave a 24" end at end of the 112th row. With both wrong sides of each section facing you, join centers with yarn needle, according to Joining instructions in Part I.

Make a sl kn, leaving a 5" end, and, with right side of belt facing you, work reverse st (see Reverse Stitch instructions in Part I) all around edges of belt, starting near an end, ending with sl st to first reverse st. Knot yarn and cut, leaving a 5" end.
Finishing Hide all loose ends, according to Finishing instructions in Part I.
Choker Make a sl kn, leaving a 5" end. Ch 8; turn.
Row 1 Sk first ch, sc in each ch sp across. Ch 1; turn.
Row 2–end Sc in every sc across. Ch 1; turn. Repeat until choker fits snugly on neck when held end to end, then do 2 more rows.

Edge choker all around with reverse st as for belt. Knot yarn and cut, leaving a 5" end.
Finishing Hide all loose ends according to Finishing instructions in Part I. Sew snap fasteners to extreme corners at one end with matching sewing thread.

Men's Lounge Jacket

A luxurious and warm wraparound three-quarter-length jacket suitable for après-ski or any wintry setting.

Materials

12 skeins (3½ oz. each) of 4-ply wool or acrylic yarn for *each* of 2 complementary colors (Suggested: ecru and light tan.)
1 size J crochet hook
1 size K crochet hook
yarn needle
Gauge   5 sc=2"; 6 rows=2"; 2 strands of yarn; size K hook.

Crochet

NOTE: Two strands are used throughout (unless otherwise specified), 1 in each color.

Instructions are given for men's Small size; Medium and Large sizes are in parentheses.
Back   Make a sl kn with 2 strands on size K hook, leaving 5" ends. Ch 43 (46, 49), ch 1 more; turn.
Row 1   Sc in 2nd ch sp from hook and sc all across row. Ch 1; turn.
Row 2   Sc in every sc across. Ch 1; turn.
Row 3, etc.   Repeat 2nd row for 60 (66, 72) rows in total.
Armholes
First Dec Row   Sl st for 7 sts, sc across to 8th-from-last st of pr r. Ch 1; turn.
Second Dec Row   Dec 1 sc at beg of row, sc across, dec 1 sc in last 2 sc of pr r. Ch 1; turn.
Third Dec Row   Repeat 2nd Dec Row.
Row 4   Sc in every sc across. Ch 1; turn (even row).
Row 5, etc.   Repeat 4th row 19 (20, 21) more times. End last row by knotting yarn and cutting, leaving 5" ends.

Front (left side)   Make a sl kn on same hook, leaving 5" ends. Ch 26. Ch 1 more; turn.
Row 1   Sc in 2nd ch sp from hook and in every ch across. Ch 1; turn.
Row 2   Sc in each of first 2 sc of pr r, make hazelnut st in next sc with 6 (double-strand) lps on hook to close. * Sc in each of next 2 sc of pr r, make hazelnut st as before in next sc. Repeat from * across row (8 hazelnuts made). Ch 1; turn.
Row 3   Sc in every sc (including hazelnut sc) across. Ch 1; turn.
Rows 4 and 5, 6 and 7, etc.   Repeat 2nd and 3rd rows alternately, to complete 59 (65, 71) rows, ending on a sc row.
Row 60 (66, 72)   Sl st 3 sc, * sc in next 2 sc, hazelnut in next sc, sc in next 2 sc. Repeat from * across row (7 hazelnuts made). Ch 1; turn.
Row 61 (67, 73)   Sc in every sc across. Ch 1; turn.

Rows 62, 63, etc. (68, 69, etc.; 74, 75, etc.) Repeat from * in 60th and 61st rows alternately to complete 76 (82, 88) rows.
Row 77 (83, 89) Sc in first 2 sc of pr r, * hazelnut in next sc, sc in next 2 sc. Repeat from * 2 more times (3 hazelnuts made). Ch 1; turn.
Rows 78–80 (84–86, 90–92) Sc in every sc across. Ch 1; turn. End 80th row (86th, 92nd) by knotting yarn and cutting, leaving 18″ ends.
Front (right side) Repeat as for Front (left side) up to 59th row (65th, 71st).
Row 60 (66, 72) Repeat from * in 60th row of left side for 7 times only, then sc in each of next 2 sc. Ch 1; turn.
Row 61 (67, 73) Sc in every sc across. Ch 1; turn.
Rows 62, 63, etc. (68, 69, etc.; 74, 75, etc.) Repeat 60th and 61st rows alternately to complete 76 (82, 88) rows.
Row 77 (83, 89) Sl st 12 sc of pr r, * sc in next 2 sc, hazelnut in next sc, sc in next 2 sc. Repeat from * 2 more times (3 hazelnuts made). Ch 1; turn.
Rows 78–80 (84–86, 90–92) Repeat same-numbered rows as for left side.
Sleeve Make a sl kn, leaving 5″ ends. Ch 18 (19, 20), ch 1 more; turn.
Row 1 Sk first ch, sc in every ch across. Ch 1; turn.
Row 2 Inc 1 sc at beg of row, sc across, inc 1 sc at end of row. Ch 1; turn.
Rows 3–5 Repeat 2nd row (inc row).
Rows 6, 7 Sc in every sc across. Ch 1; turn (even rows).
Row 8 Repeat 2nd row.
Rows 9–12 Even rows.
Row 13 Inc row.
Row 14 Even row.
Row 15 Inc row.
Row 16 Even row.
Row 17 Inc row.
Rows 18–21 Even rows.
Rows 22–26 Inc rows.
Rows 27–33 Even rows.
Row 34 Dec 1 sc at beg of row, sc across, dec 1 sc at end of row. Ch 1; turn.
Row 35 Repeat 34th row (dec row).
Row 36–end Work 4 even rows and 1 dec row repeatedly to complete 76 (80, 84) rows. At end of last row, knot yarn and cut, leaving 6′ ends.

Repeat Sleeve instructions for other sleeve.
Joining Match up upper left- and upper right-hand corners of left and right fronts to upper right- and left-hand corners of last row of back (Figure III-12). Using yarn needle and 18″ ends, join the 9-st lengths of the fronts to the back according to Joining instructions in Part I.

Join sleeves along their side seams from last row up to 28th row, using the 6′ ends; then join tops of sleeves to armhole openings of fronts and back. Finally, join fronts to back along side seams.

Collar and Front Border
Row 1 Make a sl kn with 2 strands of the darker colored yarn, leaving 5″ ends. Starting at bottom of the unjoined corner of right front, sc in every row sp up right front until you reach the last row that contains 7

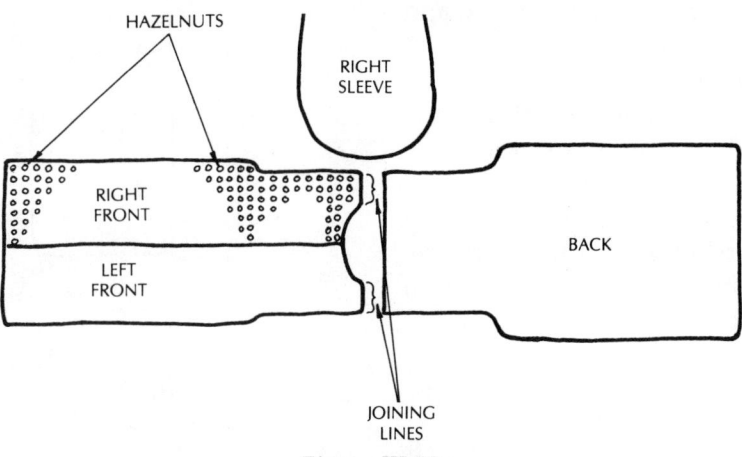

Figure III-12

hazelnuts. Work 3 sc in this corner sp, then continue single-crocheting across the remainder of the right front, across the back, and down the left front. Work 3 sc in the corresponding corner sp of left front at the first row that contains 7 hazelnuts, then continue down left front. Ch 1; turn.

Rows 2, 3 Continue to sc, making 3 sc in the center sc at both corners. Ch 1; turn.

Rows 4–8 Repeat 2nd row, using 1 strand of each color (see instructions for changing colors in Part I), and leaving a 5" end of the darker color. At end of 8th row, drop lighter color and, using 2 strands of darker color, ch 4.

Row 9 Trc up to corner st, 2 trc in this st, ch 1, 2 trc in same st. Then trc across, repeating this sequence in other corner st. Trc down to other end; then drop 1 strand of the darker color and pick up 1 strand of the lighter color, leaving a 5" loose end. Ch 1; turn.

Row 10 Sc again in every st, make 2 sc in ch-1 sp at corners. End by knotting yarn and cutting, leaving 6" ends.

Pocket Make a sl kn with mixed colors, leaving 4" ends. Ch 15, ch 1 more; turn.

Row 1 Sk first ch sp and sc in every ch sp across. Ch 1; turn.

Rows 2–22 Sc in every sc across. Ch 1; turn.

Row 23 Sl st loosely in every sc across. Knot lighter colored yarn and cut, leaving a 4" end. Pick up 1 strand of the darker color and, using 2 strands of the darker color, sc in first 2 row sp, hazelnut (with 5 lps to close) in next row sp along edge of piece, * sc in next 2 row sp, hazelnut (with 5 lps to close) in next row sp. Repeat from * along edge, across bottom, and up other edge. Ch 1; turn.

Sc in every st along all 3 sides for 3 more border rows; then knot yarn and cut, leaving 6' ends. Repeat all of the above for other pocket.

Join pockets to fronts on sc rows by pinning in position shown in Figure III-13, 2 hazelnuts in from border and 8 hazelnuts up from bottom, using yarn needle and 6' ends.

Belt Make a sl kn with 2 strands of the darker color on size J hook, leaving 5" ends. Ch 138.

Round 1 Sk first ch sp and sc in every ch across. Drop 1 strand of the lighter color and pick up 1 strand of the darker color in last sc. Sc again in last sc, 2 sc in last ch sp with mixed colors. Sc in every ch sp on other side of ch, work 2 sc in last sc and 2 sc in last ch sp.

Round 2 Work 2 sc in first sc of first rnd, sc in every sc around. Complete last sc with the darker color, dropping 1 strand of the lighter color.

Round 3 Work reverse st all around, ending with sl st to first reverse st.

Belt Loop Make a sl kn on size J hook with 2 strands of mixed colors, leaving 7" ends. Ch 10; turn.

Row 1 Sc in 2nd ch from hook and in every ch across. End row by knotting yarn and cutting, leaving an 8" end. Repeat for other belt loop.

Attach belt loops right at side seams to encompass 18th, 19th and 20th hazelnuts from bottom (Figure III-13). Start join at bottom of loop, using shorter pair of loose ends, then travel other pair of loose ends up through side seam to be used as joining yarn for the top of the loop. Join so that belt loop does not lie flat, but assumes a "C" shape.

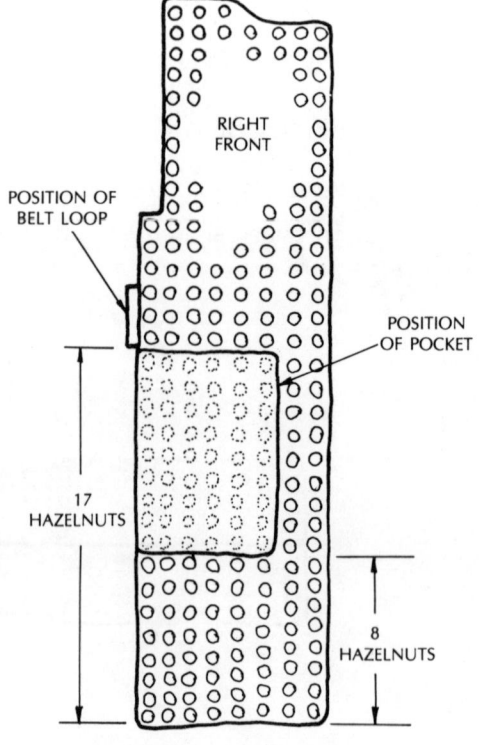

Figure III-13

Two-Piece Bikini

Materials

4 skeins (2 oz. each) of 2-ply acrylic or wool sport yarn, 2 skeins for color A, 2 for contrasting color B (Suggestion: aqua and bright red.)
1 size C crochet hook
3 yds. of thin elastic
yarn needle
small safety pin
Gauge 5 sts = 1"; 7 rows = 2"; size C hook.

Crochet

NOTE: Instructions given are for Small size; Medium and Large instructions are in parentheses.

Much of the crochet calls for single-crocheting in a hdc, and half-double-crocheting in a sc. When single-crocheting in a hdc of the pr r, insert hook into front and 1 top lp *only*, as indicated by the arrow in Figure III-14.
Bottom Make a sl kn on size C hook with color A yarn, leaving a 4" end. Ch 104 (107, 110); turn.

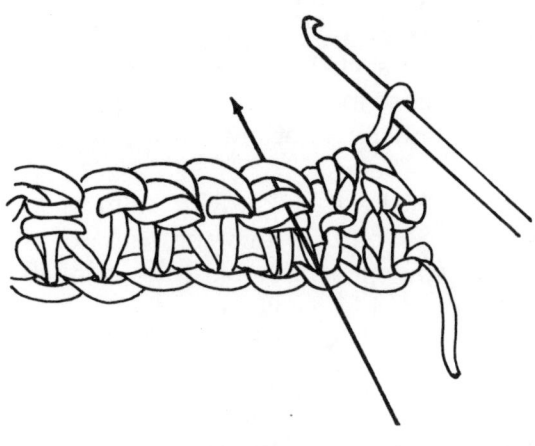

Figure III-14

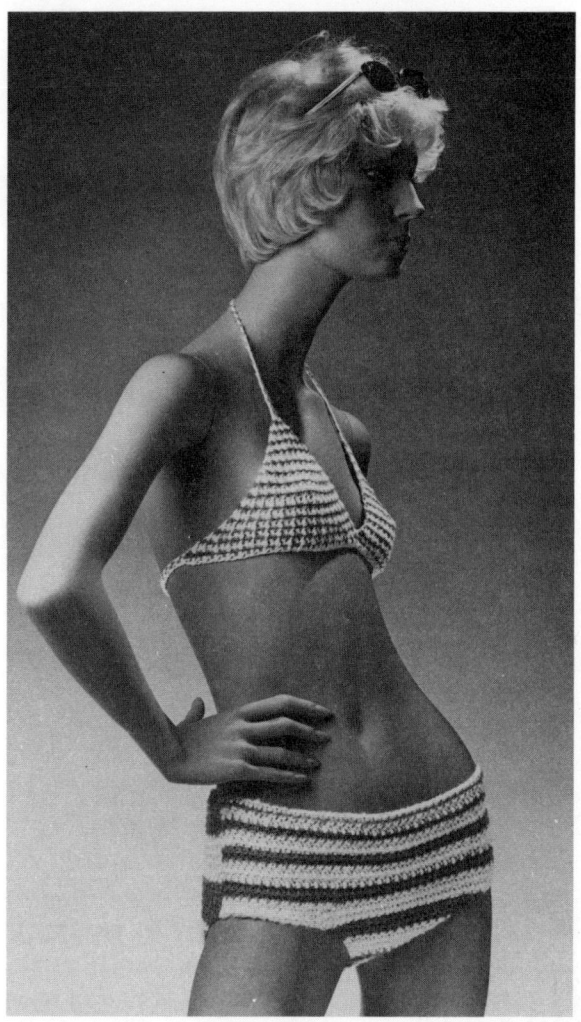

Row 1 Sc in 2nd ch from hook, * hdc in next ch, sc in next ch. Repeat from * across row. Ch 1; turn.
Row 2 Sc in first hdc (Figure III-14) of pr r, hdc in first sc of pr r (this order may have to be reversed, depending on the number of chs in cast row). * Sc in next hdc, hdc in next sc. Repeat from * across row. Ch 1; turn.
Rows 3–10 Repeat 2nd row. At end of the 10th row, change to color B (see instructions for changing color in Part I), leaving a 5" cut end of color A. The following chart summarizes the color changes required during the remainder of the crochet for the bottom. Refer to it while following the inc and dec instructions below. Leave 5" ends for all color changes.

Rows	Color
1–10	A
11–20	B
21–29	A
30–38	B
39–46	A
47–54	B
55–61	A
62–68	B
69–74	A
75–80	B
81–85	A
86–90	B
91–94	A
95–98	B
99–101	A
102–104	B
105, 106	A
107, 108	B
109	A
110	B

Rows 11–24 Repeat 2nd row (work even), making proper color changes according to chart.

Row 25 Dec 1 st at beg of row by skipping first st and working a sc (or hdc) in next st. Continue reg pat across; dec 1 st at end of row by skipping next-to-last st of pr r and working a sc in last st if your st just made was a hdc; or a hdc if your last-made st was a sc, *regardless* of what the last st of pr r is. Ch 1; turn.

Rows 26–60 Repeat 25th row, making 2 dec per row and the proper color changes.

Rows 61–73 Work even, making the proper color changes.

Row 74 Inc 1 st at beg of row by working a sc and then hdc in first st of pr r if it is a sc; or by working a hdc and then sc in this st if it is a hdc. Work reg pat across, then inc similarly in the last st of this row. Ch 1; turn.

Rows 75–84 Repeat 74th row, making 2 inc, following the color chart.

Row 85 Work even.

Rows 86, 87 Inc 1 st at each end.

With color B yarn still on hook, ch 22 (24, 25). Ch 1 more.

Row 88 Sc in 2nd ch from hook, hdc in 3rd, * sc in next ch, hdc in next. Repeat from * across chs, making sure it doesn't twist, and continue pat across 87th row, then ch 22 (24, 25) as before, ch 1 more. Sc in 2nd ch from hook, hdc in 3rd, repeat from * above across chs only. Knot yarn and cut, leaving a 5" end.

Row 89 Make a sl kn with color B yarn, leaving a 4" end. Starting at right-hand end of 88th row (with right side of work facing you), continue sc–hdc pat across entire row. Ch 1; turn.

Rows 90–110 Work even, changing colors at proper rows. At end of 110th row, knot yarn and cut, leaving a 5" end.

Hide all loose ends according to Finishing instructions in Part I. Using yarn of either color and yarn needle, join front to back at side seams according to Joining instructions in Part I. Thread the thin elastic through the yarn needle and weave through sts at bottoms of leg openings. Knot elastic for a snug fit to legs and cut, leaving 5" ends for further hiding. Repeat this procedure for elastic into waistline.

Bikini Top

First Cup Make a sl kn with color A yarn, leaving a 4" end, ch 37 (39, 40), and place a small safety pin in last ch made. Ch 90 (88, 88) more; turn.

Row 1 Sc in 2nd ch from hook, * sk next ch, ch 1, sc in next ch. Repeat from * across row until you reach safety-pinned ch. Sc in this ch, hdc in next, sc in next, repeating the hdc–sc pat as for Bottom across row. Change to color B in last st of first row. Ch 1; turn.

NOTE: Colors A and B are alternated for every row of Bikini Top.

Row 2 Work hdc–sc pat up to safety pin, then sc in first ch-1 sp past safety pin. * Ch 1, sk next sc, sc in next ch-1 sp. Repeat from * across. End by knotting yarn and cutting, leaving a 4" end.

Row 3 Make a sl kn with color A yarn, leaving a 4" end. With wrong side of work facing you, insert hook into hdc above safety-pinned ch, yoh and ptl, insert hook into next sc [above 36th ch (38th, 39th)], yoh again, pull through 3 lps on hook (dec made). Continue sc–hdc pat in remainder of row, changing to color B in last st of row. Ch 1; turn.

Doily Camisole*

This lacy blouse is designed to give a stained glass–paneled look, providing a wealth of fashion applications.

Rows 4–8 Work hdc–sc pat, dec 1 st at safety-pinned end of work only, changing color every row.
Row 9 Work even, change color, ch 1, turn.
Row 10 Dec 1 st at safety-pinned end as before, change color, ch 1, turn.
Row 11 Repeat 9th row.
Row 12 Repeat 10th row.
Row 13 Repeat 9th row.
Rows 14–26 Dec 1 st at *each* end, changing color every row. End 26th row by chaining 73.
Shoulder Strap Pick up color B for 74th ch; turn. Work (sc, sk next ch, ch 1, sc in next sc) pat down ch. Making sure not to twist strap, sl st to st of color B in 26th row. Knot yarn and cut, leaving a 4" end.
Second Cup Make a sl kn with color A yarn, leaving a 4" end. Ch 90 (88, 88), placing a safety pin in last ch made. Ch 37 (39, 40) more; turn.
Row 1 Work hdc–sc pat up to safety pin, then work (sc, sk next ch, ch 1, sc in next ch) pat past pin, which is the same procedure you followed for first row of First Cup, except in reverse. Change to color B in last st of row. Ch 1; turn.
Row 2 Work (ch 1, sk next sc, sc in next ch-1 sp) pat up to pin; then work hdc–sc pat beyond, reversing the procedure of 2nd row of First Cup. Knot and cut yarn at end of row.
Rows 3–26 Repeat as for First Cup, making first dec in 3rd row with right side of work facing you, and the ensuing decs at the safety-pinned end as before.

Repeat Shoulder Strap instructions, above, for Second Cup. Join cups together with yarn needle at first 2 rows only. Then make a sl kn with color B yarn, leaving a 4" end. Sc in ch row at extreme right-hand end of back strap of the first cup, with right side of work facing you. Work (sk next ch, ch 1, sc in next ch) pat all across ch row, past join, and across other back strap. Knot yarn and cut, leaving a 4" end. Hide all loose ends according to Finishing instructions in Part I.

Materials

6 balls (53 yds. each) of No. 5 pearl cotton yarn in framing background color A (Suggestion: white.)

4 balls (53 yds. each) of same yarn in each of 3 colors, motif color B, complementary motif color C, and contrasting motif color D (Suggestion: B—yellow, C—gold, D—orange.)

*Reprinted by permission of *Woman's Day* magazine. Copyright © 1977 by CBS Publications, Inc.

1 size C crochet hook
yarn needle
Gauge Each motif should measure 7" x 7" when finished; the camisole will then fit bust sizes 32"–36".

Crochet

The camisole is composed of 10 individual square motifs, which are joined as they are made in the sequence illustrated in Figure III-15.

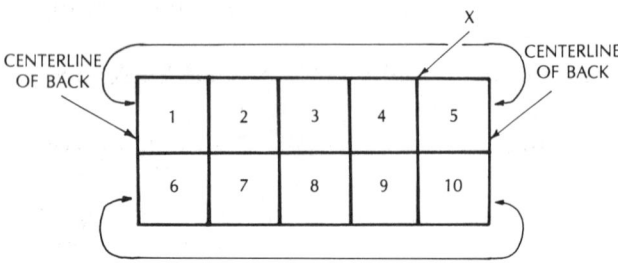

Figure III-15

Motif 1 Make a sl kn on hook with color D yarn, leaving a 5" end. Ch 8, sl st to first ch to form a ring.
Round 1 Ch 4, trc 27 times in center of ring. End with sl st to top ch sp of ch-4.
Round 2 Ch 5, trc in first trc of 1st rnd, ch 1, * trc in next trc, ch 1. Repeat from * all around, ending with sl st to 4th ch sp of original ch-5.
Round 3 Sl st to first ch-1 sp, work a ch-1 and sc in same sp. * Ch 3, sc in next ch-1 sp. Repeat from * all around, ending with ch-3. Sl st to first sc made (28 lps made).
Round 4 Sl st to first lp, ch 3, dc in same first lp. * Ch 5, sk next 2 lps, work 9 dc in next lp, ch 5, sk next 2 lps, work dc in next lp up to the next-to-last step *only* (2 lps on hook). Do *not* close this dc, but work another dc in same lp up to the next-to-last step (3 lps on hook in total). Yoh and pull through all 3 lps on hook (joined dc made). Ch 3, work joined dc in next lp. Repeat from * all around, ending with joined dc in last lp, ch 3, sl st to top ch sp of ch-3 made at beg of rnd.
Round 5 Sl st in next dc, ch 3, dc in same sp as sl st. * Ch 5, (trc in next dc, ch 1) 8 times, trc in next dc, (ch 5, joined dc in next joined dc) twice. Repeat from * all around, ending with joined dc in last joined dc, ch 5. Insert hook into top of ch-3 made at beg of rnd, yoh with color B yarn, and complete sl st. Cut color D yarn, leaving a 5" end.
Round 6 Sl st in next dc, ch 3, dc in same sp as sl st. * Ch 5, (sc in next ch-1 sp, ch 3) 7 times, sc in next ch-1 sp, ch 5, joined dc in next joined dc, ch 7, joined dc in next joined dc (ch-7 corner lp made). Repeat from * all around. After last ch-7 corner lp, sl st to ch-3 to close.
Round 7 Sl st in next dc, ch 3, dc in same sp as sl st. * Ch 5, (sc in next ch-3 lp, ch 3) 6 times, sc in next lp, ch 5, joined dc in next joined dc, ch 5. In next ch-7 lp, work (2 dc, ch 5) twice, then joined dc in next joined dc. Repeat from * all around, ending with (2 dc, ch 5, 2 dc) in last ch-7 lp. Ch 5 and sl st to ch-3 to join.
Round 8 Sl st in next dc, ch 3, dc in same sp as sl st. * Ch 5, (sc in next ch-3 lp, ch 3) 5 times, sc in next lp, ch 5, joined dc in next joined dc, ch 5, dc in each of next 2 dc, work (2 dc, ch 5, 2 dc) in next ch-5 lp. Dc in each of next 2 dc, ch 5, joined dc in next joined dc. Repeat from * all around, ending with ch-5. Sl st to ch-3 to close.
Round 9 Sl st in next dc, ch 3, dc in same sp as sl st. * Ch 5, (sc in next ch-3 lp, ch 3) 4 times, sc in next lp, ch 5, joined dc in next joined dc, ch 5, dc in each of next 4 dc, work (2 dc, ch 5, 2 dc) in next ch-5 lp, dc in each of next 4 dc, ch 5, joined dc in next joined dc. Repeat from * all around, ending with dc in last 4 dc, ch 5, sl st to ch-3 to join.
Round 10 Sl st in next dc, ch 3, dc in same sp as sl st. * Ch 9, work a trc in next ch-3 lp up to the next-to-last step *only* (2 lps on hook). Work another trc in next ch-3 lp up to next-to-last step (3 lps on hook), and 2 more trc similarly in the next 2 ch-3 lps (5 lps on hook in total). Yoh and pull through all 5 lps on hook. Ch 9, joined dc in next joined dc, ch 5, dc in each of next 4 dc, ch 5, sk next 2 dc. In next ch-5 lp, work (2 dc, ch 7, 2 dc), ch 5, sk next 2 dc, dc in each of next 4 dc, ch 5, joined dc in next joined dc. Repeat from * all around, ending with dc in last 4 dc, ch 5. Then insert hook in top of first ch-3, yoh with color A, and

complete sl st. Cut color B yarn, leaving a 5" end.

Round 11 Ch 1, * sc in next lp, ch 6, sc in 4th ch sp from hook to make picot, ch 2, sc in same lp (picot lp made). Ch 6, make picot, ch 2. Repeat from * all around, ending with sl st to first sc (56 picot lps made). Knot yarn and cut, leaving a 5" end.

Motif 2 Repeat all instructions as for Motif 1 through 5th rnd, using color C yarn. At the end of the 5th rnd, do *not* change color for last sl st, but retain color C.

Repeat Motif 1 instructions through the 8th rnd. Change to color D yarn in closing sl st of 8th rnd, and repeat 9th and 10th rnds with this color. Change to color A at end of 10th rnd.

Round 11 Ch 1, * sc in next lp, ch 6, make picot, ch 2, sc in same lp (1 picot lp made). Ch 6, make picot, ch 2. Repeat from * across, up to and including lp before corner lp.

Joining Motifs Sc in corner lp, ch 4, sl st to any corner picot lp on motif 1. * Ch 1, sc in 3rd ch sp of ch-4 on motif 2, ch 2, sc in same lp on motif 2. Ch 4, sl st in next picot lp on motif 1, ch 1, sc in 3rd ch sp of ch-4 on motif 2, ch 2, sc in next lp on motif 2, ch 4, sl st in next picot lp on motif 1. Repeat from * across, up to and including lp before next corner picot lp. Then ch 1, sc in 3rd ch sp of ch-4 on motif 2, ch 2, sc in corner lp on motif 2, ch 4, sl st in next corner picot lp on motif 1, ch 1, sc in same corner lp on motif 2 (joining completed). Ch 6, sc in 4th ch sp from hook, ch 2. Repeat from * in 11th rnd for Motif 1 and end as for Motif 1. Knot yarn and cut, leaving a 5" end.

Color Changes for Motifs 3–10 All of the remaining motifs are crocheted and joined according to previous instructions. The following summarizes the variations in color to be used, all color changes being made at the sl st closing pr rnd:

Motif 3
Rounds 1–3: A
Rounds 4–10: B
Round 11: A

Motif 4
Rounds 1–8: D
Rounds 9, 10: B
Round 11: A

Motif 5
Rounds 1–5: B
Rounds 6–10: C
Round 11: A

Motif 6
Rounds 1–10: D
Round 11: A

Motif 7
Rounds 1–3: A
Rounds 4–10: C
Round 11: A

Motif 8
Rounds 1–8: B
Rounds 9, 10: C
Round 11: A

Motif 9
Rounds 1–3: A
Rounds 4–10: D
Round 11: A

Motif 10
Rounds 1–5: C
Rounds 6–10: B
Round 11: A

Complete all remaining motifs, joining as you go, according to Figure III-15. Note that edges of motifs 5 and 10 are joined to motifs 1 and 6 to form a tube, with this join becoming the centerline of the back.

Top Edging Make a sl kn with color A yarn, leaving a 5" end.

Round 1 With right side of work facing you and starting at point X of Figure III-15, sc in joining of Motifs 4 and 5. * Ch 1, sc in top of next picot. Repeat from *, counting the join between motifs as 1 picot, all around top edge of tube, ending with sl st to first sc (70 lps made). Knot yarn and cut, leaving a 5" end. Do *not* turn.

Front Edging Make a sl kn with color A yarn, leaving a 5" end; then sl st in 5th lp past the point where you broke off yarn at end of the first rnd for Top Edging, working in the same direction as this rnd.

Row 1 Ch 6, * dc in next lp, ch 3. Repeat from * 32 times, then dc in next lp (33 lps made, counting original ch-6 as 1 dc and 1 ch-3). *Turn.*

Row 2 Sl st in first lp, ch 6, dc in next lp. * Ch 3, dc in next lp. Repeat from * 31 times; turn.

Row 3 Sl st in first lp, ch 5, dc in next lp, * ch 2, dc in next lp. Repeat from * 30 times; turn.

First Shoulder Strap

Row 1 Sl st in first lp, ch 5, dc in next lp. * Ch 2, dc in next lp. Repeat from * 7 times (8 lps made); turn.

Row 2 Repeat first row, repeating from * 6 times only.

Row 3 Repeat first row, repeating from * 5 times only.

Row 4 Repeat first row, repeating from * 4 times only.

Row 5 Repeat first row, repeating from * 3 times only.

Row 6 Repeat first row, repeating from * twice; then ch 4; turn.
Row 7 Sk first lp, dc in next dc, ch 1, dc in next dc, ch 1, sk next ch, dc in next ch, ch 4; turn.
Row 8, etc. Repeat 7th row until strap measures 5½" from first row, then omit last ch-4. Knot yarn and cut, leaving an 8" end.
Second Shoulder Strap Make a sl kn with color A yarn, leaving a 5" end. Sl st to 14th lp past end of first shoulder strap on 3rd row of Front Edging.
Row 1 Ch 5, dc in next lp, * ch 3, dc in next lp. Repeat from * 7 times (8 lps made); turn.
Row 2, etc. Repeat from 2nd row as for first strap.
Back Edging Lay tube out on flat surface with join at back centered, right side of work facing you, and front shoulder straps equidistant from each edge of tube. Make a sl kn with color A yarn, leaving a 5" end. Sl st to 8th lp in from right-hand edge at top of tube.
Row 1 Ch 6, dc in next lp, * ch 3, dc in next lp. Repeat from * 20 times (21 lps made); turn.
Row 2 Sl st in first lp, ch 6, dc in next lp, * ch 3, dc in next lp. Repeat from * 19 times; turn.
Row 3 Sl st in first lp, ch 5, dc in next lp, * ch 2, dc in next lp. Repeat from * 18 times; turn.
First Shoulder Strap
Row 1 Sl st in first lp, ch 5, dc in next lp. * Ch 2, dc in next lp. Repeat from * 7 times (8 lps made); turn.
Row 2, etc. Repeat from 2nd row as for first Shoulder Strap on Front Edging; break off yarn with 5" end.
Second Shoulder Strap Make a sl kn with color A yarn, leaving a 5" end. Sl st to 2nd lp from right on 3rd row of Back Edging.
Row 1 Ch 5, dc in next lp, * ch 2, dc in next lp. Repeat from * 7 times (8 lps made); turn.
Row 2, etc. Repeat as for first strap.

Join straps, using 8" ends and yarn needle, according to Joining instructions in Part I.
Neck and Armhole Edging Make a sl kn with color A yarn, leaving a 5" end, and sc in any ch-1 sp of top edging at either armhole, with right side of work facing you. * Ch 4, sc in 3rd ch sp from hook (1 picot made), ch 1, sc in next ch-1 sp. Repeat from * all around armhole, up and down outer edge of shoulder strap, using the row sp, and back to the start, ending with sl st to first sc. Knot yarn and cut, leaving a 5" end. Repeat for other armhole and also for neck opening, including inner edges of shoulder straps.
Bottom Edging With color A yarn, work 2 rnds of the same edging pat around bottom of tube, working sc into picot lps instead of sp.
Finishing Hide all loose ends according to Finishing instructions in Part I.

Multicolor Ski Muffler

Materials

1 skein (4 oz.) of 4-ply wool or acrylic yarn in 4 contrasting variegated colors (color V) (Suggestion: tan, green, orange and brown.)
1 skein (2 oz.) of same type yarn in each of the 4 solid colors in the variegated skein (colors A, B, C and D) (Suggestion: as above—tan, green, orange and brown.)
1 size G crochet hook
yarn needle

Crochet

Make a sl kn on size G hook with color V yarn, leaving a 6" end. Ch 35; turn.
Row 1 Dc in 2nd ch from hook, then dc across row. Ch 3; turn.
Row 2 Dc in 2nd dc and in every dc across until you reach the next-to-last st (32 dc made). In this st work a dc up to the next-to-last step (2 lps on hook), then yoh with color A yarn and complete dc. Cut color V yarn, leaving a 6" end. Ch 1; turn.
Row 3 Sc in next sc, * sk next st, sc in next st. Then in same st (yoh, insert hook in st, yoh, pull through st) twice, yoh, pull through 4 lps, yoh, pull through last 2 lps (cluster made). Repeat from * across row. After last cluster, end with dc in last st. Ch 1; turn.
Row 4 Repeat 3rd row, changing to color V yarn in last dc as described in 2nd row. Ch 3; turn.
Row 5 Dc in 2nd dc and in every st across. Ch 3; turn.
Row 6 Dc in 2nd dc and in every dc across. Change to color B yarn in last dc. Ch 1; turn.
Rows 7, 8 Repeat 3rd and 4th rows.
Row 9, etc. Repeat this pat of 2 rows of dc in color V, then 2 rows of clusters in alternate solid colors (color C is next for 11th and 12th rows), A, then B, then C, then A, etc. Change colors in last dc of pr r in which the color is to be used, ch 3 to turn at end of first dc row, ch 1 for the 2nd.

When muffler length reaches 70", end with 2 rows of dc. Knot yarn and cut, leaving a 6" end. Cut 14" lengths of 2 strands of color D yarn and attach to every st at either end of the muffler according to instructions set out in Tassels and Fringes in Part I.
Finishing Hide all loose ends according to Finishing directions in Part I.

Winter Sweater, Skirt and Hat Ensemble

A bulky turtleneck sweater, matching ribbed skirt, and hat combine fashion and warmth in this three-piece set.

Materials

23 skeins (1 7/10 oz. each) of wool-acrylic-rayon blend knobby tweed yarn in color of your choice for sweater
16 skeins of same yarn for skirt
4 skeins of same yarn for hat
1 skein (3½ oz.) of 4-ply wool or acrylic yarn in black for hat
1 skein (1 oz.) of 67% mohair–33% acrylic frosted yarn in black for hat
1 yd. of cotton batting (5" wide) or equivalent for stuffing brim
sewing needle and heavy-duty thread in black
1 size J crochet hook
yarn needle
safety pin

Gauge for Sweater and Skirt 5 sts = 2"; 5 rows = 2¼"; tweed yarn; size J hook.

Crochet

NOTE: The instructions are for size Medium; however, the bulky ribbed nature of these garments will encompass a wide range of sizes above and below. All sc in the following instructions are to be worked in the back lp only of the sts in pr r (see Ribbed Crochet instructions in Part I). When working past a sl st in pr r, sc in (back lp of) st below the sl st.

Sweater The sweater is made in 2 identical halves, then joined.

Make a sl kn on hook, leaving a 5" end. Ch 81; turn.

Row 1 Sc in 2nd ch from hook and in every ch across (80 sc made). Ch 1; turn.
Row 2 Sc (in back lp only) in first sc and 27 sts more for a total of 29 sts (counting turning ch as 1 st), sl st in 30th st; turn.
Row 3 Sc (back lp) for 17 sts (counting sl st as 1 st), sl st in 18th st; turn.
Row 4 Sc for 39 sts, sl st in next st; turn.
Row 5 Sc to end (52 sts made). Ch 1; turn.
Row 6 Sc for 41 sts (counting ch-1 as 1 st), sl st in next st; turn.
Row 7 Sc for 29 sts (counting sl st as 1 st), sl st in next st; turn.

NOTE: Count sl sts and ch-1s as 1 st in all of the following.

Row 8 Sc for 47 sts, sl st in next st; turn.
Row 9 Sc to end (60 sts made). Ch 1; turn.
Row 10 Sc for 29 sts, sl st in next st; turn.
Rows 11–15 Repeat rows 3–7.
Row 16 Sc for 55 sts, sl st in next st; turn.
Row 17 Sc for 56 sts. Ch 1; turn.
Row 18 Dec 1 sc in first 2 sc (see Decreasing instructions in Part I), sc for 16 sts total, sl st in next st; turn.
Row 19 Sc to end. Ch 1; turn (17 sts made).
Row 20 Dec 1 sc at beg of row (as in 18th row), sc for 37 sts, sl st in next st; turn.
Row 21 Sc to end. Ch 1; turn.
Rows 22–52 For all even-numbered rows, dec 1 sc at beg, sc for number of sts given in Table below, sl st in the next st; turn. For all odd-numbered rows, sc to end of row. Ch 1; turn.

Row	Number of Stitches
22	26
24	43
26	12
28	33
30	22
32	59
34	8
36	29
38	18
40	35

WINTER SWEATER, SKIRT AND HAT ENSEMBLE 113

42	6
44	25
46	14
48	39
50	6
52	12

Row 53 Sc to end of row. Ch 21; turn.
Row 54 Sc in 2nd ch from hook and in every ch. Continue to sc past ch for a total of 41 sts, sl st in next st; turn.
Row 55 Sc for 21 sts, sl st in next st; turn.
Row 56 Sc to end. Ch 1; turn (50 sts made).
Row 57 Sc to end. Ch 1; turn (70 sts made).
Row 58 Sc for 41 sts, sl st in next st; turn.
Row 59 Repeat 55th row.
Row 60 Sc for 29 sts, sl st in next st; turn.
Row 61 Repeat 56th row.
Row 62 Repeat 58th row.
Row 63 Repeat 55th row.
Row 64 Sc for 37 sts, sl st in next st; turn.
Row 65 Repeat 56th row (58 sts made).
Row 66 Repeat 58th row.
Rows 67–79 Repeat rows 55, 60, 61, 58, 55, 56, 57, 58, 55, 60, 61, 58 and 59, respectively.
Rows 80–87 Repeat rows 56–63.
Rows 88, 89 Repeat 56th and 57th rows.
Rows 90–105 Repeat rows 58–73.
Rows 106–158 Repeat 52nd row, increasing 1 sc at beg of row instead of decreasing (see Increasing instructions in Part I). Then repeat all rows in reverse numerical order back to the first row, substituting "inc" for "dec" in each case.

Repeat all of the above instructions for other matching half of sweater; then join halves, wrong sides out, with yarn needle according to Joining instructions in Part I. Turn inside out.

Skirt Make a sl kn on hook, leaving a 5" end. Ch 71; turn.
Row 1 Sc in 2nd ch from hook and in every ch across. Ch 1; turn.
Row 2 Sc for 43 sts (back lp only, as before), sl st in next st; turn.
Rows 3–7 Sc across row. Ch 1; turn.
Row 8 Sc for 29 sts, sl st in next st; turn.
Rows 9–11 Repeat 3rd row.
Row 12 Sc for 57 sts, sl st in next st; turn.
Row 13 Repeat 3rd row.
Row 14 Sc for 13 sts, sl st in next st; turn.
Rows 15, 16 Repeat 3rd row.
Row 17, etc. Repeat 3rd row, then rows 2–16 to complete 2nd section of skirt. Repeat this pat 4 more times to total 6 sections, then join with yarn needle to complete skirt. You may want to run elastic through top of waistband to provide for extra firmness in waist, if you are much smaller than a Medium.

Hat

Crown

NOTE: Instructions for sizes are given within text. All sc in crown are done in back lps; those in brim are conventional.

Make a sl kn on hook with 1 strand each of black yarns, leaving 5" ends. Ch 3, sl st to back lp of first ch to form ring.

Round 1 Ch 1 (counts as 1 sc), place a safety-pin marker in ch just made, sc (in back lp) of first ch of ring, sc twice in (back lps of) each of the next 2 chs (6 sts made).
Round 2 Remove marker, sc twice in (back lp of) marked ch-1 sp, replace marker in first sc made, sc twice in each of the next 5 sts.
Round 3 Sc twice in every sc around (24 sts made), replace marker in last sc made. For future rnds, move marker to last st of each rnd.
Round 4 Sc in first sc, * 2 sc in next sc, sc in next sc. Repeat from * all around. Move marker (inc rnd).
Round 5 Sc in each of first 2 sc, * 2 sc in next sc, sc in each of next 2 sc. Repeat from * all around (inc rnd).
Round 6 Sc in each of first 3 sc, * 2 sc in next sc, sc in each of next 3 sc. Repeat from * all around (inc rnd).

Try crown on to determine if another inc rnd is required to fit comfortably. If not, continue with 7th rnd; if so, sc in each of first 4 sc, * 2 sc in next sc, sc in each of next 4 sc. Repeat from * all around.

Round 7, etc. Sc in every sc around until crown reaches level of top of earlobe when tried on.
Next Round Sk first sc (dec made), * sc in each of the next 9 sc, sk next sc. Repeat from * all around.
Next Round Repeat pr rnd. For last st, insert hook in back lp of last sc of pr rnd, yoh,

pull through st, yoh with 2 strands of knobby tweed yarn, leaving 5" ends, and complete sc with this yarn.

Brim

Round 1 2 sc (reg) in first sc, * sc in next 7 sc, 2 sc in next sc. Repeat from * all around.

Round 2 2 sc in first sc, * sc in each of next 3 sc, 2 sc in next sc. Repeat from * all around.

Rounds 3–7 Sc in every sc around (even rnds).

Round 8 Sk first sc (dec made), sc in each of next 7 sc, sk next sc. Repeat from * all around.

Round 9 Sk first sc, * sc in each of next 3 sc, sk next sc. Repeat from * all around. Knot yarn and cut, leaving 5" ends.

Form a ring with the cotton batting or other stuffing material to fit behind the brim. Sew last round of brim to crown, 5 rnds up, using heavy-duty sewing thread and making sure that batting is evenly distributed, giving a smooth, tubular effect.

Finishing Hide all loose ends according to Finishing directions in Part I.

Fan Shawl

Materials

6 skeins (3½ oz.) of 4-ply wool or acrylic heather-type yarn for background color A
1 skein (4 oz.) of 4-ply wool or acrylic in contrasting solid color to match cast of background yarn for fans (color B)
1 skein (1 4/10 oz.) of acrylic-nylon blend multilobal yarn in closest match to color B (color C)
1 size J crochet hook
yarn needle

Crochet

The fans are crocheted in individual square motifs against the background color, then joined. Triangular motifs of the background color are then added to complete shawl.

Square Motif Make a sl kn on hook with 1 strand each of colors B and C, leaving 5" ends. Ch 13; turn.

Row 1 Hdc in 2nd ch from hook, hdc in each of next 2 ch, dc in each of next 3 ch, trc in each of next 3 ch, dbl trc in each of next 2 ch, work 4 dbl trc in last ch. Ch 1; turn.

Row 2 Sc in back lp only (see Ribbed Crochet instructions in Part I) of every st across. Ch 1; turn (15 sc made).

Row 3 Hdc in each of first 3 sc, dc in each of next 3 sc, trc in next 3 sc, dbl trc in next 2 sc, work 4 dbl trc in next sc. Ch 1; turn (3 sc remaining).

Row 4 Repeat 2nd row.

Rows 5–10 Repeat 3rd and 2nd rows alternately. At end of 10th row, ch 5 (5 fan tips made).

Work a dbl trc into row sp at beg of 9th row up to the next-to-last step (2 lps on hook), then another dbl trc up to the next-to-last step in the row sp at base of the 8th row (3 lps on hook). Repeat this pat, double-triple-crocheting into the row sp at the base of each row, holding the last lp on your hook. After your 9th dbl trc, yoh and pull through all 10 lps on your hook. Knot yarn and cut, leaving 6" ends.

Motif Background Make a sl kn with color A yarn, leaving a 5" end.

Row 1 With right side of work facing you, work 2 sc in back lp of ch-1 sp at beg of 10th row of fan. Then work 2 dbl trc in same sp that contains the 4 dbl trc in the 9th row, then 2 trc in same sp. * Work 2 sc in back lp of ch-1 sp at next fan tip, 2 dbl trc in same sp that contains 4 dbl trc, 2 trc in same sp. Repeat from * 3 more times, ending with 2 dbl trc and 2 trc in first ch made. Ch 1; turn.

Row 2 * Sk first 2 trc, work 5 dc in next dbl trc, sk next 2 sts, sc in next st. Repeat from * 6 more times. Ch 1; turn.

Row 3 Sl st in first 2 dc, * sc in next dc, sk next 2 dc, 5 dc in next sc, sk next 2 dc. Repeat from * 4 more times, ending with sc in center of last shell (5 shells made); turn.

Row 4 Sk first 2 dc, 5 dc in next sc, sk next 2 dc. Repeat from * in 3rd row 4 times in total, ending with sc in center of last shell (4 shells made); turn.

Row 5 Repeat 4th row, repeating from * 3 times (3 shells made); turn.

Row 6 Repeat, making 2 shells.

Row 7 Repeat, making 1 shell.

Work 1 rnd of sc in every st and row sp around square, working 3 sc in each corner. End rnd with sl st to first sc. Now work a rnd of (sk 2 sc, 5 dc in next sc, sk 2 sc), working 6 dc in center sc of each 3-sc group at each corner. This pat will give you 4 shells on each side of the square. Knot yarn and cut, leaving a 3' end.

Repeat above instructions 9 more times to complete 10 motifs; then join, using yarn needle and 3' ends, according to Joining instructions in Part I, as illustrated in Figure III-16.

Triangular Motif Make a sl kn with color A yarn, leaving a 5" end. Ch 30; turn.

Row 1 5 dc in 3rd ch from hook, * sk next 2 ch, sc in next ch sp, sk next 2 ch, 5 dc in next ch sp. Repeat from *, ending with 5 dc in last

FAN SHAWL 117

ch sp (5 shells made); turn.
Row 2 Sl st in first 2 dc, * sc in next dc, sk next 2 dc, 5 dc in next sc, sk next 2 dc. Repeat from *, ending with sc in center of last shell of pr r (4 shells made); turn.
Row 3 Sk first 2 dc, 5 dc in next sc, sk next 2 dc. Repeat from * in 2nd row, above (3 shells made); turn.

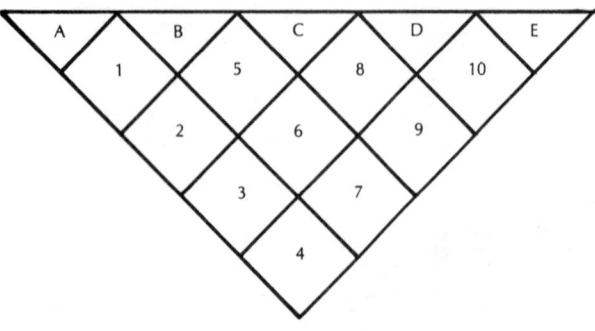

Figure III-16

Row 4 Repeat 3rd row, making 2 shells.
Row 5 Repeat 3rd row, making 1 shell.

Work 1 rnd of sc in every st and row sp around triangle, working 3 sc in each corner. End rnd with sl st to first sc. Now work a rnd of (sk 2 sc, 5 dc in next sc, sk 2 sc), working 6 dc in center sc of each 3-sc group at each corner. This pat will give you 4 shells on each side of the triangle. Knot yarn and cut, leaving a 3' end.

Repeat above instructions 4 more times to complete 5 triangular motifs; then join to shawl as before, in positions A, B, C, D and E, as shown in Figure III-16.

Children's Striped Pullover

Materials

2 skeins (2 oz. each) of 2-ply sport yarn in each of 2 bright colors: A and B (Suggestion: red and green.)
3 skeins ($1^{4}/_{10}$ oz. each) of 60% acrylic–20% wool–20% mohair-blend yarn in 3rd bright color C (Suggestion: yellow.)
1 size F crochet hook
yarn needle
safety pins
Gauge   4 sts = 1"; 4 rows = 1"; 2-ply yarn; size F hook.

Crochet

NOTE: Instructions are given for children's size 2, to measure 10½" across back at underarms. Sizes 4 and 6 are in parentheses, to measure 11½" and 12½" across back.

Waistband Border

Make a sl kn on hook with color A yarn, leaving a 5" end. Ch 9 (13, 17).
Row 1 Sc in 2nd ch from hook and in each ch across. Ch 1; turn.
Rows 2–84 (92, 100) Sc in back lp only (see Ribbed Crochet instructions in Part I) of every sc across. Ch 1; turn. Repeat this pat for 83 (91, 99) more rows. Join tube by sl st to each ch sp of ch 9 (13, 17) first made.
Body
Round 1 Ch 1, sc in same sp as last sl st, sc in every row sp at top of tube, ending with sl st to first sc [84 (92, 100) sc made].
Round 2 Ch 1 (counts as 1 hdc), sk first sc, hdc in every sc, ending with sl st to first hdc.
Round 3 Ch 1 (counts as 1 hdc), sk first hdc, hdc in every hdc around, ending with sl st to first hdc.
Rounds 4–6 Repeat 3rd rnd. At end of 6th rnd, insert hook into first hdc, yoh with color C yarn, and complete sl st with color C. Cut color A yarn, leaving a 5" end.
Rounds 7, 8 Repeat 3rd rnd. At end of 8th rnd, change to color A yarn, as described above.
Rounds 9–12 Repeat 3rd rnd, change to color C at end of 12th rnd.
Rounds 13–15 Repeat 3rd rnd. Change to color B.
Rounds 16–23 Repeat 3rd rnd. Change to color C.
Round 24 Repeat 3rd rnd. Change to color B.
Rounds 25–33 Repeat 3rd rnd. Knot yarn and cut, leaving a 5" end. Place safety-pin markers in the 4th, 39th, (43rd, 47th), 46th (50th, 54th), and 81st (89th, 97th) hdc of 33rd rnd.

Cuff Make a sl kn with color A yarn, leaving a 5" end. Ch 11; turn.
Row 1 Sc in 2nd ch from hook and in every ch across. Ch 1; turn.
Rows 2–30 Sc in back lp of every sc across row. Ch 1; turn. Join tube at end of 30th row by sl st to each ch sp of ch-11 first made.
Sleeve
Round 1 Ch 1, sc in same sp as sl st and in every row sp around top edge of cuff, ending with sl st to first sc (30 sc made).
Round 2 Repeat 2nd rnd as for Body.
Rounds 3–6 Repeat 3rd rnd as for Body.
Round 7 (inc rnd) Ch 1, hdc in first hdc of pr rnd and in every hdc around (1 hdc inc made).
Round 8, etc. Repeat hdc pat, making color changes and incs (as in 7th rnd) as summarized in the Tables below:

Rounds	Color
1–15	A
16, 17	C
18–21	A
22–24	C
25–32	B
33	C
34–42	B

Size	Increase
2	Every 7th rnd, 3 more times
4, 6	In 9th rnd and every (6th, 4th) rnd, (4, 6) more times

At end of the 42nd rnd knot yarn and cut, leaving a 5" end. Repeat all instructions for other sleeve.
Yoke
Round 1 Make a sl kn with color C yarn, leaving a 5" end. Sc in first marked st on Body, move marker to this st, and * sc in every st across body, up to the next marked st. Sc in this st, move marker, pick up sleeve, sk first 3 sts on sleeve past sl st joining, and sc across top of sleeve up to and including 4th st before joining, then sc in next marked st on Body. Repeat from * 1 more time [136 (152, 168) sc

made]. Join with sl st. Knot yarn and cut, leaving a 5" end. Mark 18th (20th, 22nd) st with a pin to indicate center of back and start all remaining Yoke rnds at this point.

Round 2 Make a sl kn with color C yarn, leaving a 5" end. Sl st to marked st at center back. Ch 1, sk first sc, hdc in every sc to marked st. * Dec 1 hdc in this st and in next st (see Decreasing instructions in Part I), then move marker to st just made. Hdc in every st up to st just before next marked st, dec 1 hdc again and move marker, hdc in each sc up to next marked st. Repeat from * 1 more time. Hdc in each remaining sc; join with sl st to first hdc.

Rounds 3–12 (14, 14) Repeat 2nd rnd above. Dec 1 hdc at each of the 4 markers.

Picot Edging * Sc for 3 sts, ch 3, sl st in 3rd sc. Repeat from * all around neckline, ending with sl st to first sc.

Using a yarn needle and color C yarn, join both underarm seams according to Joining instructions in Part I. Hide all loose ends according to Finishing instructions in Part I.

Pom-Pom Tie Make a sl kn with color A yarn, leaving an 8" end. Ch to measure 28". Knot yarn and cut, leaving an 8" end. Using a yarn needle, thread ch with running sts through sts at top of neckline, just below picot edging. With 1 strand each of colors A, B and C, make 2 pom-poms on a template 1¾" in diameter, according to instructions set out in Pom-Poms in Part I, and attach to either end of tie.

Oriental Tote and Slippers

Materials

8 balls (95 yds. each) of No. 8 pearl cotton yarn in color of your choice for tote
8 balls (95 yds. each) of same yarn for slippers
1 size F crochet hook
1 size G crochet hook (for slippers, if Large)
yarn needle
6 buttons ⅜" in diameter (for slippers)

Crochet

Tote This bag is crocheted as a rectangle and then folded, origami-style, as shown in Figure III-17, and tied to close.

Make a sl kn on size F hook with 2 strands of No. 8 pearl cotton yarn, leaving 5" ends. Ch 41; turn.

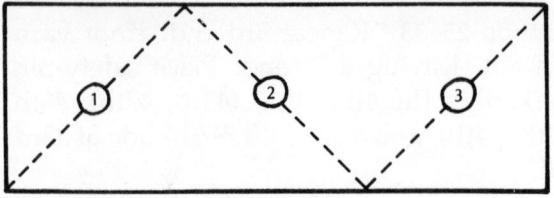

Figure III-17

Row 1 Sc in 2nd ch from hook, * hdc in next, sc in next. Repeat from * across row. Ch 1; turn.
Row 2, etc. Sc in front and 1 top lp only of first hdc (see Figure III-14), * hdc in next sc, sc in proper lps of next hdc. Repeat from * across row. Ch 1; turn.

Repeat pat of 2nd row until the length of your rectangle is exactly 3 times its width; then knot yarn and cut, leaving 5" ends.

Lay out your rectangle on a flat surface with the wrong side facing you. Fold along line 1 in Figure III-17, then line 2, then line 3, giving you the configuration shown in Figure III-18. Using a yarn needle, join along the lines indicated in Figure III-18, according to Joining instructions in Part I.

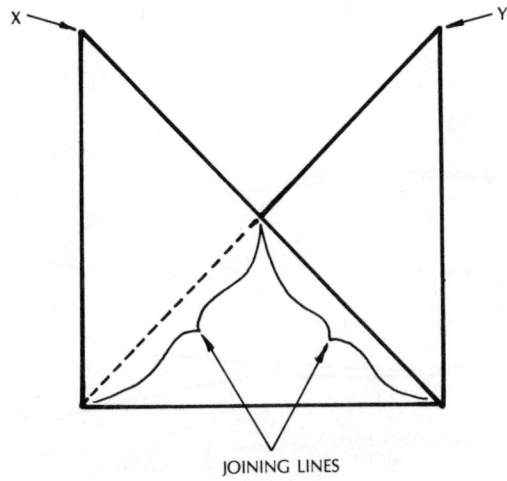

Figure III-18

Finishing Hide all loose ends according to Finishing directions in Part I. Ends X and Y are then tied in a loose double knot to close bag.
Slippers Use size F hook for women's Small and Medium; use size G hook for Large. The slippers are made in 3 separate sections, 2 uppers and 1 sole section, and then joined.
First Section of Slippers Make a sl kn with 2 strands of yarn, leaving 3' ends. Ch 13; turn.
Row 1 Sc in 2nd ch from hook, * hdc in next, sc in next. Repeat from * across row. Ch 1; turn.
Row 2 Work (sc, hdc) pat as described in 2nd row of Tote across row. Ch 9; turn.
Row 3 Sc in 2nd ch from hook and work (hdc, sc) pat across ch and then across sts of 2nd row. Ch 1; turn.

Rows 4–23 Work (sc, hdc) pat evenly across rows (20 sts made). Ch 1; turn.
Row 24 Sl st first 2 sts, work pat to end of row. Ch 1; turn.
Row 25 Dec 1 st at beg of row by inserting hook into first st, yoh, ptl, insert hook into next st, yoh, ptl, yoh, pull through 3 lps (dec made). Work even for remainder of row. Ch 1; turn (before last 2 sl sts).
Row 26 Work pat across, dec 1 st at end of row in last 2 sts according to instructions in 25th row.
Row 27 Work even row (no dec).
Row 28 Inc 1 st at beg of row by working a hdc and sc in first sc (inc on a hdc by working a sc then dc). Work pat across. Ch 1; turn.
Row 29 Work even row.
Row 30 Inc 1 st at beg (according to instructions in 28th row).
Rows 31–37 Work even rows.
Rows 38, 39 Dec 1 st at end of rows.
Rows 40–44 Work even rows.
Rows 45–49 Dec 1 st at beg *and* end of rows. At end of 49th row, knot yarn and cut, leaving a 12" end.
Button Loops of Slippers Insert hook into first ch sp of original ch-13, yoh with 3' ends, and complete sl st. Ch 6, sl st to next ch sp, sl st for 4 more chs, ch 6, sl st for next 5 chs, ch 6, sl st to last ch. Knot yarn and cut to a 5" length.
Second Section of Slippers Make a sl kn on hook, leaving a 12" end (2 strands). Ch 20; turn.
Row 1 Sc in 2nd ch from hook, work (hdc, sc) pat across. Ch 1; turn.
Rows 2–19 Work even rows.
Row 20 Dec 1 st at end of row.
Rows 21, 23, 25 Dec 1 st at beg of rows.
Rows 22, 24 Dec 1 st at end of rows.
Row 26 Inc 1 st at beg of row.
Rows 27–31 Work even rows.
Row 32 Inc 1 st at beg of row.
Rows 33–38 Work even rows.
Row 39 Dec 1 st at beg of row.
Row 40 Work even row.
Row 41 Dec 1 st at end of row.
Row 42 Work even row.
Row 43 Inc 1 st at beg of row.
Row 44 Work even row.
Row 45 Dec 1 st at beg of row.
Rows 46–49 Dec 1 st at beg *and* end of rows.

At end of 49th row, knot yarn and cut, leaving a 12" end.

Third Section of Slippers Make a sl kn with 2 strands on hook, leaving 12" ends. Ch 6; turn.

Row 1 Sc and hdc in first ch from hook, work (sc, hdc) pat across ch, sc and dc in last ch sp. Ch 1; turn (2 inc made).

Row 2 Work even row.

Rows 3–5 Inc 1 st at beg *and* end of rows.

Rows 6–15 Work even rows.

Rows 16–18 Inc 1 st at beg *and* end of rows.

Rows 19–23 Work even rows.

Rows 24, 25 Inc 1 st at beg *and* end of rows.

Rows 26–35 Work even rows.

Row 36 Inc 1 st at beg of row.

Row 37A Work even for 9 sts. Ch 1; turn.

Row 38A Work even to end (9 sts made). Ch 1; turn.

Rows 39A–43A Work even rows (9 sts made).

Row 44A Dec 1 st at beg *and* end. Knot yarn and cut, leaving a 12" end.

Row 37B Make a sl kn, leaving 5" ends. Hdc in 10th st of 36th row, just past the end of row 37A. Work pat across row, dec 1 st at end. Ch 1; turn.

Row 38B Dec 1 st at beg.

Rows 39B–42B Work even rows.

Rows 43B, 44B Dec 1 st at beg *and* end of rows. At end of row 44B, knot yarn and cut, leaving a 12" end.

Repeat all 3 sections for other slipper.

Joining Following the Joining instructions in Part I, join First Section and Second Section along the line illustrated in Figure III-19, using a yarn needle and the 12" ends. This figure and the 2 following figures depict the slippers in their final positions as worn, but all joining operations should be performed on the wrong side of the sections.

Consult Figure III-20 to determine positions and start of join of First Section and Second Section to Third Section. While joining, carefully contour the toe sections for the proper fullness and join both sections for about three-fourths of the distance to the heel tip.

Consult Figure III-21 for the method of overlapping the sections at the heel tip and continue join, with all 3 sections meeting at the base of the heel tip. Try the slippers on, placing safety-pin markers at the positions where the buttons should be sewn. Sew on buttons.

Finishing Hide all loose ends according to Finishing instructions in Part I.

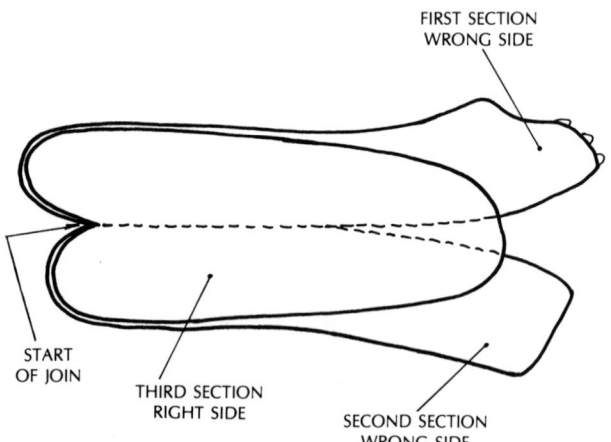

Figure III-20

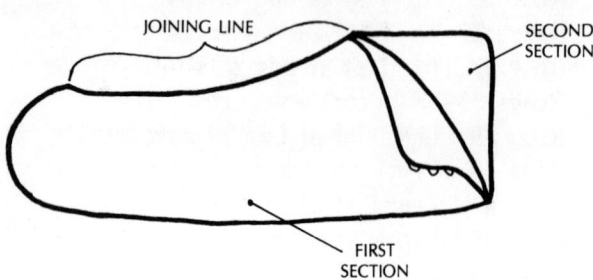

Figure III-19

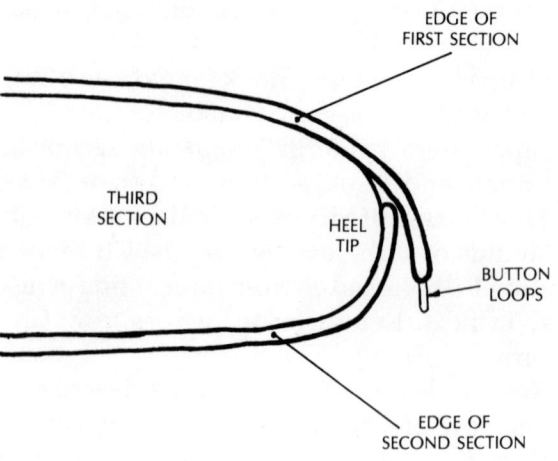

Figure III-21

Men's Cardigan

Materials

11 (12, 12) skeins (3½ oz. each) of worsted weight acrylic yarn in color of your choice
1 size K crochet hook
yarn needle
safety pins
5 buttons (1½" in diameter)
Gauge 5 sts = 2"; 3 rows = 2"; 2 strands of yarn; size K hook.

Crochet

NOTE: Instructions are for men's Small size; Medium and Large sizes are in parentheses. Two strands of yarn are used throughout.
Bottom Border Make a sl kn with 2 strands of yarn on size K hook, leaving a 5" end. Ch 9; turn.
Row 1 Sc in 2nd ch from hook and in every ch across row. Ch 1; turn.
Row 2 Sc in back lp only (see Ribbed Crochet instructions in Part I) of every sc across. Ch 1; turn.
Row 3, etc. Repeat 2nd row until border measures 39" (40", 41") when slightly stretched, being sure to make an odd number of rows. At end of last row, ch 1.
Body
Row 1 Sc (reg) in every row sp along top edge of border, ending with ch-1; turn.
Row 2 Sk first sc, (sc and dc in next sc, sk next sc) (1 moss st made). Repeat moss st 4 more times (5 moss sts made), then (sc and dc) in next 2 sc (1 moss st inc made). Work (5 moss sts, 1 moss st inc) across row. Ch 1; turn.
Row 3 Sk first 2 sts, (sc and dc in next dc, sk next sc) (moss st made). Work moss st across row. Ch 1; turn.
Row 4, etc. Repeat 3rd row to measure 15½" (16", 16½"). Place safety-pin markers 10 (11,

12) moss sts in from either end of last row. Ch 1; turn.
First Front
Row 1 (dec row) Sl st first 2 moss sts (1 moss st dec made), work moss st across row to marker. Ch 1; turn.
Row 2 (dec row) Sl st first 2 moss sts (1 moss st dec made), work moss st across row. Ch 1; turn.
Rows 3, 4 Repeat 2nd row.
Row 5 Work moss st pat across row as in 3rd row of Body (even row).
Rows 6–9 Repeat 2nd row (dec rows).
Rows 10–12 Work even rows.
Row 13 Repeat 2nd row (dec row).
Rows 14–19 Work even rows. At end of 19th row, knot yarn and cut, leaving a 5" end.
Second Front
Row 1 Make a sl kn on hook, leaving 5" ends. Sk first 2 moss sts of last row of other side of Body, sc in dc of 3rd moss st (dec made), work moss st pat across to marker. Ch 1; turn.
Rows 2–19 Repeat as for First Front.
Top of Back Make a sl kn with 2 strands on hook, leaving 5" ends.

Row 1 Sc in first dc past marker on last row of Body and work moss st across to next marker. Ch 1; turn.
Row 2 (dec row) Sl st first 2 moss sts (1 dec made), work moss st across row up to and including next-to-last moss st before marker. Ch 1; turn (2nd dec made).
Row 3 Work even.
Row 4 Repeat 2nd row, above, decreasing at beg and end of row.
Row 5 Work even.
Row 6 Repeat 2nd row.
Row 7 Work even.
Row 8 Repeat 2nd row.
Rows 9–18 Work even rows. At end of 18th row, ch 1; turn.

Shoulder and Neck Shaping
Row 1 Work 4 (5, 6) moss sts across. Ch 1; turn.
Row 2 Repeat first row.
Row 3 Work 1 (2, 3) moss sts across. Ch 1; turn.
Row 4 Repeat 3rd row, knot yarn and cut, leaving 15" ends.

Make a sl kn on hook, leaving 5" ends. Sc to first dc of 18th row of Top of Back at other side of back, and work rows 1–4, above, in toward center of back.

Using a yarn needle and 15" ends, join 4th row just made to 19th row of fronts, according to Joining instructions in Part I.

Cuff Make a sl kn on hook with 2 strands, leaving 5" ends. Ch 9; turn.
Row 1 Sc in 2nd ch from hook and in every ch across. Ch 1; turn.
Rows 2–18 Sc in back lp only of first sc and every sc across. Ch 1.

Sleeve
Row 1 Sc (reg) in first row sp at top edge of Cuff, sc in next row sp, 2 sc in next sp, 1 sc, 1 sc, 2 sc, 1 sc, 2 sc, 1 sc, 2 sc, 1 sc, 1 sc, 2 sc, 1 sc, 1 sc, 2 sc, 1 sc, and 2 sc in last row sp. Ch 1, turn (25 sc made).
Rows 2, 3 Work moss st pat. Ch 1; turn (even row).
Row 4 (inc row) Sc and dc in first dc in row (inc made), work moss st pat across. At end of row, work 1 sc and 1 dc in sc before last dc, as well as 1 sc and 1 dc in last dc (1 moss st inc made). Ch 1; turn.
Rows 5, 6 Work even.
Row 7 Repeat 4th row (2 inc made).
Row 8, etc. Repeat this pat of 2 even rows, 1 dbl-inc row, until you have completed 28 (30, 32) rows.
Row 29 (31, 33) Sl st first 2 moss sts (1 dec made), work moss st pat across row up to and including next-to-last moss st. Ch 1; turn (1 dec made).
Row 30 (32, 34) Work even.
Rows 31–36 (33–38, 35–40) Repeat 29th and 30th rows (31st and 32nd, 33rd and 34th), alternately. End last row by knotting yarn and cutting, leaving a 5" end.

Repeat Cuff and Sleeve instructions for other sleeve. Join sleeves to armhole, using yarn needle and following Joining instructions in Part I.

Neck and Front Border
Row 1 Make a sl kn with 2 strands on hook, leaving 5" ends. With right side of Right Front facing you, sc in first st at bottom of last row of Bottom Border, and in every st across, then every row sp along Right Front, around Shoulder and Neck Shaping edge, down Left Front, and, finally, first row of other edge of Bottom Border. Ch 1; turn.
Row 2 Using small safety pins, mark sts in the first row just made for 5 buttonholes, all evenly spaced on Left Front. Sc in every sc up Left Front until you reach the first marker. Ch 2, sk 2 sc, sc in next sc. Repeat this pat at each marker, then sc in every sc of first row until you reach a point 3" below level of the top shoulder seam. Then dec 1 sc in every 4th sc (see Decreasing instructions in Part I) until you reach the corresponding point 3" below the other shoulder seam. Work even down Right Front to end. Ch 1; turn.
Row 3 Sc in every sc of pr r, working 2 sc in the ch-2 sp at each buttonhole. Knot yarn and cut, leaving 5" ends.
Finishing Hide all loose ends according to Finishing instructions in Part I; sew on buttons.

Victorian Blouse

This charming style, which appeared in *Good Housekeeping*'s *Needlecraft*, features the classic Victorian yoke front.

Materials

30 (34, 36) balls (53 yds. each) of No. 5 pearl cotton yarn (Suggestion: white.)
1 size B crochet hook
1 size D crochet hook
8 buttons (½" in diameter)
yarn needle
safety pins
Gauge 6 sc = 1"; 10 rows = 3"; size B hook.

Crochet

NOTE: Instructions given are for sizes 8–10; instructions for sizes 12 and 14 are in parentheses.

Front Make a sl kn on size B hook, leaving a 5″ end. Ch 92 (98, 104); turn.

Row 1 Sc in 2nd ch from hook and in every ch across.

Row 2 Ch 4; turn. Yoh 3 times, insert hook into first sc, * yoh, pull through sc, yoh, pull through 2 lps on hook (4 lps now on hook). Yoh, sk next sc, insert hook into next sc, yoh, pull through st, yoh, pull through 2 lps on hook (5 lps now on hook). (Yoh, pull through 2 lps) 4 times (inverted Y made). Ch 1, dc in sp made by arms of inverted Y (X st made). Yoh 3 times, insert hook into next sc. Repeat from * across row, making 30 (32, 34) X sts. Then ch 1, trc in last sc, ch 1; turn.

Row 3 Sc in first ch-1 sp, * 2 sc in ch-1 sp of next X st, sc in sp between X sts. Repeat from * across row, ending with sc in ch-4 sp.

Row 4, etc. Repeat 2nd and 3rd rows alternately until your work measures 4″, ending on a sc row.

Next Row (dec row) Sl st in first sc, ch 4, sk next 2 sc, work X-st pat, beg with next sc up to 5th-from-last sc. Ch 1, sk next 2 sc, yoh twice, insert hook into last sc, yoh, pull through st, (yoh, pull through 2 lps) 4 times (dec made) [28 (30, 32) X sts made]. Ch 1; turn.

Next 10 Rows Repeat 3rd and 2nd rows alternately, 5 times each.

Next Row (inc row) 2 sc in first ch-1 sp, (2 sc in next ch-1 sp, 2 sc in sp between X sts) twice (3-sc inc). * 2 sc in next ch-1 sp, sc in sp between X sts. Repeat from * until you have 5 sp remaining in row, then (2 sc in sp between X sts, 2 sc in ch-1 sp) twice, 2 sc in ch-4 sp (3-sc inc) [91 (97, 103) sc made].

Next 5 Rows Repeat 2nd and 3rd rows alternately.

Next Row Repeat inc row, above.

Next 5 Rows Repeat 2nd and 3rd rows alternately.

Next Row Repeat inc row [103 (109, 115) sc made].

Next Rows Repeat 2nd and 3rd rows alternately until work measures 13″, or desired length, to underarm, ending with a sc row.

Armhole Shaping

Row 1 Ch 1; turn. Sl st in first 5 (8, 8) sc, ch 4, sk 1 sc, X st across, beg in next sc, until 7 (10, 10) sc remain. Ch 1, sk first sc, trc in next sc [30 (30, 32) X sts made].

Row 2, etc. Work 3 (5, 7) even rows of 3rd row–2nd row pat.

Yoke Opening, Left Side

Next Row Work 5 (5, 6) X sts, ch 4, sl st in next sc; turn.

Next Row Sc in each ch of ch-4, sc in sp before first X st. * 2 sc in next ch-1 sp, 1 sc in sp between X sts. Repeat from * across, ending with sc in ch-4 sp; turn.

Next 16 Rows Repeat last 2 rows alternately.

Yoke Opening, Right Side Make a sl kn on hook, leaving a 5″ end. Sk 58 sc on last full row at end of Armhole Shaping, sl st to next sc, ch 4, work X-st pat, beg with next sc, to end [5 (5, 6) X sts made]. Continue pat as for Left Side until work is same length as Left Side. Knot yarn and cut, leaving a 5″ end.

Yoke

Row 1 Make a sl kn on size D hook, leaving a 5″ end. With right side of Front facing you, sl st in last st at lower left corner of Yoke Opening, ch 6, sl st in bottom half of last X st on 2nd X-st row of Yoke Opening, Left Side; turn. Working across bottom of opening, dc in every sc of Front, drawing up first lp of each dc to match height of ch-6 first made. When you reach the edge of Yoke Opening, Right Side, sl st in bottom half sp of last X st on 2nd X-st row of Yoke Opening, Right Side, to correspond with first sl st.

Row 2 Replace size D hook with size B hook. Sl st to next st along side edge; turn. * Sc in each of the next 6 sc, dec 1 sc (see Decreasing instructions in Part I) in next 2 sc. Repeat from * across row, ending with sl st in side edge (50 sc made).

Row 3 Sl st up edge to bottom half sp of 3rd X-st row; turn. Replace size B hook with size D hook and, working across center Front, again dc in each of the first 3 sc, * ch 2, sk 2 sc, dc in next 4 sc. Repeat from * across, ending with 3 dc; sl st in side edge.

Row 4 Sl st in next ch on edge; turn. Working across center Front, * ch 2, sk 2 dc, dc

in next dc, dc in each of next 2 ch, dc in next dc. Repeat from * across, ending with ch 2; sl st in side edge.
Row 5 Sl st along side edge to end of next sc row; turn. Sc in each dc and each ch across; sl st in side edge.
Row 6 Ch 6, sk next 2 rows on side edge, sl st in bottom half sp of next X-st row; turn. Work a long dc in each st across; sl st to side edge.
Row 7 Using size B hook, sl st in next st at edge; turn. Sc in each dc; sl st to side edge.
Rows 8–13 Repeat rows 3–7, then 3rd row again, ending with sl st to edge of Yoke Opening, Right Side.
Neck and Shoulder Shaping, Right Shoulder
Row 1 Turn. (Ch 2, sk 2 dc, dc in next dc, dc in each of next 2 ch, dc in next dc) twice (12 sts made). Ch 3; turn.
Row 2 Dc in next 3 sts, hdc in next 4 sts, sc in next 4 sts, ending with sl st in side edge. Knot yarn and cut, leaving a 5" end.
Neck and Shoulder Shaping, Left Shoulder
Row 1 With wrong side of work facing you, make a sl kn on hook, leaving a 5" end. Sk 26 sts on 13th row of Yoke past Right Shoulder Shaping, sl st in next st, ch 3, (dc in each of next 2 ch, dc in next dc, ch 2, sk 2 dc, dc in next dc) twice. Ch 3; turn.
Row 2 Repeat 2nd row as for Right Shoulder. Knot yarn and cut, leaving a 5" end.
Back, Right Side
NOTE: Back is made in 2 sections to be joined at the center with a row of buttons.
  Make a sl kn on size B hook, leaving a 5" end. Ch 50 (53, 56). Work an even X-st pat as for Front until work measures same length as Front to underarm, ending with a sc row [16 (17, 18) X sts made].
Armhole Shaping Ch 1; turn. Sl st to first 5 (8, 8) sc, ch 4, sk 1 sc, work X-st pat, beg with next sc, across [14 (14, 15) X sts made]. Work in pat until same length as Front to shoulder at side edge. Knot yarn and cut, leaving a 5" end.
Back, Left Side
Make a sl kn on size B hook, leaving a 5" end. Work as for Back, Right Side, reversing Armhole Shaping so as to be symmetrical to right side.

Sleeves
Make a sl kn on size B hook, leaving a 5" end. Ch 42 (45, 48) and, making sure not to twist ch, sl st to first ch sp to form ring.
Round 1 Ch 1, sc in same ch sp and each ch around [42 (45, 48) sc made]; sl st to first sc.
Round 2 Ch 4, work X-st pat around, beg in st at base of ch-4 just made; end with sl st in top of ch-4 [14 (15, 16) X sts made].
Round 3 Ch 1, * sc in sp before next X st, 2 sc in ch-1 sp of next X st. Repeat from * around, ending with sl st to first sc.
Rounds 4–18 Repeat 2nd and 3rd rnds alternately (even rnds).
Round 19 Ch 1, (2 sc in sp before next X st, 2 sc in next ch-1 sp) 3 times, * sc in next sp between X sts, 2 sc in next ch-1 sp. Repeat from * until you have 6 sps remaining in rnd, then (2 sc in sp between X sts, 2 sc in next ch-1 sp) 3 times; sl st to join [6-st inc; 48 (51, 54) sc made].
Rounds 20–24 Repeat 2nd and 3rd rnds alternately.
Round 25 Repeat 19th rnd (inc rnd).
Round 26, etc. Work 5 even rnds and then 1 inc round 1 (2, 2) more time(s) [60 (69, 72) sc made]. Then work even until work measures 17" from beg, or the desired length to underarm, ending with a sc row.
Cap Shaping
Row 1 Sl st in first 5 (8, 8) sc, ch 4, sk first sc, work X-st pat, beg with next sc, until you have 7 (10, 10) sts remaining in row, ch 1, sk first sc, trc in next sc [16 (17, 18) X sts made]. Ch 1; turn.
Row 2 (sc row) Work even. Ch 4; turn.
Row 3 (dec row) Repeat dec row as for Front after 4th row [14, (15, 16) X sts made].
Row 4, etc. Work 3 even rows in pat, then 1 dec row 3 (4, 4) times more, then an even and a dec row 3 (2, 3) times more [2 (3, 2) X sts made], ending with a sc row. Knot yarn and cut, leaving a 5" end.
Cuff
Round 1 Make a sl kn on size B hook, leaving a 5" end. Sl st to any sc at bottom of sleeve, work 2 sc in base of each sc around [84 (90, 96) sc made].
Round 2 Ch 4, work X-st pat in base of ch-4 and around, making 2 chs at top of each X st

instead of the usual ch-1, and making a ch-1 between X sts. End with sl st in top of ch-4 [28 (29, 30) X sts made].

Round 3 Ch 1, 2 sc in sp before first X st, * 3 sc in next ch-2 sp, 2 sc in next ch-1 sp. Repeat from * all around; join with sl st.

Round 4 Ch 1, sc in first sc, * ch 3, sc in next sc. Repeat from * all around; join with sl st. Knot yarn and cut, leaving a 5" end.

Yoke Ruffle Make a sl kn on size B hook, leaving a 5" end. Ch 116, or enough to outline *entire* yoke opening.

Row 1 Sc in 2nd ch from hook, * 2 sc in next ch, sc in next ch. Repeat from * across (172 sc made).

Row 2 Ch 4; turn. Repeat pat of 2nd rnd of Cuff across, ending with trc in last sc.

Row 3 Ch 1; turn; 2 sc in first ch-1 sp. Repeat from * in 3rd rnd of Cuff, ending with 2 sc in last sp. *Do not join.*

Row 4 Ch 3; turn; sc in first sc. Repeat from * in 4th rnd of Cuff, ending with sc in last sc. Knot yarn and cut, leaving a 3' end.

Using a yarn needle and starting with the 3' end just left, join ruffle to yoke along sides and bottom according to Joining directions in Part I.

Neck Edging Join side and shoulder seams, using yarn needle.

Row 1 Make a sl kn on size B hook, leaving a 5" end. Sl st to corner st on right half of back at neck. Ch 1, then work 74 evenly spaced sc around neck edge.

Rows 2, 3 Ch 1; turn. Sc in every sc across.

Row 4 Ch 4; turn. Work X-st pat across.

Row 5 Repeat 2nd row, above.

Row 6 Repeat 4th row, above.

Rows 7, 8 Repeat 3rd and 4th rows of Yoke Ruffle. Knot yarn and cut, leaving a 5" end.

Back Edging, Left Side

Row 1 Make a sl kn on size B hook, leaving a 5" end. With right side of work facing you, sl st to lower corner st at center of left back. Work approximately 4 sc at end of each X-st row and 1 sc at end of each sc row, working along edge of back opening up to 7th row of neck edging.

Rows 2–5 Ch 1; turn. Sc in each sc. Knot yarn and cut, leaving a 5" end. Using small safety pins, mark this edge for 8 evenly spaced buttons, the first to be located about $\frac{1}{2}$" below the upper edge, the last to be located 2" above the lower edge.

Back Edging, Right Side Beginning at neck edge, work as for left side. On 3rd row, ch 3 and sk 2 sc at each corresponding marked position for buttonholes. On 4th row, work 3 sc in each ch-3 sp.

Finishing Hide all loose ends according to Finishing instructions in Part I; sew on buttons in marked positions.

Men's Cossack Hat

Materials

2 skeins (4 oz. each) of homespun Irish tweed wool in basic variegated color V (Suggestion: gray and tan.); 1 skein of same yarn in each of 2 colors: A and B (Suggestion: black and white.)
1 size K crochet hook
yarn needle
safety pin
Gauge 2 sts = 1"; 2 rows = 1"; 4 strands of yarn; size K hook.

Crochet

NOTE: Instructions given are for men's size Small; Medium and Large sizes are in parentheses. Four strands of yarn are used throughout: 2 of color V and 1 each of colors A and B.

Make a sl kn on size K hook with 2 strands of color V and 1 each of colors A and B, leaving 5" ends. Ch 24; turn.
Row 1 Sc in 2nd ch from hook and in every ch across. Ch 1; turn.
Row 2 Sc in back lp only (see Ribbed Crochet instructions in Part I) of first 12 sts, then sc in usual manner for remaining 11 sts. Ch 1; turn.
Row 3 Sc (reg sc) in first 11 sts, then sc in back lp for remaining 12 sts. Ch 1; turn.
Row 4, etc. Repeat 2nd and 3rd rows alternately, so that ribbing appears only at bottom of hat. Work until length measures 24" (25", 26"), ending last row at bottom of hat; to join, sl st loosely to every ch sp of ch-24 first made.
Top Section
Round 1 Work a sc in every row sp at top of hat, working all around top edge and ending with sl st to first sc. Mark this sl st with a small safety pin to identify back of hat, and mark corresponding point halfway around top edge to identify front.
Round 2 (dec rnd) Dec 1 sc in first 2 sc (see Decreasing instructions in Part I). Sc in every sc around (work even) up to next-to-last sc before next (front) marker. Dec 1 sc in last 2 sts before marker; turn; dec 1 more sc in first 2 sts on other side of marker. Work even, then dec 1 sc in last 2 sts before next (back) marker. End with sl st to first sc.

Close remaining opening with a row of sc, inserting hook into top strands of sts on either side of the gap and lining them up carefully to correspond. Knot yarn and cut, leaving 5" ends.
Finishing Hide all loose ends according to Finishing instructions in Part I. Turn hat inside out and fold ribbed section up to form brim.

Rainbow Hooded Cape

Materials

6 skeins (1 oz. each) of frosted 67% mohair–33% acrylic blend yarn in white
3 skeins (3½ oz. each) of 4-ply acrylic yarn in rainbow variegated colors
7 skeins (4 oz. each) of 4-ply worsted acrylic yarn in basic cape color B (Suggestion: dark blue.)
1 size H crochet hook
yarn needle
safety pins
Gauge 3 sts=1"; 3 rows=1"; 1 strand frosted yarn and 1 strand variegated yarn; size H hook.

Crochet

NOTE: The instructions allow for making the cape to any desired length.
Yoke Make a sl kn on size H hook with 1 strand of white and 1 strand of variegated yarns, leaving 5" ends. Ch 51; turn.
Row 1 Sc in 2nd ch from hook and in every ch across. Ch 1; turn. Place safety-pin markers in 6th sc from end, 13th, 19th, 25th, 31st, 37th and 44th sc.
Row 2 (inc row) Sc in back lp only (see Ribbed Crochet instructions in Part I) of every sc across, working 2 sc in every marked st (inc made). Move marker to last st made after every inc (57 sc made). Ch 1; turn. (NOTE: All sc in Yoke and Hood are in back lp only.)
Row 3 (inc row) Repeat 2nd row, increasing 1 sc at each marker. Move markers (64 sc made). Ch 1; turn.
Row 4 (even row) Sc (in back lp) of every sc across. Ch 1; turn.
Rows 5, 6 Repeat 2nd row (inc rows).
Rows 7–22 Repeat 4th and 2nd rows alternately (134 sc made). At end of the 22nd row, knot yarn and cut, leaving 5" ends.
Hood
Row 1 (inc row) Make a sl kn with same strands as for yoke, leaving 5" ends. With front of yoke facing you, sc in base of first ch of original ch-51 and in every ch across, up to and including 20th ch. Inc 1 sc in 21st ch. (sc in next ch, inc 1 sc in next ch) 5 more times (6 inc made). Continue to sc across remainder of ch. Ch 1; turn.
Rows 2–8 Work even.
Row 9 Work even to center of back (28th st). Ch 1; turn.
Row 10 (dec row) Dec 1 sc in first 2 sc (see Decreasing instructions in Part I), then work even across row. Ch 1; turn.
Rows 11, 12 Work even.
Row 13 (dec row) Work even up to next-to-last sc, dec 1 sc in last 2 sc. Ch 1; turn.
Rows 14–38 Work (2 even and 1 dec rows) 8 more times (18 sts in last row). Knot yarn and cut, leaving 3' ends.

Make a sl kn on hook with same strands, sc into 29th st on 8th row of Hood, work even across remainder of row. Ch 1; turn. Work even for 26 sts, then dec 1 sc in last 2 sts. Ch 1; turn. Repeat the pat as for other half of hood: 2 even rows, then 1 row with 1 dec at center of back, until same length as other section (18 sts in last row). Knot yarn and cut, leaving 5" ends. Join seam at center back, using yarn needle and 3' end, according to Joining instructions in Part I.
Ties Make a sl kn with same strands, leaving 5" ends. Sl st to bottom strands of 4th st from end in first row of Yoke, with right side of work facing you. Dc in top strands of same 4th st. * Yoh, insert hook into back lp of top 2 strands of dc just made, and complete another dc. Repeat from * 14 more times (ch of dc made). Knot yarn and cut, leaving 5" ends.

Repeat the above, inserting chs of dc in the 4th st in from ends of the 10th and 20th rows of the Yoke, and then in the corresponding sts of the first, 10th and 20th rows on the other side of the Yoke.

RAINBOW HOODED CAPE 131

Body

Row 1 Make a sl kn on hook with 1 strand of color B yarn, leaving a 5" end. With right side of yoke facing you, sc (reg, not back lp) in first st at left end of last row of hood, dc in same st, * sk next st, sc and dc in next st (moss st made). Repeat from * across row to end. Ch 1; turn.

Row 2 Sk first dc and sc, * sc and dc in next dc, sk next sc (moss st made). Repeat from *, making moss st across row. Ch 1; turn.

Row 3 (inc row) Sk first moss st and work moss st pat up to first marker. At marker, sc and dc in next sc instead of skipping it (1 moss st inc made). Move marker to dc of moss st just made. * Work moss st across to next marker, inc 1 moss st at marker, move marker. Repeat from * across row, working moss st pat past last marker to end of row. Ch 1; turn.

Rows 4–15 Work 2 even rows of moss st (as 2nd row, above) and 1 row of 1 moss st inc (as 3rd row, above) at each marker.

Armhole Opening, Right Front
Row 16A Work even for 12 moss sts. Ch 1; turn.

Rows 17A–36A Sk first moss st and work moss st across. Ch 1; turn (even rows). Knot yarn and cut at end of row 36A, leaving a 5" end.

Armhole Opening, Center
Row 16B Make a sl kn on hook, leaving a 5" end. Sk first moss st on the 15th row of Body past last moss st of row 16A. Work moss st pat across center of back to left edge, until 12 moss sts remain in the 15th row. Ch 1; turn.

Rows 17B–36B Work even, as for rows 17A–36A. At end of row 36B, knot yarn and cut, leaving a 5" end.

Armhole Opening, Left Front
Row 16C Make a sl kn on hook, leaving a 5" end. Skipping first moss st on the 15th row of Body past last moss st of row 16B, work moss st pat across to left edge. Ch 1; turn.

Rows 17C–36C Work even, as for other 2 sections. At end of row 36C, ch 1; turn.

Armhole Joining and Remainder of Body
Row 1 Work moss st pat across, joining bottoms of armhole openings. Ch 1; turn.

Row 2, etc. Work even until cape is desired length. Knot yarn and cut, leaving a 5" end.

Armhole Edging Make a sl kn with same yarn, leaving a 5" end. With right side of work facing you, sc in top st of Armhole Opening, Right Front, and sc in every row sp down opening to bottom. Turn. Dc up edge of center section to top, ending with sl st to first sc. Knot yarn and cut, leaving a 5" end.

Repeat Armhole Edging for left armhole opening, starting first sc at bottom of left front, single-crocheting up left front and double-crocheting down center.

Yoke and Hood Edging Make a sl kn on hook with 1 strand of variegated and 1 strand of white yarns, leaving 5" ends. Sc in yoke where it meets body at right front, and sc in every row sp up yoke, around hood, down yoke, ending where yoke meets left front of body. For this last sc, insert hook into last row sp, yoh, ptl, yoh with color B yarn, and complete sc with color B yarn. Cut variegated and white yarns, leaving 5" ends.

Body Edging Dc in every row sp around entire body, finishing at points where body meets yoke. Knot yarn and cut, leaving a 5" end.

Pom-Poms for Ties Make 6 looped pom-poms, using 1 strand each of variegated and white yarns, according to instructions set out in Looped Pom-Poms in Part I, and attach to ties.

Finishing Hide all loose ends according to Finishing instructions in Part I.

Deco Clutch

This is an all-purpose handbag reminiscent of the Art-Deco era.

Materials

- 12 balls (53 yds. each) of No. 5 pearl cotton yarn in dark color of your choice
- 1½ yds. (36" wide) of lining material in matching color
- ¾ yd. buckram or other stiffening material
- 1 9" zipper in matching color
- 1 size E hook
- yarn needle
- sewing needle and thread in matching colors
- felt-tipped pen or chalk
- sewing scissors
- straight pins

Crochet

"Tail" Ornament Make a sl kn on size E hook with 2 strands of yarn, leaving 5" ends. Ch 6; sl st to first ch to form a ring.

Round 1 Sc in every ch around.

Rounds 2–7 Sc in every sc of pr rnd (6 sc made).

Body

Round 8 Ch 3, dc in first sc of 7th rnd, * ch 2, dc in next sc. Repeat from * 4 more times (6 dc made).

Round 9 Ch 2, dc in ch-3 sp, dc in first dc, dc in next ch-2 sp. * Ch 2, dc in same ch-2 sp, dc in next dc, dc in next ch-2 sp. Repeat from * to end of rnd, ending with dc in first ch-2 sp.

Round 10 Ch 2, dc in same ch-2 sp (as ended pr rnd), * dc in each st of next dc group, dc in next ch-2 sp, ch 2, dc in same ch-2 sp. Repeat from *, ending with dc in first ch-2 sp of rnd.
Rounds 11–27 Repeat 10th rnd 17 times.
Round 28 Ch 2, sc in each st of 27th rnd, working 3 sc in each ch-2 sp. End with 3 sc in first ch-2 sp made.
Round 29 Sc in every sc of 28th rnd. Knot yarn and cut, leaving 5" ends.
"Tail" Ornament for Zipper Follow instructions for "Tail" Ornament on bag up to and including the 7th rnd; then work 1 more rnd of sc. Knot yarn and cut, leaving an 8" end.
Lining Lay out lining material on a flat surface and fold in half with wrong sides facing out. Place the hexagonal crocheted bag on top of the lining, and trace around the outline with felt-tipped pen or with chalk. Pin both layers together all around, just inside the marked lines. Cut both layers simultaneously along marked lines with sewing scissors.

Repeat the above procedure for the buckram, this time cutting only 1 layer, about $\frac{1}{2}$" inside the marked lines so that the buckram piece is slightly smaller than the lining.

Sandwich the buckram between the 2 lining layers, this time facing right sides out, and fold in half along a line joining any pair of opposite corners. Sew all 4 layers together at each side seam, about $\frac{3}{8}$" in from the raw edges and to within 1" of the tops.

Sandwich about $\frac{1}{4}$" of the fabric edge of 1 side of the zipper between the 2 layers of lining at the top of the bag, with zipper closure facing out. Pin in place along top, folding each lining layer in toward zipper fabric to form $\frac{1}{4}$" hems. Sew zipper fabric to lining layers with 2 lines of stitches, as close to the top edge of the lining as possible. Repeat this procedure to attach other edge of zipper fabric to lining layers at other side of bag opening. Remove pins.

Fold the crocheted bag in half and join the 2 side seams, using a yarn needle and following instructions set out in Joining in Part I.
Finishing Hide all loose ends according to Finishing directions in Part I. Insert the lining into the bag and sew the 2 fabric edges of the zipper to the bag at each side of the top opening. Attach "tail" ornament to zipper closure with 8" end.

Mesh Rosette-Bordered Shawl*

Materials

35 balls (53 yds. each) of No. 5 pearl cotton yarn (Suggestion: white or ecru.)
1 No. 1 crochet hook (steel)
yarn needle
safety pins

*Reprinted by permission of *Woman's Day* magazine. Copyright © 1976 by CBS Publications, Inc.

Crochet

Make a sl kn on hook, leaving a 5" end. Ch 325; turn.
Row 1   Dc in 4th ch from hook and in every ch across (count ch-3 as 1 dc). Ch 5; turn.
Row 2   Trc in 5th ch from hook, ch 5, trc in 5th ch from hook, pulling trc lps to equal the height of the ch-5. * Sk next 6 dc, sc in next dc, ch 5, trc in same dc where sc was just made, ch 5, trc in 5th ch from hook (mesh st made). Repeat from * until 7 sts remain in row, sk next 6 dc, sc in last st (46 mesh sts made). Ch 5; turn.
Row 3 (dec row)   Sc in center-pointed apex of first mesh st, * ch 5, trc in same apex, ch 5, trc in 5th ch from hook, sc in next apex. Repeat from * across row (45 mesh sts made). Ch 5; turn.
Rows 4–47   Repeat 3rd row, dec 1 mesh st in each row until only 1 remains. At end of 47th row knot yarn and cut, leaving a 5" end.

Border

Row 1   Make a sl kn on hook, leaving a 5" end. With right side of work facing you, sc in last dc of first row at upper left-hand corner of shawl. Ch 7. Work a triple-triple crochet in 7th ch from hook as follows: yoh 4 times, insert hook in ch sp, yoh, pull through st, (yoh and pull through 2 lps on hook) 5 times (trp trc made). Ch 7, trp trc in 7th ch from hook (long mesh st made). Sc in apex of mesh st at beg of 2nd row. * Work long mesh st, sk apex at end of next row, sc in apex at beg of next row. Repeat from * along left edge of the shawl up to the next-to-last row, work long mesh st in apex at center bottom of shawl, then up right edge of shawl, ending with ch-7 in upper right-hand corner; turn.
Rows 2–5 (dec rows)   Sc in apex of first long mesh st, * ch 7, trp trc in same apex, ch 7, trp trc in 7th ch from hook, sc in next apex. Repeat from * down right edge, up left edge, turn, down left edge, etc., until 5th row is completed. Place a small safety pin in apex of last long mesh st made. Knot yarn and cut, leaving a 5" end.
Motif 1   Make a sl kn on hook, leaving a 5" end. Ch 4; join with sl st to first ch to form ring.

Round 1 Ch 4, (trc in center of ring) 17 times. End with sl st to top of ch-4.
Round 2 *[Ch 10, sl st in 4th ch from hook (1 picot made), ch 6, sc in next trc] twice. Ch 10, make picot, ch 6, sk next trc and sc in next trc. Repeat from * 5 more times (12 picots made).
Round 3 Sl st first 6 chs to first picot, ch 3, work (3 dc, ch 1, 4 dc) in center of picot (first picot tip made). Ch 1, * work (4 dc, ch 1, 4 dc) in next picot lp (2nd picot tip made), ch 1. Repeat from * 7 more times (9 picot tips made). Mark the first 3 picot tips made with small safety pins. Work 4 dc in next picot lp, then pick up shawl and sl st in apex of marked long mesh st (st X in Figure III-22). Work 4 more dc in same picot lp, ch 1. Work each of next 2 picot tips as for last picot tip worked, slip-stitching them to apexes of long mesh sts Y and Z, as shown in Figure III-22. End with sl st to ch-3 on first picot tip (12 picot tips made; 3 attached to shawl). Knot yarn and cut, leaving a 4" end.
Motif 2 Work as for Motif 1 up to and including the 6th picot tip of the 3rd rnd. Work each of the next 3 picot tips as for the 10th picot tip of Motif 1, joining each to its corresponding tip of Motif 1 with sl sts. Work the last 3 tips in a similar manner, joining them to the apexes of long mesh sts A, B and C (Figure III-22) with sl sts. Knot yarn and cut, leaving a 4" end.
Motifs 3–7 Work as for Motif 2, joining 3 tips to previous motif and 3 tips to shawl.
Motif 8 Work as for Motif 2, but join only the 9th and 10th tips to the first 2 tips of Motif 7 and the 11th and 12th tips to the 2 corner long mesh sts on shawl.
Motif 9 Join 8th and 9th tips to first 2 tips of Motif 8 and next 3 tips to shawl.
Motifs 10–15 Work to correspond to Motifs 6 through 1.
Edging Make a sl kn on hook, leaving a 5" end. Sc in bottom of first ch sp of original foundation ch at top corner of shawl. Working across ch, * ch 2, sk next ch, sc in next ch. Repeat from * across, ending with sc in last ch.

Continue edging down left side of shawl by working a long mesh st (as in first row of Border), sc in apex of long mesh st at end of first row of Border, work another long mesh st, sc in apex of long mesh st at end of next row. Continue this pat down left side of shawl, working sc in ch-1 sps of each of the unattached picot tips, then up right side to top corner. Knot yarn and cut, leaving a 5" end.
Tassels Make a tassel for each long mesh st in the edging according to instructions set out in Tassels and Fringes in Part I, and using a 13" template and 21 turns of yarn. Do not cut ends of tassel.
Finishing Hide all loose ends of shawl according to Finishing directions in Part I.

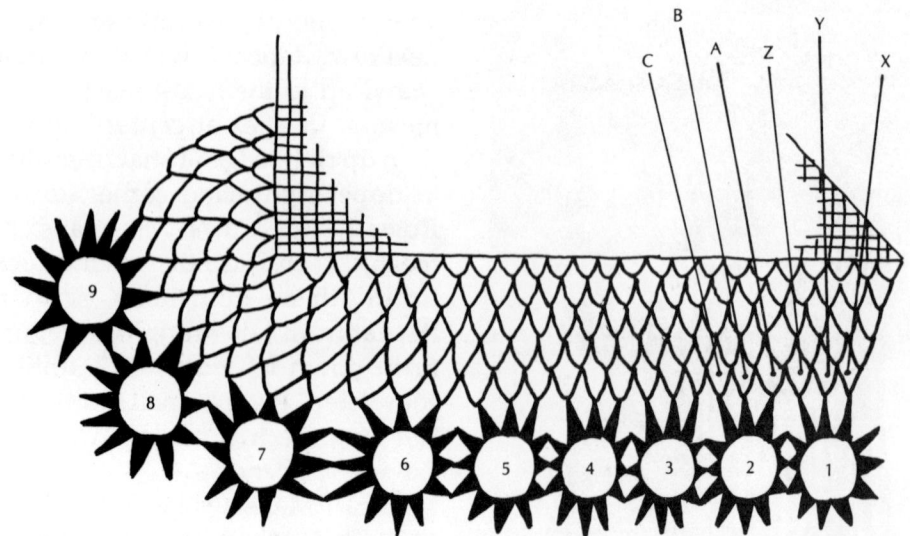

Figure III-22

Men's Winter Gloves

Materials

1 skein (4 oz.) of 4-ply wool or acrylic yarn in basic glove color of your choice (for men's Small or Medium size), 4-ply bulky yarn for Large size (color A)
40 yds. of same type yarn in contrasting color B for trim
1 size E crochet hook
yarn needle
Gauge 4 sts = 1"; 4 rows = 1"; reg 4-ply yarn; size E hook. 4 sts = 1 1/16"; 4 rows = 1 1/16"; bulky 4-ply yarn; size E hook.

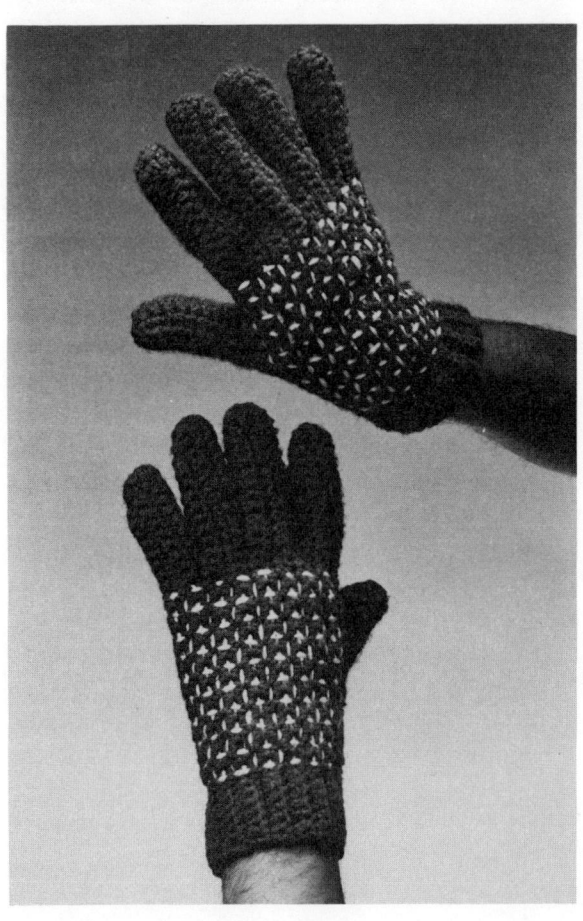

Crochet

Right Glove Make a sl kn on size E hook, leaving a 5" end of color A yarn. Ch 36; turn.
Row 1 Sc in 2nd ch from hook and in every ch across.
Row 2 Ch 1; turn. Work a reg sc in first sc and sc in back lp only of each of next 5 sc (see Ribbed Crochet directions in Part I). Sc (reg) in remaining sts up to next-to-last st. Work 2 sc in last st (1 inc made) (36 sc made).
Row 3 Ch 1; turn. Dec 1 sc in first 2 sc (see Decreasing directions in Part I), sc (reg) across row until you have 6 sts remaining. Sc in back lps of next 5 sc, reg sc in last.

NOTE: The ribbed crochet will form the cuff of the glove. Always work the 6 cuff sts as in 2nd and 3rd rows, above; all other sc is done in both top strands.

Row 4 Ch 1; turn. Work 6 cuff sts, sc in each of next 21 sts, then ch 11.
Row 5 Turn; sc in 2nd ch from hook and in remainder of ch. Continue to sc to end, working cuff sts as before (37 sts made).
Row 6 Ch 1; turn. Sc in every sc, inc 1 sc in last st.
Row 7 Ch 1; turn. Dec 1 sc at beg of row, sc to end.
Row 8 Ch 1; turn. Work cuff, sc in each of next 21 sts, then ch 13.
Row 9 Turn; sc in 2nd ch from hook and in remainder of ch. Continue to sc to end (39 sc made).
Row 10 Ch 1; turn. Work cuff, sc in each of next 11 sts, then ch 11 (for thumb); turn. Sc in 2nd ch from hook and in each remaining ch. Continue to sc in every sc of pr r, working in opposite direction to cuff, up to the next-to-last st. Work 2 sc in last st (51 sts made).
Row 11 Ch 1; turn. Dec 1 sc at beg, sc in each of next 32 sts, bringing you to the tip of the thumb. Work 10 sc in other side of ch on thumb, then sc in each st to end (60 sts made).
Row 12 Ch 1; turn. Work 48 sts, including thumb, then ch 12 (for forefinger).
Row 13 Turn; sc in 2nd ch from hook and in remainder of ch. Continue to sc in each st to end.
Row 14 Sc in every sc, inc 1 sc in last st (60 sts made).

Row 15 Ch 1; turn. Dec 1 sc, sc in each of next 31 sts to tip of thumb. Fold thumb flat and join with a row of sc by inserting hook into next st and last st worked. Work 9 more such sts through both edges of thumb, then sc in each st to end.
Row 16 Ch 1; turn. Sc in every st to end of forefinger (39 sts made).
Gussets Work a sc in end row sps of each of the 3 rows at the tip of the forefinger. Continue to sc down the side of the forefinger toward the middle finger. Continue up the side of the middle finger, working 3 sc at the top, etc. Finish off down the side of the glove, ending at the cuff.
Back of Glove, Fourth Finger
Row 1 Ch 1; turn. Work 6 cuff sts, sc in each of the next 27 sts.
Row 2 Ch 1; turn. Work even to end.
Row 3 Ch 1; turn. Work 33 sts, then, skipping side edge of rows, sc in next st on finger, 2 sc in next (36 sts made).
Row 4 Ch 1; turn. Dec 1 sc at beg, work even to end.
Row 5 Ch 1; turn. Work 35 sts, then work a sc on side edge of last st made and a sc in the end sts of each of the last 2 rows (38 sts made).
Row 6 (joining row) Fold finger flat and join as for thumb with a row of sc, working up to base of next finger (27 sts of hand left free).
Back of Glove, Third Finger
Row 1 Work a sc in each of the 9 sts on side of finger.
Row 2 Ch 1; turn. Sc in each of 9 sts on finger, then 27 sts of hand.
Row 3 Ch 1; turn. Work 36 sts, sk side edge of rows, sc in next st on finger, 2 sc in next st (39 sts made).
Row 4 Ch 1; turn. Dec 1 sc at beg, work even until end.
Row 5 Ch 1; turn. Work 38 sts, sc in side edge of last st, sc in each end st of last 2 rows (41 sts made).
Row 6 Repeat 6th row as for fourth finger.
Back of Glove, Middle Finger Work as for third finger, working 10 sc on side of finger.
Back of Glove, Forefinger Work similarly, working 9 sc on side of finger. Continue joining row on finger to end of cuff. Knot yarn and cut, leaving a 5" end.
Trim Using a yarn needle and color B yarn and beg at first st above cuff of first row of forefinger, weave yarn under 1 st and over 1 st up to base of the forefinger; then, alternately, over 1 st and under the next in the next row, until you reach the cuff. Repeat up next row and down next until you reach side of the glove. Then repeat pat across rows, crossing the sts you originally made. Knot yarn and cut right at knot.
Finishing Hide other loose end according to instructions set out in Finishing in Part I. Turn glove inside out.
Left Glove Work palm the same as for Right Glove up to and including the 14th row. Begin 15th row as for Right Glove, but fold thumb in opposite direction. Finish to correspond, joining fingers from same side as for thumb.

Toddlers' Hooded Coat

Materials

6 skeins (3 oz. each) of 4-ply worsted wool yarn in variegated colors of your choice (color V)
1 skein (2 oz.) of same type yarn in solid color to match one of the variegated tones for band (color B)
1 size G crochet hook
1 separated zipper, 12" (14", 14"), in color B
1 button (1" in diameter) in color B
yarn needle
sewing needle and thread
Gauge 7 sts = 2"; 4 rows = 1"; size G hook.

Crochet

NOTE: Instructions are given for size 12 mos.; toddlers' sizes 1 and 2 are in parentheses.
Back Make a sl kn on size G hook with color V yarn, leaving a 5" end. Ch 38 (41, 45) to measure 10¾" (11¾", 12¾").
Row 1 Sc in 2nd ch from hook and in every ch across. Ch 1; turn.
Row 2 Work a short lp st as follows: insert hook into first sc, yoh, pull through st (2 lps on hook), insert hook into same sc, form a ½" long lp with yarn and hold in place at back of work with middle finger of left hand. Yoh (with forefinger) and pull through st (3 lps on hook). Yoh again and pull through 3 lps (short lp st made). To continue, insert hook into next sc, etc. Repeat short lp st across row. Ch 1; turn (even row).
Row 3 Sc in every short lp st across row. Ch 1; turn.
Rows 4–19 Repeat 2nd and 3rd rows alternately. For last st of 19th row, insert hook into last st of 18th row, yoh, ptl, yoh with color B yarn and complete sc with color B yarn. Cut color V yarn, leaving a 5" end. Ch 1; turn.
Rows 20–25 Repeat 2nd and 3rd rows alternately. At end of 25th row, change back to color V as described in the 19th row. Ch 1; turn.
Row 26, etc. Repeat 2nd and 3rd rows alternately until work measures 8¼" (9½", 10¼"), ending with a short lp st row; turn.
Armhole Shaping
Row 1 Sl st in each of first 2 (2, 3) sts, ch 1, sc in next st and every st across until 2 (2, 3) sts remain in row. Ch 1; turn.
Row 2 Work short lp st in every sc across. Ch 1; turn.
Row 3 (dec row) Dec 1 sc in first 2 sc (see Decreasing instructions in Part I), sc in every st across until 2 sts remain, dec 1 sc in last 2 sts. Ch 1; turn.

Rows 4, 5 Repeat 2nd and 3rd rows, above [29 (32, 34) sts made].
Row 6, etc. Repeat pat as for 2nd and 3rd rows of Back alternately, until length from first row of Armhole Shaping measures 4½" (5", 5½"), ending with a short lp st row; turn.
Shoulder Shaping
Row 1 Sl st in first 4 sts, ch 1, sc in every st across until 4 sts remain in row; turn.
Row 2 Sl st in first 3 (4, 4) sts, ch 1, work short lp sts across until 3 (4, 4) sts remain. Ch 1; turn.
Row 3 Sc in each of remaining 15 (16, 18) sts for back of neck. Knot yarn and cut, leaving a 5" end.
Left Front Make a sl kn with color V yarn, leaving a 5" end. Ch 19 (21, 23).
Row 1, etc. Work as for back, inserting a band of color B at end of the 19th row, etc., until same number of rows have been completed to Armhole Shaping, ending with a short lp st row; turn.
Front Armhole Shaping
Row 1 Sl st in first 2 (2, 3) sts, ch 1, sc in each remaining st across. Ch 1; turn.
Row 2 Work short lp st across. Ch 1; turn.
Row 3 Dec 1 sc in first 2 sts, sc in each remaining st across. Ch 1; turn.
Rows 4, 5 Repeat 2nd and 3rd rows.
Row 6, etc. Work even in pat on remaining 14 (16, 17) sts until same number of rows have been completed as on Back up to Shoulder Shaping, ending with a short lp st row (at armhole edge); turn.
Shoulder Shaping
Row 1 Sl st in first 4 sts, ch 1, sc across. Ch 1; turn.
Row 2 Lp st across until 3 (4, 4) sts remain. Ch 1; turn.
Row 3 Sc across. Knot yarn and cut, leaving a 5" end.
Right Front Work as for Left Front up to Armhole Shaping.
Armhole Shaping
Row 1 Sc across until 2 (2, 3) sts remain. Ch 1; turn.
Row 2 Lp st across. Ch 1; turn.
Row 3 Sc across, dec 1 sc in last 2 sts. Ch 1; turn.
Rows 4, 5 Repeat 2nd and 3rd rows.

Row 6, etc. Repeat as for 6th row, etc., of Left Front.
Shoulder Shaping
Row 1 Sc across until 4 sts remain. Ch 1; turn.
Row 2 Lp st across. Ch 1; turn.
Row 3 Sc across. Knot yarn and cut, leaving a 5" end.
Sleeves Make a sl kn on hook with color V yarn, leaving a 5" end. Ch 22 (25, 26); turn.
Row 1 Sc in 2nd ch from hook and in each ch across. Ch 1; turn.
Rows 2, 3 (even rows) Sc in every sc across. Ch 1; turn.
Row 4 (inc row) [Sc in next sc, 2 sc in next sc (1 inc made), sc in next sc] 7 (8, 8) times. For toddlers' size 2, work 2 sc in last sc. Ch 1; turn.
Row 5, etc. Work even in short lp st–sc pat as for Back over these 28 (32, 34) sts, until total sleeve length measures 7" (7½", 8"), ending on a lp st row; turn.
Top Shaping
Row 1, etc. Sl st in first 2 (2, 3) sts, ch 1, sc in each st across until 2 (2, 3) sts remain. Ch 1; turn. Continue in pat, dec 1 sc at each end of every sc row until 14 (14, 15) sts remain; turn.
Next Row Sl st in first 4 sts, ch 1, work across until 4 sts remain. Ch 1; turn.
Next Row Work even across row. Knot yarn and cut, leaving a 5" end.
Hood
Row 1 Make a sl kn on hook with color V yarn and, with wrong side of work facing you, sc in every sc around entire neck edge.
Row 2 (inc row) Sc in each of the first 2 sc, (2 sc in next sc, sc in each of the next 2 sc) 3 times, 2 sc in each sc until 11 sts remain, sc in each of the next 2 sc, (2 sc in next sc, sc in each of the next 2 sc) 3 times. Ch 1; turn.
Row 3 Work short lp st in each sc across. Ch 1; turn.
Row 4 Sc across. Ch 1; turn.
Row 5, etc. Repeat 3rd and 4th rows alternately, until hood measures 7" (7½", 8"), ending with a lp st row. Knot yarn and cut, leaving a 5" end.

Join side and sleeve seams, using a yarn needle and following instructions set out in Joining in Part I. Similarly, join sleeves to armholes. With right side of work facing you, work a row of sc up right front edge, around front of hood, and down left front edge. Knot yarn and cut.

Work a rnd of sc in bottom of foundation ch at each sleeve, ending with sl st to first sc. Knot yarn and cut. Attach a ch lp of correct length to act as a buttonhole on right front at neck. Sew on button and zipper with matching thread.

Finishing Hide all loose ends according to Finishing directions in Part I.

Disco Scarf

A glittering costume-type accessory to swirl with the rhythm as you dance.

Materials

4 skeins ($7/10$ oz. each) of 80% acetate–20% metallic plastic blend yarn, 1 each in green, red, brown and silver
1 size I hook
yarn needle

Crochet

Make a sl kn on size I hook with brown yarn, leaving a 6" end. Ch 99; turn.

Row 1 Sc in 15th ch from hook, * ch 7, sk next 6 ch, sc in 7th ch. Repeat from * across ch. Ch 7; turn.

Row 2 Sc in first sc, * ch 7, sc in next sc. Repeat from * across row, ending with sc in 8th ch sp of ch-14 lp. Ch 7; turn.

Row 3 Sc in first sc, * ch 7, sc in next sc. Repeat from * across row. Ch 7; turn.

Row 4 Repeat 3rd row up to last sc. For last sc, insert hook into last sc of pr r, yoh, pull through st, yoh with red yarn and complete sc with red. Cut brown yarn, leaving a 6" end.

Rows 5–7 Repeat 3rd row. For last sc of 7th row, change back to brown.

Rows 8–10 Repeat 3rd row; change to silver.

Rows 11, 12 Repeat 3rd row; change to brown.

Rows 13–15 Repeat 3rd row; change to green.

Rows 16–18 Repeat 3rd row; change to brown.

Rows 19–21 Repeat 3rd row; change to silver.

Row 22 Repeat 3rd row. At end of the 22nd row, sl st to first st of 21st row.

Border and Fringe Edging

Row 1 Working along edge of scarf, sc in every *other* row sp to corner, sc in corner st, * ch 7, sc in back of next ch that contains a sc of first row of body of scarf. Repeat from * along ch, sc in next corner and in every other row sp along last edge.

Round 1 * Ch 7, sc in next sc. Repeat from * across length of scarf to corner, sl st to first sc along next edge, ch 14, sl st to sc at base of ch-14 just made, * sl st to next sc, ch 14, sl st to base of ch. Repeat from * along edge. Sc in next corner, * ch 7, sc in next sc of first row of border. Repeat from * until next corner, then sc in this corner. * Ch 14, sl st to base sc, sl st to next sc. Repeat from * along remainder of edge.

Fringe Extension

Row 1A Sl st through 7 chs of last ch-14 lp made, * ch 14, sl st back in same ch-14 sp, sl st in ch-14 sp of next lp. Repeat from *, ending with sl st to last lp on edge; turn.

Row 2A Repeat row 1A. Knot yarn and cut, leaving a 6" end.

Row 1B Make a sl kn on hook with silver yarn, leaving a 6" end. Sl st to first ch-14 lp of first rnd at other edge of scarf. Repeat from * in Row 1A.

Row 2B Repeat row 2A.

Chain Fringe Make a sl kn with silver yarn on hook, leaving a 6" end. Sl st to first ch-14 lp of row 2A or row 2B at edge of scarf. (Ch 50, sl st in same lp) 3 times. Knot yarn and cut, leaving a 6" end.

Repeat the above for each lp of rows 2A and 2B, using colors to correspond to rows in the body of the scarf.

Finishing Hide all loose ends according to Finishing directions in Part I.

Summer Playsuit

Materials

3 skeins (2 oz. each) of 2-ply acrylic sport yarn in color A
3 skeins of same yarn in lighter contrasting color B
1 No. 8 crochet hook (steel)
1 size F crochet hook
1 snap fastener 3/8" in diameter.
yarn needle
Gauge 4 sts = 1"; 4 rows = 1½"; size F hook.

Crochet

NOTE: Instructions are for a ladies' Small size; Medium and Large sizes are in parentheses.
Shorts The shorts are made in 4 sections, then joined and bordered.
Right Front Make a sl kn on size F hook with color A yarn, leaving a 5" end. Ch 45 (46, 47); turn.
Row 1 Sc in 2nd ch from hook and in each of the next 2 (3, 4) chs. Insert hook into next ch, yoh, pull through st, then yoh with color B yarn, leaving a 5" end, and pull through 2 lps, completing sc with color B yarn. Do not cut color A yarn, but "strand" for next 3 sts (see instructions set out in Changing Colors in Mid-Row in Part I). Work a dc in each of the next 3 chs, and a 4th dc up to the next-to-last step (2 lps on hook). Yoh with strand of color A (without pulling) and complete 4th dc. Strand color B to await next color change, * sc in next 3 chs, complete 4th sc with color B, dc in next 3 chs, complete 4th dc with color A. Repeat from * until end of row. End row with 4th sc of color A. Ch 2 (counts as 1 dc); turn.
Rows 2–7 Sk first sc, dc in every sc of pr r, sc in every dc of pr r, changing colors in last st of each group. Ch 1 for even-numbered rows to turn, ch 2 for odd-numbered rows (even rows).

Row 8 (dec row) Work pat as in pr r, dec 2 sts in last 4 sts (see Decreasing instructions in Part I). Do *not* ch; turn.
Row 9 (dec row) Dec 2 sts in first 4 sts, work even for remainder of row. Ch 2; turn [40 (41, 42) sts made].
Rows 10, 11 Repeat 8th and 9th rows, but do not ch at end of 11th row [36 (37, 38) sts made].
Row 12 Dec 1 st in first 2 sts, work pat even to end. Ch 1; turn.
Row 13 Work pat, dec 1 st in last 2 sts. Do not ch; turn.
Rows 14, 15 Repeat 12th and 13th rows [32 (33, 34) sts made].
Rows 16–22 (22, 23) Work pat even, as in rows 2–7. At end of the last row, knot working color yarn and cut both colors, leaving 5" ends.
Left Back Repeat all of the above.

Left Front Repeat as for Right Front up to and including the 7th row.
Row 8 Repeat 9th row as for Right Front.
Row 9 Repeat 8th row as for Right Front.
Rows 10, 11 Repeat 8th and 9th rows, above.
Row 12 Repeat 13th row as for Right Front.
Row 13 Repeat 12th row as for Right Front.
Rows 14, 15 Repeat 12th and 13th rows, above.
Rows 16–22 (22, 23) Repeat as for Right Front.

Right Back Repeat Left Front. Using a yarn needle and the proper color yarn for each striped section, join (according to Joining instructions in Part I) all 4 sections together, with the dec areas forming the crotch and center seams and the even sections forming the side seams.

Border at Waist
Round 1 Make a sl kn with color A yarn on size F hook, leaving a 5" end. Sc in first st at either side seam at top of shorts. Sc for 0 (1, 2) more sts, then insert hook into top strands of next 2 sts and work a sc (1 dec made). Sc in next st. * Sc in next st, 1 sc in next 2 sts together (dec as before), sc in next st. Repeat from * up to stripe at next side seam. For Medium and Large sizes, add (1, 2) sc in each color A band at side seam, then work same pat around to last color A band. For Medium and Large sizes, add (1, 2) extra sc in this band. End with sl st to first sc made.
Round 2 Ch 1; turn. Sc in every sc of pr rnd. End with sl st to ch-1 sp.
Round 3 Repeat 2nd rnd.
Round 4 Ch 3, dc in sc at base of ch-3, * ch 2, sk next 2 sc, dc in next sc up to the next-to-last step (2 lps on hook), dc in next sc up to next-to-last step (3 lps on hook), yoh, pull through 3 lps (1 joined dc made). Repeat from * all around, ending with sl st in top of ch-3. Ch 1; turn.
Round 5 Sc in first joined dc, * sc in each ch sp of next ch-2, sc in next joined dc. Repeat from * all around, ending with sl st in first sc. Ch 1; turn.
Round 6 Sc in every sc around, sl st to first sc; turn.
Round 7 Sl st loosely in every sc around. Knot yarn and cut, leaving a 5" end.

Belt Make a sl kn on No. 8 steel hook with color A yarn, leaving a 5" end. Ch 5; turn.
Row 1 Sc in 2nd ch from hook and in each ch across. Ch 2; turn.
Row 2 Sk first sc and dc in each sc across. Ch 1; turn.
Row 3 Sc in every dc across. Ch 2; turn.
Row 4, etc. Repeat 2nd and 3rd rows alternately until belt fits comfortably on hipline when woven through the joined dc in Border at Waist, allowing a ½" overlap for snap. Knot yarn and cut, leaving a 5" end.
Finishing Hide all loose ends according to Finishing instructions in Part I. Sew snap parts to ends of belt with matching sewing thread.

Halter Instructions given are for bust sizes 30–32; 34–36 and 36–38 are in parentheses.

Make a sl kn on size F hook with color A yarn, leaving a 5" end. Ch 27 (28, 29); turn.
Left Side
Row 1 Sc in 2nd ch from hook and in next 0 (1, 2) chs. Change to color B in next ch, as in the first row of Shorts, "stranding" color A behind work. Dc in each of the next 3 chs, change back to color A in the 4th ch, repeating the pat as for Shorts to end of row. Ch 2 (counts as 1 dc), turn.
Rows 2–16 (18, 18) Work pat as for Shorts, double-crocheting in every sc of pr r, single-crocheting in every dc of pr r, skipping first sc when beg a row with dc, chaining 1 to turn for a row that begins with sc, chaining 2 for one that begins with dc, counting the ch-2 as 1 dc, and changing colors in the last st of each band. At the end of the last row, knot yarn and cut, leaving a 12" end.
Right Side Make a sl kn on size F hook with color A yarn, leaving a 5" end. Ch 27 (28, 29); turn.
Row 1 Sc in 2nd ch from hook and in each of the next 2 chs. Change to color B in next ch. Repeat pat as for Left Side [26 (27, 28) sts made]. Ch 2; turn.
Rows 2–16 (18, 18) Repeat as for Left Side, except at the end of the last row, ch 1; turn.
Neckstrap
Row 1 Still with color A, sc in each of first 4 sts. Ch 2; turn.

Row 2 Sk first sc, dc in next 3 sc. Ch 1; turn.
Row 3 Sc in top of ch-2 and in each dc across. Ch 2; turn.
Row 4, etc. Repeat 2nd and 3rd rows alternately until strap measures 11¾" (12", 12½"). At the end of the last row, knot yarn and cut, leaving a 12" end.

With wrong sides of both sections facing you, join color A band at end of the last row of Left Side to color A band at beg of last row of Right Side, using a yarn needle and the 12" end of color A yarn. Then, being careful not to twist Neckstrap, join its end to the corresponding color A band at beg of last row of Left Side with the 12" end.

Edging Make a sl kn on size F hook with color A, leaving a 5" end. With right side of halter facing you, sl st to *bottom* of first st on foundation ch at beg of the first row of Right Side.

Row 1 Dc in same st (in top strands), * ch 1, sk next st along foundation ch, work a joined dc as in 4th rnd of Border at Waist in bottoms of next 2 sts. Repeat from * along ch row, round corner, and work same pat, skipping a row sp and working a joined dc in next 2 row sp. Work a joined dc centered on the seam that joins both sections and work the same pat along the Left Side, ending at end of the first row of Left Side. Knot yarn and cut, leaving a 5" end.

Halter Ties Make a sl kn on No. 8 hook with color A yarn, leaving a 5" end. With wrong side of work facing you, sc in the top of 1 st of the joined dc of Edging at the center seam of Halter. Sc again in bottom of the same st, ch 2, turn, sk the last sc made, dc in first sc, ch 1, turn, sc in dc, sc in top of ch-2, * ch 2, turn, sk first sc, dc in next sc, ch 1, turn, sc in dc, sc in top of ch-2. Repeat from * until tie measures 18" (19", 20"). Knot yarn and cut, leaving a 5" end.

Repeat above for the other tie, working first 2 sc in other st of joined dc at center seam.

Finishing Hide all loose ends according to Finishing directions in Part I. Thread Halter Ties by weaving them over and under joined dc of Edging of their corresponding sides.

Ladies' Three-Season Gloves

Materials

9 balls (53 yds. each) of No. 8 pearl cotton yarn in color of your choice
1 size B crochet hook
yarn needle
Gauge 6 sts = 1"; 3 rows = 1"; 3 strands of yarn; size B hook.

Crochet

NOTE: Instructions are for a ladies' Medium size. Three strands of yarn are used throughout.
Right Glove Make a sl kn on size B hook with 3 strands of No. 8 pearl cotton yarn. Ch 39; turn.

Row 1 (wrong side) Hdc in 2nd ch from hook and in each ch across.
Row 2 (inc row) Ch 1; turn. Hdc in every hdc up to last st, 2 hdc in last st (1 inc made).
Row 3 (dec row) Ch 1; turn. Sk first hdc (1 dec made), hdc in next hdc and across row (38 sts made).
Row 4 Ch 1; turn. Hdc in first st and in each of next 28 sts. Ch 14; turn.
Row 5 Hdc in 2nd ch from hook and in each ch, continuing hdc to end of row (42 sts made).
Row 6 (inc row) Repeat 2nd row.
Row 7 (dec row) Repeat 3rd row (42 sts made).
Row 8 Ch 1; turn. Hdc for 29 sts. Ch 15; turn.
Row 9 Hdc in 2nd ch from hook, hdc in each ch, hdc in each of next 14 sts, ch 13 (for thumb), work 2 hdc in 2nd ch from hook, hdc in each of the next 11 sts, hdc in last hdc worked (on palm) before the ch-13 for the thumb; hdc in each of the remaining 15 sts on palm.
Row 10 Ch 1; turn. Hdc in 15 sts of palm and 14 sts of thumb; hdc in each of the 12 chs on thumb. Sk next st on palm, hdc in each of the next 26 sts, 2 hdc in last st (69 hdc made).

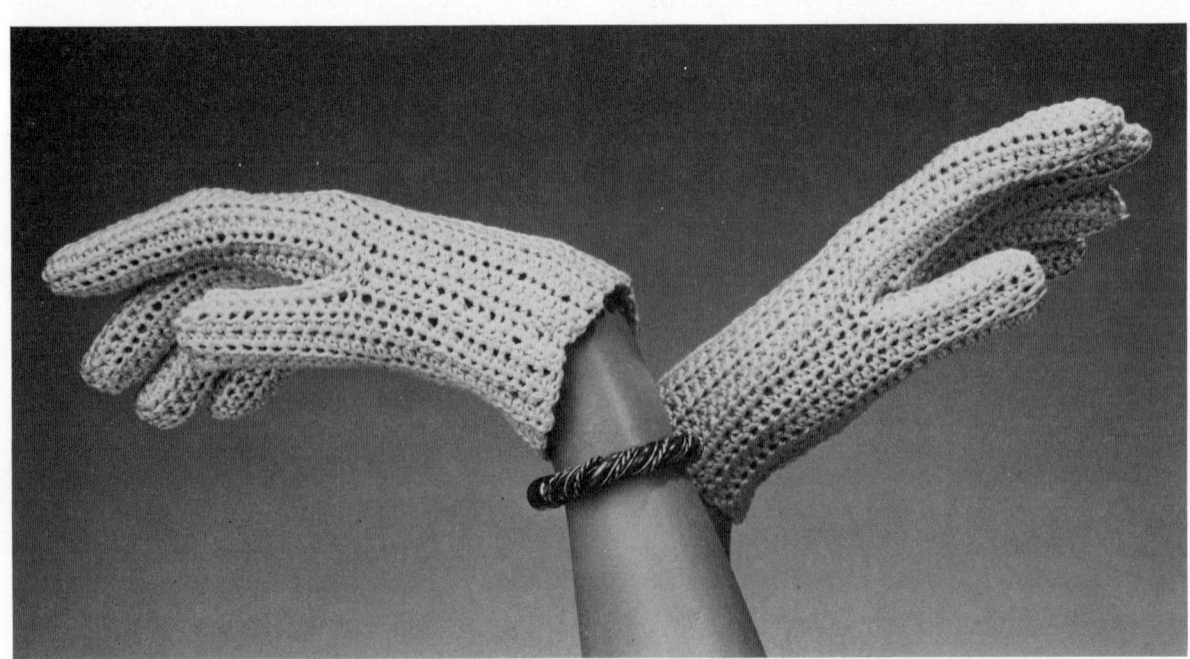

Row 11 Ch 1; turn. Sk first hdc, hdc in each of the remaining 68 sts.
Row 12 Ch 1; turn. Hdc for 54 sts, ch 14 (for forefinger); turn.
Row 13 Hdc in 2nd ch from hook and in every ch; continue to hdc to end of row (67 hdc made).
Row 14 Ch 1; turn. Hdc in 28 sts to tip of thumb, sk next st, hdc to end.
Row 15 Ch 1; turn. Sk first st, hdc in next 37 sts, fold thumb so that it is on the wrong side of palm. Sk 1 st at tip of thumb, insert hook in next hdc and in last hdc worked and work a sl st. Work 11 *sc* through top strands of each st on either side of thumb opening to join; hdc in remaining 16 sts of palm.
Row 16 Ch 1; turn. Work a hdc in each st and row sp around entire glove, excluding thumb and cuff end, making 2 hdc at center of each fingertip. Knot yarn and cut, leaving a 5″ end. Turn thumb right side out.
Back of Hand Repeat above instructions up to and including the 8th row (this time the first row will be on the right side).
Row 9 Turn. Hdc in 2nd ch from hook and in each ch; continue to hdc to end of row (43 hdc made).
Row 10 Ch 1; turn. Hdc across, 2 hdc in last st.
Row 11 Ch 1; turn. Sk first st, hdc across.
Row 12 Ch 1; turn. Hdc for 29 sts, ch 14 (for forefinger); turn.
Row 13 Hdc in 2nd ch from hook, hdc to end of row.
Row 14 Repeat 10th row, above (inc row).
Row 15 Repeat 11th row, above (42 hdc made).
Row 16 Repeat as for 16th row of palm.

Match up both sections of glove with both wrong sides out. Make a sl kn on hook with 3 strands of yarn and, inserting hook through top strands of the first pair of corresponding hdc at cuff end, join both sections with a row of *sc* around entire glove, ending at the other cuff end. Knot yarn and cut, leaving 5″ ends.
Finishing Hide all loose ends according to Finishing instructions in Part I.
Left Glove Repeat as for Right Glove, noting that the first row of the palm will be on the right side and working up to and including the 14th row.
Row 15 Ch 1; turn. Sk first hdc, work a hdc in each of the next 37 sts, fold thumb so that it is on the wrong side of palm. Sk 1 st, turn, insert hook in hdc just worked and in hdc after skipped hdc and work a sl st. Complete thumb joining and rest of row as for Right Glove.
Back of Hand Work the same as for Right Glove, noting that the first row will be wrong side for joining operation. Turn gloves inside out so that joined seams are on inside.

Men's Ski Sweater

Materials

6 skeins (4 oz. each) of 4-ply acrylic knitting worsted in main body color A (Suggestion: tan.)
2 skeins (4 oz. each) of same yarn in yoke color B (Suggestion: brown.)
2 skeins (4 oz. each) of same yarn in stripe color C (Suggestion: dark brown.)
1 size F crochet hook
1 size I crochet hook
yarn needle
Gauge 6 sts = 2"; 5 rows = 2"; 2 strands of yarn; size I hook.

Crochet

NOTE: Instructions are for a men's Small size; Medium and Large sizes are in parentheses.
Ribbed Border Make a sl kn on size F hook with 1 strand of color A yarn, leaving a 5" end. Ch 15; turn.
Row 1 Sc in 2nd ch from hook and in each ch across. Ch 1; turn.
Row 2, etc. Sc in back lp only (see Ribbed Crochet directions in Part I) of every sc across. Ch 1; turn. Repeat until strip measures 16½" (16¾", 17¼") when stretched slightly. Ch 1; turn.
Back
Row 1 Replace size F hook with size I hook. Working in row sp along top edge of Ribbed Border and yarning over hook with an additional strand of color A to complete first st with 2 strands of color A, * (2 sc (reg) in first row sp, sc in next) twice, 2 sc in next row sp. Repeat from * to end, producing 8 sc for every 5 rows of ribbing. The total number of sc must be odd. Ch 1; turn.
Row 2 Sc in first sc, * ch 1, sk next sc, sc in next sc. Repeat from * across row. Ch 1; turn.
Row 3 (first pat row) Sc in first sc, * sc in next ch-1 sp, ch 1, sk next sc. Repeat from * across, ending with sc in last ch-1 sp, sc in last sc. Ch 1; turn.
Row 4 (2nd pat row) Sc in first sc, * ch 1, sk next sc, sc in next ch-1 sp. Repeat from * across, ending with sc in last sc. Ch 1; turn.
Row 5, etc. (even rows) Repeat pat rows 3 and 4 alternately, until Back measures 8½" (9", 9"), excluding Ribbed Border.
Next Row (inc row) Inc 2 sc by working 2 sc in first and last sts of row. Ch 1; turn.
Next Rows Work even in pat rows for 2" more in length, then 1 more inc row as described above. Work even until length measures 11¾" (12¼", 12¼") (excluding ribbing), and then 1 more inc row. Work 1 more even row and, in the last st, change to 2 strands of color B yarn (see instructions set out in Changing Colors in Part I).
Armhole Shaping
Rows 1–6 (dec rows) Dec 1 st at beg of row (see Decreasing instructions in Part I), work pat across, dec 1 st at end of row. Change to 2 strands of color C in last st of 6th row.

Rows 7–9 Repeat dec rows in color C. Change to color B at end of 9th row.
Rows 10, 11 Repeat dec rows in color B. Change to color C.
Rows 12–14 Repeat dec rows in color C. Change to color B.
Rows 15–20 Repeat dec rows in color B.
Row 21A Work even in pat for 11 (10, 10) sts only. Knot yarn and cut, leaving 5" ends.
Row 21B Make a sl kn on size I hook with 2 strands of color B, leaving 5" ends. Sc to 11th (10th, 10th) st in on 20th row at other side of Back and work pat to end to match row 21A. Knot yarn and cut, leaving 5" ends.
Front Work as for Back, starting with Ribbed Border, up to and including the 17th row of Armhole Shaping.
Neck Shaping
Row 18A Work pat even for 16 (15, 15) sts. Ch 1; turn.
Row 19A Dec 1 st at beg, work pat, dec 1 st at end. Ch 1; turn.
Row 20A Dec 1 st at neck edge only, the remainder of row to be worked even in pat.
Row 21A Repeat row 19A. Knot yarn and cut, leaving 5" ends.
Rows 18B–21B Make a sl kn on hook with 2 strands of color B yarn. Sc in 16th (15th, 15th) st in on 17th row of other side of Front, then repeat rows 18A–21A.
Sleeves Using size F hook and 1 strand of color A yarn, repeat instructions for Ribbed Border, stopping crochet when strip measures 7¼" (7½", 7¾"). Ch 1; turn.
Rows 1, 2 Repeat as for rows 1 and 2 for Back.
Rows 3–15 Repeat pat rows. Inc 1 st at beg and end of rows 3, 6, 9, 12 and 15.
Row 16, etc. Work pat even until sleeve measures 12¼" (12¾", 13½"), excluding Ribbed Border. Then work 2 more inc rows as in 3rd row. Pick up color B in last st of last row.
Armhole Shaping
Rows 1–6 Work pat in color B. Dec 1 st at beg and end of rows 1, 3 and 5. Change to color C at end of 6th row.
Rows 7–9 Work as for rows 1–6 in color C. Dec in 7th and 9th rows. Change to color B.
Rows 10, 11 Work pat in color B. Dec in 11th row. Change to color C.
Row 12 Work pat in color C. Dec 1 st at beg and end of row.
Row 13 Dec 2 sts at beg and end.
Row 14 Repeat 12th row, above. Change to color B.
Rows 15–19 Repeat 12th and 13th rows, alternately. Knot yarn and cut, leaving 5" ends.

Repeat all of the above for other sleeve. Using a yarn needle, join sleeve seams for each sleeve; then join front to back with side and shoulder seams, according to Joining instructions in Part I. Join sleeves to armholes.
Collar Make a sl kn on size I hook with 2 strands of color B yarn. With right side of sweater facing you, sc in the center of the 20th row on Back. Work 42 (45, 45) sc around neckline, with dec at both shoulder seam areas to form a smooth collar line. End rnd with sl st to first sc made. Work 2 more rnds of sc. Knot yarn and cut, leaving 5" ends.
Finishing Hide all loose ends according to Finishing instructions in Part I.

Boys' Hooded Sweater

Materials

4 (4, 5) skeins (4 oz. each) of 4-ply wool or acrylic yarn in color of your choice
1 size I crochet hook
1 size J crochet hook
1 separating zipper [16" (17", 17")] in matching color
sewing needle and thread
yarn needle
Gauge 4 sts = 1¾"; 4 rows = 1¼"; size J hook.

Crochet

NOTE: Instructions are given for a boys' size 8; sizes 10 and 12 are in parentheses.
Ribbed Border Make a sl kn on size I hook, leaving a 5" end. Ch 8; turn.
Row 1 Sc in 2nd ch from hook and in each ch across. Ch 1; turn.
Rows 2–66 (68, 70) Sc in back lp only (see Ribbed Crochet instructions in Part I) of every sc across. Ch 1; turn.
Body
Row 1 Replace size I hook with size J hook. Sc (reg) in every row sp along top edge of Ribbed Border [67 (69, 71) sc made]. Ch 1; turn.
Row 2 (pat row) Sc in first sc, * sc in *base* of next sc (see arrow in Figure III-23), sc (reg) in next sc. Repeat from * across row, ending with sc (reg). Ch 1; turn.
Row 3, etc. (even rows) Repeat pat row 2 until work measures 6½" (7", 7½"). Place 2 safety-pin markers 16 (17, 18) sts in from each edge.
Next Row Work pat to marked st, then work a reg and base sc in marked and next sts (2-st inc made). Work in pat to next marker

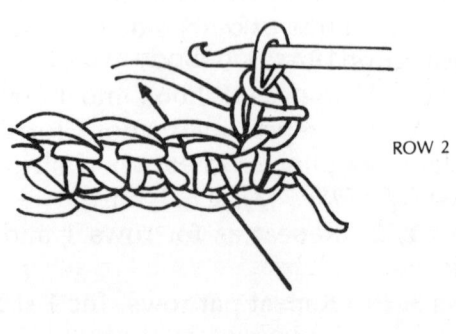
ROW 2

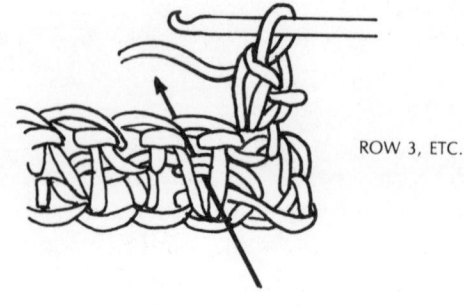
ROW 3, ETC.

Figure III-23

and inc 2 sts at this marker. Work even to end. Ch 1; turn.
Next Rows Work even in pat until work measures 11½″ (12″, 12½″).
Armhole Shaping
Row 1 Work pat for 14 (15, 16) sts, dec 1 st in next 2 sts (see Decreasing instructions in Part I). Ch 1; turn.
Rows 2–4 Work even in pat.
Row 5 Work even. Dec 1 st at armhole.
Rows 6–17 Repeat rows 2–5 three times more.
Row 18, etc. Work even in pat until height measures 15½″ (16½″, 17½″), ending last row at neck edge.
Neck Shaping
Row 1 Sk 2 sts at beg, dec 1 st in next 2 sts, work pat to end. Ch 1; turn.
Row 2 Work even in pat.
Row 3, etc. Work 1 row, decreasing 1 st at neck edge, 1 row even, until 7 (8, 9) sts remain. Knot yarn and cut, leaving a 5″ end.

Make a sl kn on hook, leaving a 5″ end. Sc in first sc at other edge of last row of Body and repeat Armhole Shaping and Neck Shaping to match.
Back
Row 1 Make a sl kn on hook, leaving a 5″ end. Insert hook into 19th (20th, 21st) st in from edge on last row of Body in back. Dec 1 st in first 2 sts, work pat across, dec 1 st at other end in 19th and 20th (20th and 21st, 21st and 22nd) sts in from other edge. Ch 1; turn.
Rows 2–4 Work even in pat.
Row 5 Dec 1 st at each armhole end.
Rows 6–17 Repeat rows 2–5 3 times. Mark the group of 4 center sts on 17th row with 2 safety pins, 1 at each end of group.
Neck Shaping
Row 1 Work pat to st before first marker, dec 1 st in this and next st. Ch 1; turn.
Row 2 Work even in pat.
Row 3, etc. Work 1 row, decreasing 1 st at neck edge, 1 row even, until 7 (8, 9) sts remain. Knot yarn and cut, leaving a 5″ end.

Make a sl kn on hook, leaving a 5″ end. Sc to st at other end of 17th row of Back and repeat Neck Shaping. Using a yarn needle, join front to Back according to Joining instructions in Part I.

Hood
Row 1 Make a sl kn on hook, leaving a 5″ end. Sc in first st at upper corner of right front and work in pat up to first shoulder seam. Continue in pat, making 2 sts in every st across back of neck up to next shoulder seam; then work even in pat to other end. Ch 1; turn.
Row 2, etc. Work even in pat until hood measures 8¾″ (9″, 9¼″). Knot yarn and cut, leaving a 5″ end.

Join ends of last row tog and then back to the point of the hood.
Sleeve Using size I hook, repeat instructions for Ribbed Border for 14 rows. Ch 1; turn. Replace with size J hook.
Row 1 Work 2 sc (reg) in each of the first 2 row sp along top edge of Ribbed Border, 1 sc in next sp, then (2 sc in next sp, 1 sc in each of next 2 sps) 3 times, 1 sc in each of next 2 sp, 2 sc in last sp (19 sc made). Ch 1; turn.
Rows 2–5 Work even in pat.
Row 6 Inc 1 st at beg and end of row.
Rows 7–24 Work 5 even rows, 1 row of inc (6th row), 3 more times.
Row 25, etc. Work even in pat until sleeve measures 13¾″ (14¼″, 14¾″).
Next Row Sk first st, dec 1 st in next 2 sts, work pat until 3 sts remain. Dec 1 st in next 2 sts, sk last st. Ch 1; turn.
Next Rows Work 1 even row, 1 row decreasing 1 st at each end, until 8 (9, 10) sts remain. Knot yarn and cut, leaving a 5″ end.

Repeat Sleeve instructions, above, for the other sleeve. Join sleeve seams; then join sleeves to armhole openings.
Pocket Make a sl kn on hook, leaving a 5″ end. Ch 14; turn.
Row 1 Sc (reg) in 2nd ch from hook and in each ch across. Ch 1; turn.
Rows 2–7 Work even in pat.
Row 8 Work in pat until 5 sts remain, dec 1 st in next 2 sts. Ch 1; turn.
Rows 9–17 Work 1 even row, 1 row decreasing 1 st at same edge as dec in 8th row. Ch 1; turn.
Row 18, etc. Work even until pocket measures 6″ (6″, 6½″) high, ending at dec edge.

Work 2 rows of reg sc along dec edge, chaining 1 to turn at end of first row. Knot yarn and cut, leaving a 5" end. Repeat all of Pocket instructions for other pocket. Join pockets to fronts, right at ribbed border and front edge, with both curved sections facing back.

Edging Make a sl kn on hook, leaving a 5" end. Sc in first st at bottom corner of ribbed border. Work 2 rows of reg sc around both front edges and hood, chaining 1 to turn at end of first row. Knot yarn and cut, leaving a 5" end.

Ties Make a sl kn on hook, leaving a 5" end. Ch to measure 39" (40", 42"). Tie a double knot at end of ch and cut yarn, leaving a 5" end. Thread ch through last sc row in hood edging, beg and ending in first row of Hood.

Finishing Sew zipper to front edging. Hide all loose ends according to Finishing instructions in Part I.

Part IV
Crochet for the Home

Fruit Basket

Materials

2 balls (105 yds. each) of 2-ply jute wrapping twine
1 size J crochet hook
yarn needle
safety pin

Crochet

Make a sl kn on size J hook with twine. Ch 4 loosely, then sl st to first ch to form ring.
Round 1   2 sc in each ch around (8 sc made).
Rounds 2, 3   2 sc in each sc around (32 sc made).
Round 4   Sc in every sc around. Mark last sc with a small safety pin which will be moved to the last st of each subsequent rnd.
Round 5   Sc in first sc, * hdc in next sc, sc in next sc. Repeat from * all around. Move marker.
Round 6   Hdc in first sc, * sc loosely in left vertical strand only of next hdc (see arrow in Figure IV-1), hdc in next sc. Repeat from * all around. Move marker.

Figure IV-1

Round 7 (inc rnd)   Sc (reg) in first hdc, * hdc in next sc, [1 sc (reg) and 1 hdc in next st] twice (1 inc made), sc (reg) in next hdc. Repeat from * all around, ending with (sc and dc) in last sc (48 sts made).
Round 8   Repeat 6th rnd.
Round 9   Repeat 7th rnd (72 sts made).
Round 10 (even rnd)   Sc (reg) in first hdc, * hdc in next sc, sc (reg) in next hdc. Repeat from * around.
Rounds 11–18   Repeat 6th and 10th rnds alternately.
Round 19 (dec rnd)   Sc (reg) in first st, * sk next st, hdc in next st (dec made), sc in next st. Repeat from * all around (48 sts made).
Round 20   Repeat 6th rnd, then sl st to first st of 20th rnd. Turn.
Round 21   Work a rnd of reverse st (see instructions in Part I), then join with sl st to first reverse st. Knot twine and cut, leaving an 8" end.
Finishing   Hide end according to Finishing instructions in Part I.

Op-Art Bedspread / Wall Hanging

Based on an original Spyros Horemis design, this ambitious project will completely transform any room that it decorates with its hypnotic eye-catching qualities.

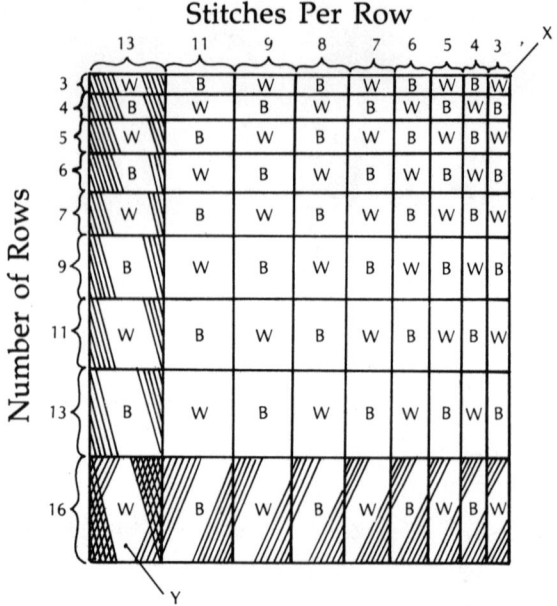

Figure IV-2

Materials

27 skeins (3½ oz. each) of 4-ply wool or acrylic yarn in black
27 skeins of same yarn in pure white
1 size D crochet hook
yarn needle
81 envelopes

Preparation and Construction

Before starting the crochet, it is important that you become completely familiar with the way this bedspread is constructed. Comprised of 2,916 individually crocheted black-and-white rectangles which are joined, using a yarn needle, the main consideration presented is one of bookkeeping, rather than crochet.

Figure IV-2 illustrates the pat layout of a quarter-section of 1 panel, the entire piece consisting of 9 panels. The number of sts in each row and the number of rows in each rectangle are easily determined from Figure IV-2. Rectangles X and Y indicate the smallest and largest rectangles in the quarter-section and in the panel.

Figure IV-3 shows how 4 quarter-sections are assembled to produce 1 panel. Note that the quarter-section of Figure IV-2 appears as section 1, which is larger than any of the other quarter-sections. The shaded areas of Figure

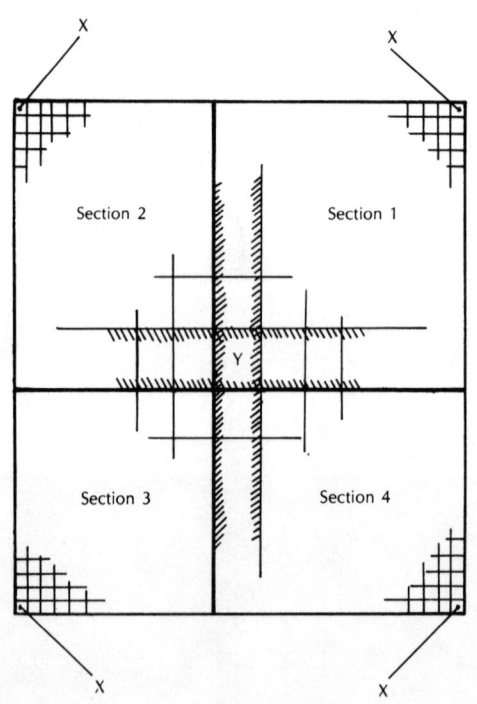

Figure IV-3

IV-3 correspond to the shaded areas of Figure IV-2, representing the bands of rectangles with the largest number of sts per row and largest number of rows. The important fact to note from Figure IV-3, which is the key to the assembly process, is that starting from rectangle X in the upper right-hand corner of section

OP-ART BEDSPREAD / WALL HANGING

1, the number of sts per row increases as you move to the left, reaches a maximum in the shaded area, and then decreases in the same symmetrical pat until you reach rectangle X again in the upper left-hand corner. Similarly, the number of rows in each rectangle increases as you move down from rectangle X, reaches a maximum, and then decreases in the same pat back to rectangle X.

Figure IV-4 illustrates the final arrangement of the 9 panels, indicating that rectangles X and Y are white in 5 of the panels, black in 4.

Three general rules should suffice to prevent any confusion in the joining operation:

1. Black edges should always be joined to white edges, and vice versa.
2. Rectangles with the same number of rows should always be joined when joining row edges; rectangles with the same number of sts per row should be joined when joining st edges.
3. Rectangle X should be the same color in all 4 corners of a panel, and should also be the same color as rectangle Y.

To simplify the bookkeeping operation, label 81 ordinary stationery envelopes (preferably the large size) with the st and row dimensions of each rectangle given in Figure IV-2, i.e., 3S x 3R, 4S x 3R, 5S x 3R, etc. In addition, the number of pieces required of each rectangle to make 1 panel should appear on each envelope, this number being 4 for all rectangles in Figure IV-2 with the exception of the shaded rectangles. Only 2 pieces are required for each of these except rectangle Y, in which only 1 is required.

Finally, each envelope should be labeled with either the letter B or the letter W to indicate whether the rectangles should be in black or in white. To begin with, label them in accordance with the B and W pattern shown in Figure IV-2. It is recommended that you first crochet all of the rectangles to complete 1 panel, storing them in the proper envelopes as labeled. Then, taking 1 rectangle from each envelope, join them in accordance with Figure IV-2. Again taking 1 piece from each envelope, with the exception of the vertical shaded band in Figure IV-2, join to form section 2; then join section 2 to section 1. Assemble section 3 without using any of the rectangles in either of the shaded bands; then join to section 2. Finally, assemble section 4 with the remaining rectangles and complete your first panel.

Repeat the above procedure 4 more times to complete the 5 panels in which rectangles X and Y are white. Then change the labeling of each envelope, crossing out the letter B and substituting the letter W, and vice versa. Work the 4 remaining panels as before; then join all 9 panels in accordance with Figure IV-4.

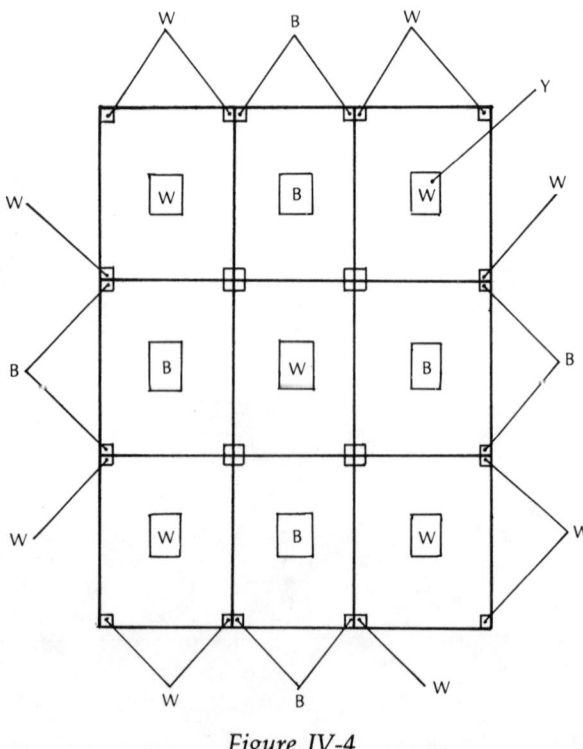

Figure IV-4

Gauge 4 sts = 1"; 4 rows = 1"; size D hook.

Crochet

NOTE: The bedspread measures approximately 9' x 7', which will generously fit a standard-size double bed.

Make a sl kn on size D hook with the proper color yarn for the rectangle you are working, leaving a 6" end for rectangles up to 7S x 7R, an 8" end for rectangles between 7S x 7R and 9S x 11R, or a 10" end for larger rectangles. Ch the amount equal to the number of sts per row required for your rectangle; then ch 1 more. Turn.

Row 1 Sc in 2nd ch from hook and in each ch across. Ch 1; turn.

Row 2, etc. Sc in every sc across. Ch 1; turn.

Work until the proper number of rows has been completed. Knot yarn and cut, leaving an end equal to the length of your sl kn end.

Join, using yarn needle and loose ends left, according to Joining instructions in Part I.

Finishing Hide loose ends according to Finishing instructions in Part I.

NOTE: For conversion to a wall hanging, see instructions under Scintillating Blanket/Wall Hanging.

Grid Curtain

Materials

1 ball (95 yds.) of No. 8 pearl cotton yarn in variegated colors
1 ball (53 yds.) of No. 5 pearl cotton yarn in solid color to match 1 tone of variegated yarn
1 ball (53 yds.) of No. 5 pearl cotton yarn in solid color to match another tone of variegated yarn
1 size J crochet hook
yarn needle

NOTE: The above amounts apply for every 90 square inches of curtain area. To compute the total amount of yarn needed, multiply the length of the curtain in inches by the width in inches. Double this figure if 2 curtains are required; then divide the result by 90. This will give the number of balls needed for each of the 3 colors specified above.

Crochet

Make a sl kn on size J hook with 2 strands of variegated No. 8 pearl cotton yarn and 1 strand each of the No. 5 yarns in the solid colors, leaving 6" ends. Ch amount to measure the desired width of your curtain, avoiding any stretching of the ch while measuring.

Row 1 Sc in 2nd ch from hook and in each ch across. Ch 1; turn.
Row 2 Sc in every sc across. Ch 1; turn.

Row 3 Sc in every sc across. Ch 6 (counts as 1 trc); turn.
Row 4 Sk first st, long trc in next st to match the length of ch-6, and long trc in every sc across. Ch 1; turn.
Rows 5, 6 Sc in every st across. Ch 1; turn.
Row 7 Sc in every sc across. Ch 6; turn.
Row 8 Repeat 4th row.
Rows 9–11 Repeat rows 5–7.
Row 12, etc. Repeat rows 4–7 until curtain measures desired length, ending with 3 sc rows. Knot yarn and cut, leaving 5" ends.
Finishing Hide all loose ends according to Finishing instructions in Part I. Hang curtain by threading a tubular-type curtain rod over and under the trc in the 4th row.

New York Skyline Wall Hanging

This is an interesting wall decoration that makes use of those leftover scraps of yarn and expresses your own color-blending creativity.

Materials

1 skein (3½ oz.) of 4-ply acrylic yarn in sky blue
various yarn scraps in up to 19 colors, including, if possible, silvers, golds, purples, grays, and browns
1 piece of 3-ply stiff cardboard, 2' x 2', for mounting
1 size I crochet hook
yarn needle
safety pins
yardstick
pencil
heavy scissors or utility knife

Crochet

Use 1 strand of the 4-ply yarns and 2 strands of the 2-ply yarns. All sts are sc, ch 1 to turn at the end of each row. Consult Figure IV-5 for the number of sts in each color for each row, 1 square in the figure representing 1 st. Change to new color in the last st of previous color (see instructions for changing colors in Part I). In the few cases where a small part of a building covers part of the building behind it, thus requiring only a few sts in the foreground color before returning to the background color, "strand" the background color behind your work (see instructions on Changing Colors in Mid-Row in Part I). Otherwise, just let each ball dangle behind your work, pinning it with a safety pin to prevent unraveling, until required again in the next row. After completing a building, knot yarn and cut, leaving a 5" end.

Begin crochet by making a sl kn on your hook with the color you are going to use for the building at the extreme lower right-hand corner of Figure IV-5, leaving a 5" end. Ch 55 (do not count ch row as part of Figure IV-5). Turn. Work 3 sc in this color, beg in 2nd ch from hook. Complete 4th sc with next color, etc.

Mounting

Before mounting, be sure that all loose ends are on wrong side of work. Lay out crocheted piece on stiff cardboard so that it is flat and rectangular. Using a pencil and the yardstick as a straightedge, mark a rectangle on the cardboard that is ½" longer and ½" wider than the crocheted piece, making sure that the corners are perfect right angles. Cut out

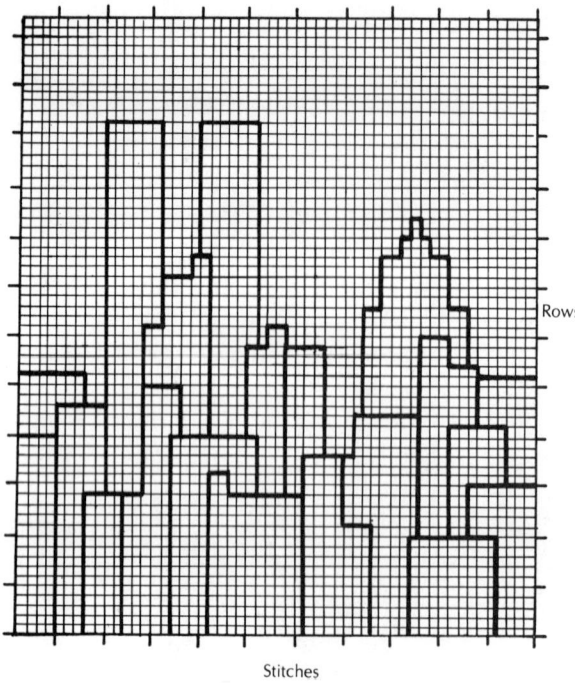

Figure IV-5

bring both edges of crochet over the cardboard so that about ¼" overlaps in back.

When reaching the left edge, weave around the corner and continue the same procedure horizontally. End by knotting firmly to the crocheted piece. Turn work over and adjust it so that the building lines are vertical.

The mounted piece may then be custom-framed or glued to a larger white cardboard rectangle to act as a mat border for standard framing.

rectangle with heavy scissors or utility knife and place it behind the crochet.

Knot a 36" piece of scrap yarn to a lp on the wrong side in the lower right-hand corner, as shown in Figure IV-6. Thread the other end through a yarn needle and weave it through the lps at the extreme top for about 1¼". Then bring it down and weave it through the bottom lps for the same distance. Repeat this process across, knotting in new yarn as needed and applying sufficient tension to

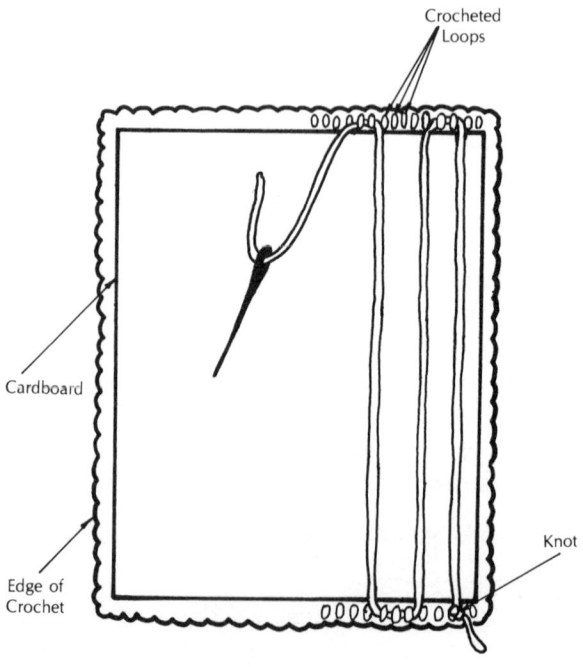

Figure IV-6

Scintillating Blanket / Wall Hanging

The scintillating effect in this blanket is produced by your selection of color blends in yarns of variegated tones.

Materials

54 skeins (4 oz. each) of 4-ply wool or acrylic yarn in variegated tones, with at least 2 skeins in each tone combination, and as many different tone combinations as possible (up to 27)
4 skeins (4 oz. each) of same type yarn, 2 in solid black and 2 in solid gold
1 size I crochet hook
yarn needle

Crochet

The blanket measures approximately 9' x 7', which will generously fit a standard-size double bed. Two strands are used throughout. It is recommended that each strand be from a different skein of variegated tones, but warm tones (i.e., reds, oranges, yellows) should be used together and cool tones (i.e., blues, greens, violets) should be used together. After finishing a band in a pair of warm-toned strands, the next band should contain cool tones, etc. All sts are sc; ch 1 to turn at the end of each row.

Skein changes should occur only in the last st of a row (see instructions on changing colors in Part I) so that all color bands will be completely homogeneous. With the yarns, hook and dimensions specified, you should easily get 5 rows per skein pair, with some yarn left over.

Begin crochet by selecting your first pair of variegated skeins. Make a sl kn on hook with 1 strand from each skein. Ch 335, or the amount to measure 8'6". Turn. Sc in 2nd ch from hook and in each ch across. Ch 1; turn; sc

in every sc across, etc. Leave 5" ends when changing skeins and at the end of crochet.
Edging
Round 1 Make a sl kn on hook with black yarn, leaving a 5" end. Sc in any ch base in center of ch row, with right side of work facing you. Sc across ch row to corner, work 3 sc in corner st, continue sc in row sps up edge and around entire blanket, working 3 sc in each corner. End by inserting hook into first sc of rnd, yoh with gold yarn, and complete sl st with gold. Cut black yarn, leaving a 5" end.
Round 2 Dc in every sc of first rnd. Complete last dc with black yarn. Cut gold yarn, leaving a 5" end.
Round 3 Sc in every dc, ending with sl st to first sc. Knot yarn and cut, leaving a 5" end.
Finishing Hide all loose ends according to Finishing instructions in Part I.

Conversion to Wall Hanging

Mark wall on which hanging is to be placed with 4 dots to indicate the corners of a rectangle that is 1' longer and 1' wider than the actual crocheted piece (points 1–4 in Figure IV-7). Drive 4 1" masonry, plasterboard, or ordinary headed nails (depending on the type of wall) into these locations, leaving about ¼" of the nailhead protruding. Then drive a series of nails in a similar manner, evenly spaced at a distance of 1' to 1½' in line with the corners, as illustrated in Figure IV-7.

Thread a section of black 4-ply yarn (or other material desired to suspend the hanging) about twice as long as the crocheted piece through a yarn needle. Tie the unthreaded end to nail 1 with a firm knot. Using the yarn needle, weave the yarn through 2 or 3 crocheted stitches 1 row in from the edge in the zigzag pattern shown in Figure IV-7, starting at the upper left-hand corner. The stitches caught by the yarn should be centered between the 2 nails above them, and the yarn should just be draped over the nails, without any wrapping or knotting. After completing top edge, tie yarn to nail 2 with a temporary single knot. The top edge of the

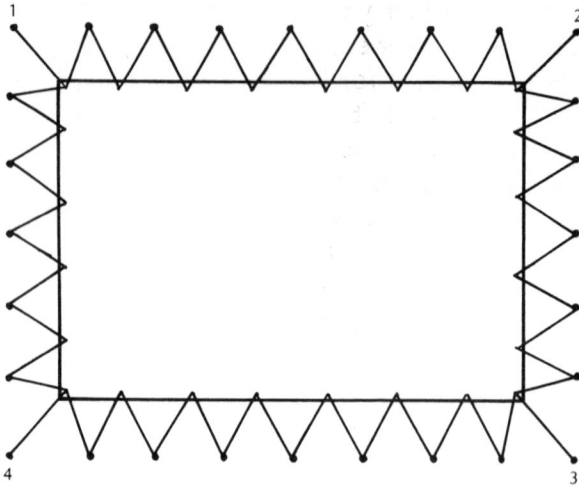

Figure IV-7

crocheted piece should be level and at a distance of 5" below a line formed by the nails. Adjust the tension and length of the yarn to achieve this, untying the knot at nail 2 if necessary. When properly adjusted, tie a firm knot at nail 2.

Thread another section of yarn through your needle, about twice the height of the hanging, and tie a firm knot to the upper right-hand corner of the crocheted piece with the unthreaded end. Zigzag this yarn down the right edge as before, tying a temporary knot at nail 3. Adjust yarn tension/length so that edge is 5" from nail line, and secure knot at nail 3.

Start bottom edge by tying another section of yarn to the crocheted piece at the lower right-hand corner and repeating the same

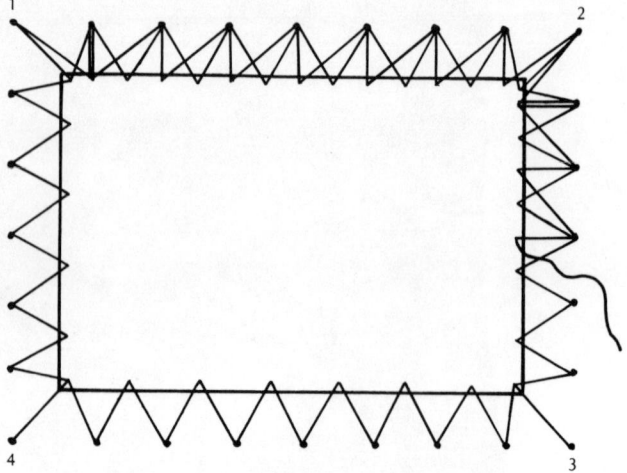

Figure IV-8

process. Adjust yarn tension/length so that upper and lower edges are level and hanging lies flat. Repeat for left edge, ending with a knot in upper left-hand corner of hanging.

Start a second round of weaving with a firm knot at nail 1, this time catching the edge of crocheted piece at a point directly below the next nail (Figure IV-8). Run the yarn over the nail, back through the same point, then over the next nail. Pull this yarn just firmly enough to alleviate some of the tension of the original yarn, but not so firmly as to cause sagging. Then catch the edge directly below this nail, then on to the next. After wrapping around nail 2, catch the edge of the hanging directly to the left of the next nail down the right edge, then over this nail, back to the same point in the hanging, then on to the next nail. Repeat this pattern all around, adding yarn as needed and ending back at nail 1.

Repeat the second round once more, again starting at nail 1 but working counterclockwise, to produce the final configuration illustrated in Figure IV-9.

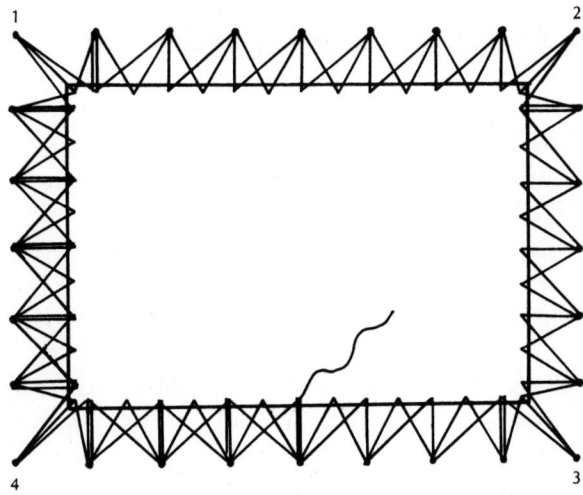

Figure IV-9

Oval Floor Mat

Suitable as a bath mat, this colorful shaggy mat will brighten any room in which it is used.

Materials

12 skeins (2 oz. each) of rug yarn for background color A (Suggestion: bright orange.)
5 skeins (2 oz. each) of same type yarn for outer stripe color B (Suggestion: lavender.)
2 skeins (2 oz. each) of same type yarn for inner stripe color C (Suggestion: aqua.)
1 size N crochet hook (3/8" diameter)
yarn needle
safety pins

Crochet

NOTE: Instructions are for an oval mat, approximately 42" x 30". Two strands of yarn are used throughout.

Make a sl kn on hook with 2 strands of color A, leaving 7" ends. Ch 23; turn.

Round 1 Work 2 lp sts (see instructions in Part I) with 1" lps in 2nd ch from hook. Mark first lp st with a small safety pin. Lp st in each ch across, 3 lp sts in last ch sp. Mark center st of this 3-st group with another safety pin. Continue lp st in base of chs, ending with lp st in same ch as first marked st (48 lp sts made).

Round 2 Work 2 lp sts in marked st, replace marker in first st made, lp st for next 10 sts. Work 2 lp sts in the next st (1 inc made), then work even in lp st until marker. Inc 1 st in marked st, move marker to first st in inc, work even for 10 more sts, inc 1 st in next st. Work even until next-to-last st (before marker). Insert hook into last st, yoh, pull through st, yoh with 2 strands of color C, and complete lp st with color C yarn. Cut color A yarn, leaving 7" ends (52 sts made).

Round 3 * Inc 1 st in marked st, move marker to 2nd st in inc, (work even for 8 sts, inc 1 st in next st) twice. Repeat from * 1 more time (58 sts made).

Round 4 * Inc 1 st in marked st, move marker to first st in inc, (work even for 4 sts, inc 1 st in 5th st) 4 times, work even to marked st. Repeat from * 1 more time (68 sts made).

Round 5 * Inc 1 st in marked st, move marker to 2nd st in inc, work even for 14 sts, inc 1 st in each of next 5 sts, work even to marked st. Repeat from * 1 more time (80 sts made).

Round 6 * Inc 1 st in marked st, move marker to first st, work even to next marker. Repeat from * 1 more time (82 sts made).

Round 7 * Inc 1 st in marked st, move marker to 2nd st, (work even for 3 sts, inc 1 st in 4th st) 9 times, work even to next marker. Repeat from * 1 more time, up to st before marker. Change back to color A in last st, as described in the 2nd rnd (102 sts made).

Round 8 * Inc 1 st in marked st, move marker to first st, (work even for 9 sts, inc 1 st in 10th st) 4 times, work even to next marker. Repeat from * 1 more time (112 sts made).

Round 9 * Inc 1 st in marked st, move marker to 2nd st, work even for 23 sts, inc 1 st in each of next 7 sts, work even to next marker. Repeat from * 1 more time (128 sts made).

Round 10 * Inc 1 st in marked st, move marker to first st, (work even for 8 sts, inc 1 st in 9th st) 6 times, work even to next marked st. Repeat from * 1 more time (142 sts made).

Round 11 * Inc 1 st in marked st, move marker to 2nd st, (work even for 9 sts, inc 1 st in 10th st) 7 times. Repeat from * 1 more time (158 sts made).

Round 12 * Inc 1 st in marked st, move marker to first st, (work even for 18 sts, inc 1 st in 19th st) 3 times, work even to next marker. Repeat from * 1 more time, up to st before marker. Change to color B in this st (166 sts made).

Round 13 * Inc 1 st in marked st, move marker to 2nd st, (work even for 19 sts, inc 1 st in 20th st) 3 times, work even to next marker.

Repeat from * 1 more time (174 sts made).
Round 14 * Inc 1 st in marked st, move marker to first st, work even for 39 sts, inc 1 st in each of next 6 sts, work even to marker. Repeat from * 1 more time (188 sts made).
Round 15 * Inc 1 st in marked st, move marker to 2nd st, work even to marker. Repeat from * 1 more time (190 sts made).
Round 16 * Inc 1 st in marked st, move marker to first st, (work even for 23 sts, inc 1 st in 24th st) 3 times, work even to marker. Repeat from * 1 more time (198 sts made).
Round 17 Repeat 15th rnd. Change to color A in last st (200 sts made).
Round 18 * Inc 1 st in marked st, move marker to first st, (work even for 19 sts, inc 1 st in 20th st) 4 times, work even to marker. Repeat from * 1 more time (210 sts made).
Rounds 19, 20 Work even, moving marker to st made in marked st.
Round 21 * Inc 1 st in marked st, (work even for 25 sts, inc 1 st in 26th st) 3 times, work even to next marker. Repeat from * 1 more time (218 sts made).
Round 22 Work 2 dc in every lp st around. End with sl st to first dc. Knot yarn and cut, leaving 7" ends.
Finishing Hide all loose ends according to Finishing instructions in Part I. To produce a pile effect, lps may be cut at the top with sewing scissors.

Shopping/Laundry Bag

Materials

6 skeins (2 oz. each) of rug yarn, 3 skeins each in 2 colors of your choice
1 size H crochet hook
1 size K crochet hook
1 size N crochet hook (3/8" diameter)
yarn needle
safety pins

Crochet

Make a sl kn with 1 strand of each color on size N hook, leaving 7" ends. Ch 50; turn.
Row 1 Sc in 2nd ch from hook, * ch 3, sk 3 chs, sc in next ch, ch 2, sl st in same sc. Repeat from * across, ending with sc in last ch. Ch 2; turn.
Row 2 Sc in first sc, * ch 3, sk 3 ch, sc in ch-2 sp, ch 2, sl st in same ch-2 sp. Repeat from * across, ending with sc in last sc. Ch 2; turn.
Rows 3–17 Repeat 2nd row. Fold bag in half, sl st to first sc of 17th row to join, ch 2, sl st to same sc. Knot yarn and cut, leaving 36" ends.

Using a yarn needle and the ends just left, join sides and bottom according to Joining instructions in Part I. Turn bag inside out.
Border Make a sl kn with 2 strands of 1 color on size K hook, leaving 7" ends.
Round 1 With right side of work facing you, sc in ch-2 sp above seam, * ch 3, sc in next ch-2 sp. Repeat from * all around, ending with sl st in first sc.
Round 2 Ch 3, sc in first sc, * ch 3, sc in next sc. Repeat from * all around, ending by inserting hook into first sc, yoh with 2 strands of other color, complete sl st with new color. Cut original color, leaving 7" ends.

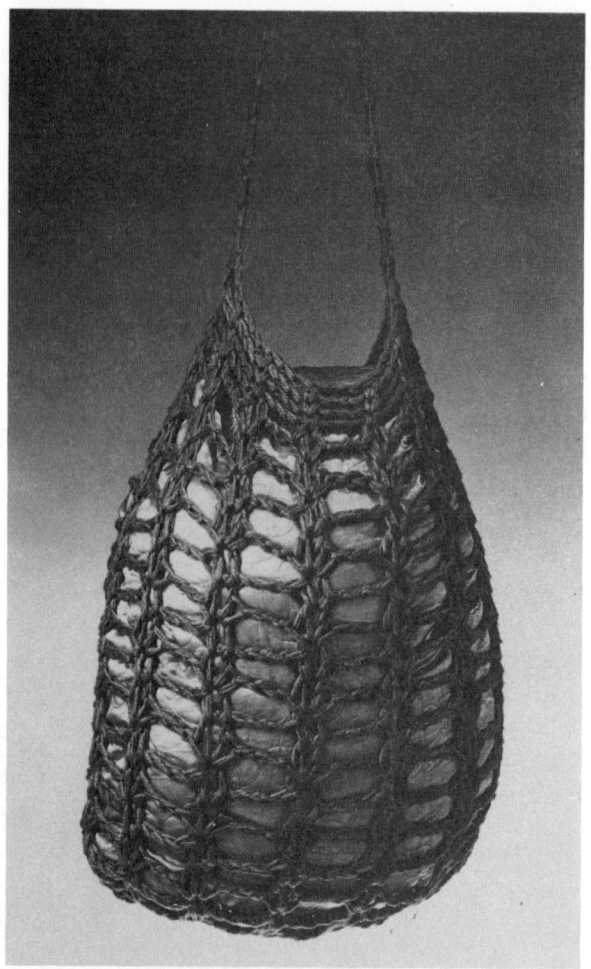

Rounds 3, 4 Ch 3, sc in first sc, * ch 3, sc in next sc. Repeat from * around, ending with sl st in first sc. At end of 4th rnd knot yarn and cut, leaving 7" ends.
Strap Fold work flatly in half so that seam is in center of back and each folded edge aligns with a sc of the 4th rnd of Border. Place a safety-pin marker in each of the edge sc. Make a sl kn with 2 strands of same color used for last rnd of Border on size H hook, leaving 5" ends.
Row 1 Sc in 3rd ch sp of ch-3 lp just before marked sc, sc in first ch sp of ch-3 lp just after marked sc, ch 1; turn.
Rows 2–53 Sc in each sc of pr r. Ch 1; turn.

Being careful not to twist strap, join to other side of bag by single-crocheting in first ch sp of ch-3 lps on either side of other marked sc. Knot yarn and cut, leaving 5" ends.
Finishing Hide all loose ends according to Finishing instructions in Part I.

Jute Planter

A macramelike appearance can be achieved with your crochet hook to dress up an ordinary ceramic flowerpot with this decorative planter.

Materials

1 ball (105 yds.) of 2-ply jute wrapping twine
1 size I crochet hook
safety pin
yarn needle
sewing scissors

Crochet

NOTE: Instructions are given for a standard 5" tall flowerpot with a top 6½" in diameter.

Make a sl kn on hook, leaving a 5" end. Ch 12, sl st to first ch to form ring.

Round 1 Ch 5, work a long dc to equal the length of the ch-5 in first ch just slip-stitched. Ch 1, * 2 long dc in next ch, ch 1. Repeat from * around, ending with sl st to top of ch-5 (23 long dc made).

Round 2 Ch 3, sk first dc, sc in first ch-1 sp, * ch 3, sk next dc, sc in next dc. Repeat from * around, ending with sl st to first ch sp of original ch-3.

Round 3 Sc in 2nd ch sp, * ch 3, sc in 2nd ch sp of next ch-3. Repeat from * around, ending with sl st to first ch sp of first ch-3 of this rnd.

Rounds 4–6 Repeat 3rd rnd.

Round 7 Sl st to 2nd ch sp, ch 5, long dc in every ch sp and sc around, ending with sl st to top of original ch-5 (52 long dc made).

Suspension Ch 100, sk 8 dc, sl st in 9th dc. Knot twine and cut, leaving a 5" end. Make a sl kn on hook, leaving a 5" end. Sk 7 dc past the point where your first ch is joined and sl st in 8th dc. Ch 100, sk 8 dc, sl st in 9th dc. Knot twine and cut, leaving a 5" end. Make a sl kn, sk 7 dc past last joining point, sl st in 8th dc, ch 100, sk 7 dc, sl st in 8th dc. Knot twine and cut, leaving a 5" end. Hide all loose ends according to Finishing instructions in Part I.

Bottom Decoration

Round A Make a sl kn on hook, leaving a 5" end. Sl st to any ch-1 sp of first rnd. Ch 13. Knot twine and cut, leaving a 20" end. * Make a sl kn on hook, leaving a 5" end. Sk 3 ch-1 sps past the last joining point and sl st to 4th ch-1 sp. Ch 13. Knot twine and cut, leaving a 20" end. Repeat from * once more.

Round B * Make a sl kn on hook, leaving a 5" end. Sk 1 ch-1 sp past the joining of a ch-13 of rnd A, sl st to next ch-1 sp. Ch 13. Knot twine and cut, leaving a 20" end. Repeat from * twice.

Ball Make a sl kn on hook, leaving a 20" end. Ch 3. Sl st to first ch to form ring.

Round 1 Ch 1. Place a safety-pin marker in this ch-1, sc in first ch just slip-stitched, 2 sc in each of next 2 ch, sl st to ch-1 that began rnd.

Round 2 Ch 1. Replace marker in this ch-1, sc in ch-1 just slip-stitched, 2 sc in each sc around, sl st to ch-1 that began rnd (11 sc made).

Round 3 Repeat 2nd rnd (23 sc made).

Round 4 Ch 1. Replace marker in this ch-1, * 2 sc in next sc, sc in next sc. Repeat from * around, ending with sl st to ch-1.

Round 5 Ch 1. Replace marker in this ch-1, sc in every sc around, sl st to ch-1.

Round 6, etc. Ch 1. Remove marker, sk first sc, * sc in next sc, sk next sc. Repeat from * until ball has an opening 1" in diameter. Stuff ball with scraps of jute or other material through this opening to form an oblate ball shape. Continue from * until ball is almost completely closed, leaving a small opening for bringing tassel strands through. Knot twine and cut, leaving a 20" end.

Attach ball to planter by inserting 20" ends left from rnds A and B through top of ball (first rnd sts), using your crochet hook or yarn needle. Knot these strands securely to sts which closed bottom opening, letting the ends hang down to form part of final tassel. Insert your hook through the ball from top to bottom and pull a pair of 20" strands of twine through the ball, knotting them tightly to each other on top of the ball at the point where the ch-13 ends meet. Cut excess ends close to knot. Repeat this process 8 times.

Bring the sl kn end made previous to the first rnd of Bottom Decoration through the ball to add to the tassel. Pull each individual tassel end down firmly, then trim tassel to an even length with sewing scissors. The planter may then be hung from a hook or bracket by the 3 suspension ch lps.

Finishing Hide all unused loose ends according to Finishing instructions in Part I.

Show Kitchen Towel

While it may never actually be used to dry dishes, this show towel will certainly improve the looks of your towel bar.

Materials

10 balls (95 yds. each) of No. 8 pearl cotton yarn in background color A
8 balls (95 yds. each) of same type yarn for trim and design in color B
1 size B crochet hook
yarn needle

Crochet

NOTE: Two strands of yarn are used throughout.

Make a sl kn on hook with (2 strands of) color A yarn, leaving 5″ ends. Ch 78; turn.
Row 1 (right side) Dc in 2nd ch from hook and in every ch across. Ch 1; turn (77 dc made).
Row 2 Sc in first dc, * (sc, ch 1, sc) in next dc (cluster made), sk next dc. Repeat from * to end of row, ending with sc in last dc. Ch 1; turn.
Row 3 (pat row) Sc in first sc, (sc, ch 1, sc) in first sc of 1st cluster, * (sc, ch 1, sc) in first sc of next cluster. Repeat from * across, ending with sc in last sc. Ch 1; turn.
Rows 4–16 Work in pat, repeating 3rd row. End 16th row with ch 3; turn.
Row 17 Sk first sc, dc in first sc of first cluster, sk ch-1 sp, dc in next sc of first cluster. * Dc in first sc of next cluster, sk ch-1 sp, dc in 2nd sc of same cluster. Repeat from * across, ending with dc in last sc. Knot yarn and cut, leaving 5″ ends.
Row 18 Make a sl kn on hook with (2 strands of) color B yarn and, with right side of work facing you, dc in ch-3 sp that began pr r. * Dc in sp between next 2 dc. Repeat from * across row. Ch 1; turn.
Row 19 Sc in first dc, * work (sc, ch 1, sc) cluster in next dc, sk next dc. Repeat from * across, ending with sc in last dc.
Rows 20, 21 Repeat pat row 3. End 21st row with ch 3; turn.
Row 22 Repeat 17th row.
Row 23 Repeat 18th row with color A instead of color B.
Row 24 Repeat 19th row.
Rows 25, 26 Repeat pat row 3. At end of the 26th row, ch 3; turn.
Row 27 Repeat 17th row.

Rows 28, 29 Repeat 18th and 19th rows.
Rows 30, 31 Repeat 3rd row, ending 31st row with ch 3; turn.
Row 32 Repeat 17th row.
Row 33 Repeat 18th row with color A yarn.
Row 34 Repeat 19th row.
Rows 35–55 Work in pat (3rd row).
Row 56 Work in pat, completing 7 clusters. For last sc of 8th cluster, insert hook into st, yoh, pull through st, yoh with color B yarn, and complete sc with color B. Cut color A yarn, leaving 5" ends. Work in pat until 9 clusters remain in row. Change back to color A, as described above, in next cluster and complete row in color A. Ch 1; turn.
Rows 57–62 Repeat 56th row, bringing all loose ends to wrong side with your crochet hook as you work.
Row 63 Work in pat, completing 4 clusters. Change to color B in 5th cluster and work in pat until 6 clusters remain in row. Change back to color A in next cluster and complete row in color A. Ch 1; turn.
Rows 64–94 Repeat 63rd row, bringing all loose ends to wrong side of work.
Rows 95–101 Repeat 56th row.
Rows 102–112 Repeat pat row 3 in color A, ending 112th row with ch 3; turn.
Rows 113–130 Repeat rows 17–34.
Rows 131–146 Repeat pat row 3, ending 146th row with ch 3; turn.
Row 147 Repeat 17th row. Knot yarn and cut, leaving 5" ends.
Finishing Hide all loose ends according to Finishing instructions in Part I.

Interwoven Tablecloth

This beautiful and versatile patterned piece can also be used as a curtain or bedspread.

Materials

1 skein (1¾ oz.) of acrylic perle twist yarn in each of 3 complementary colors
1 size F crochet hook
yarn needle
NOTE: The above amount applies for every 3 square feet of tablecloth area. To compute the total amount of yarn needed, multiply the length in feet by the width in feet of the tablecloth you require. Divide this figure by 3, which will give you the number of skeins needed for each of the 3 colors specified.

Crochet

NOTE: This tablecloth is composed of individually crocheted motifs in each of the 3 colors, which are joined as illustrated in the pattern in Figure IV-10.

Make a sl kn on hook with color you are using, leaving a 5" end. Ch 13; turn.
Row 1 Sc in 2nd ch from hook and in each of the next 5 ch, 2 sc in 6th ch, sc in each ch to end (13 sc made). Ch 1; turn.
Row 2 Sc in first sc, 2 sc in 2nd, sc in each of next 9 sc, 2 sc in next sc, sc in last sc (15 sc made). Ch 1; turn.
Row 3 Sc in first sc, 2 sc in 2nd sc, sc in each of next 11 sc, 2 sc in next sc, sc in last sc (17 sc made). Ch 1; turn.
Row 4 Sc in each of first 8 sc, 2 sc in 9th sc, sc in each of next 8 sc (18 sc made). Knot yarn and cut, leaving a 4" end.

INTERWOVEN TABLECLOTH

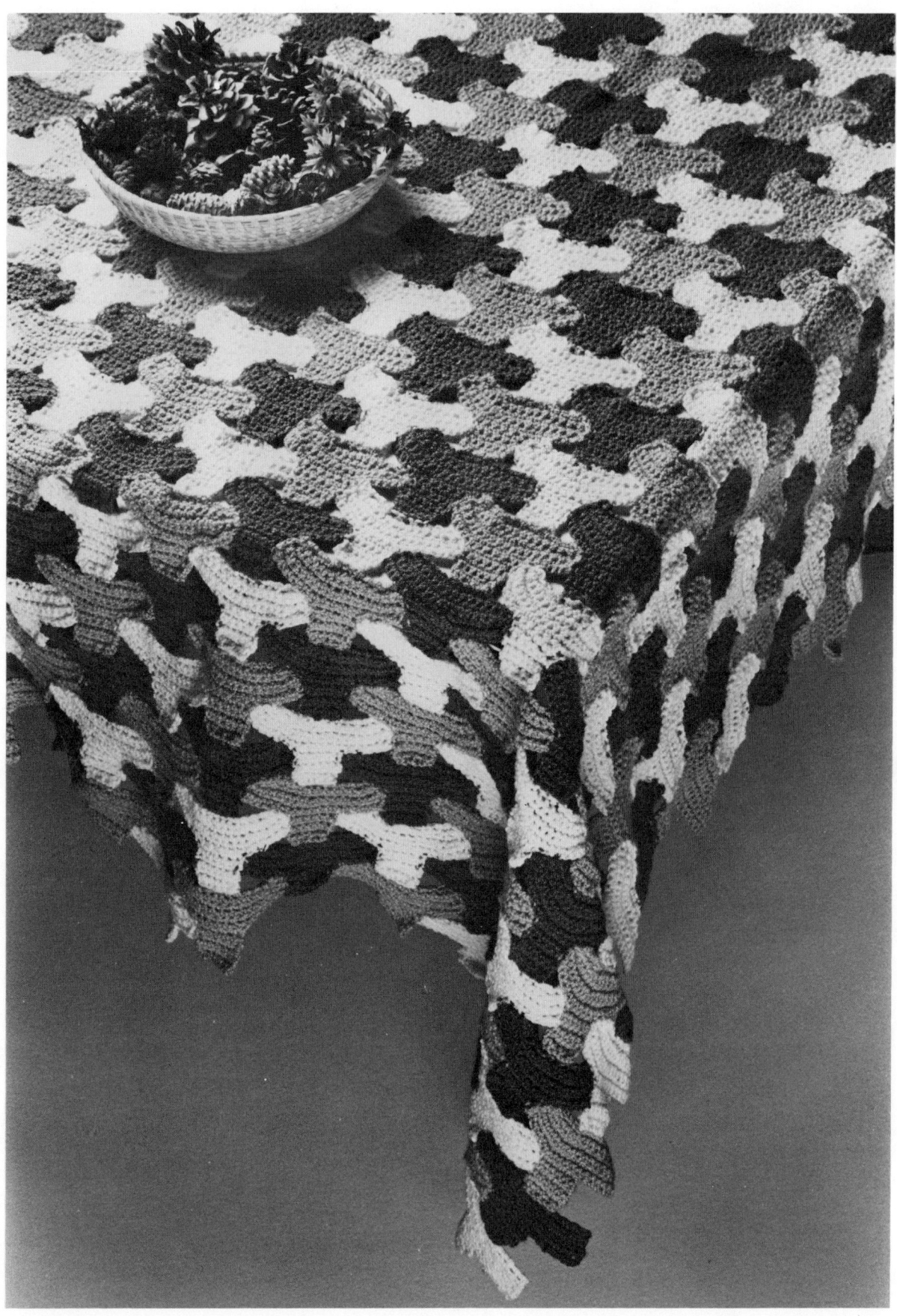

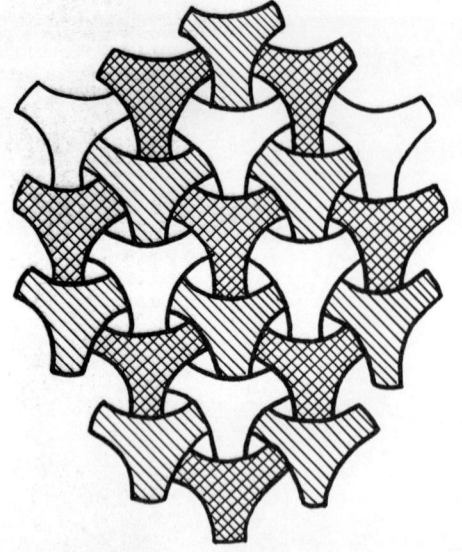

Row 5 Make a sl kn on hook with same color, leaving a 4" end. With right side of work facing you, sc in 7th st of 4th row, sc in each of next 5 sc (6 sc made). Ch 1; turn.

Rows 6–9 Sc in each sc across (6 sc made). Ch 1; turn. At end of the 9th row, knot yarn and cut, leaving a 5" end.

It is recommended that you complete 5 or 6 motifs in each of the 3 colors; then, using a yarn needle and the 5" ends left, join them according to Joining instructions in Part I.

Finishing Hide all loose ends according to Finishing instructions in Part I. Continue in this fashion until tablecloth reaches required dimensions.

☐ *Color A*

▨ *Color B*

▦ *Color C*

Figure IV-10